STONEWALLED

Police Abuse and Misconduct
Against Lesbian, Gay, Bisexual and
Transgender People in the U.S.

AMNESTY INTERNATIONAL USA

Amnesty International is a worldwide human rights activist movement with more than 1.8 million members in more than 150 countries and territories.

Amnesty International's vision is of a world in which every person enjoys all of the human rights enshrined in the Universal Declaration of Human Rights and other international human rights standards.

Amnesty International undertakes research and action focused on preventing and ending grave abuses of the rights to physical and mental integrity, freedom of conscience and expression, and freedom from discrimination, within the context of its work to promote human rights.

Amnesty International is independent of any government, political ideology, or religious creed. It does not support or oppose any government or political system. It is concerned solely with the impartial protection of human rights.

Amnesty International is funded by its worldwide membership and by donations from the public.

First published in 2005 by
Amnesty International USA
5 Penn Plaza
New York, NY 10001

www.amnestyusa.org

@ Copyright
Amnesty International Publications 2005
ISBN# 1-887204-44-X
AI Index: AMR 51/122/2005
Original language: English

CONTENTS

1

INTRODUCTION

In August 2002, Kelly McAllister, a white transgender woman, was arrested in Sacramento, California. Sacramento County Sheriff's deputies ordered McAllister from her truck and when she refused, she was pulled from the truck and thrown to the ground. Then, the deputies allegedly began beating her. McAllister reports that the deputies pepper-sprayed her, hog-tied her with handcuffs on her wrists and ankles, and dragged her across the hot pavement. Still hog-tied, McAllister was then placed in the back seat of the Sheriff's patrol car. McAllister made multiple requests to use the restroom, which deputies refused, stating, "That's why we have the plastic seats in the back of the police car." McAllister was left in the back seat until she defecated in her clothing. While being held in detention at the Sacramento County Main Jail on 6 September 2002, officers placed McAllister in a bare basement holding cell. When McAllister complained about the freezing conditions, guards reportedly threatened to strip her naked and strap her into the "restraint chair"[1] as a punitive measure. Later, guards placed McAllister in a cell with a male inmate. McAllister reports that he repeatedly struck, choked and bit her, and proceeded to rape her. McAllister sought medical treatment for injuries received from the rape, including a bleeding anus. After a medical examination, she was transported back to the main jail where she was again reportedly subjected to threats of further attacks by male inmates and taunted by the Sheriff's staff with accusations that she enjoyed being the victim of a sexual assault.[2] Reportedly, McAllister attempted to commit suicide twice. The Sheriff's Department opened an investigation into the alleged rape, and the inmate accepted a plea for "unlawful intercourse in jail" and was sentenced to three months in jail. Despite having filed a full report with the Sheriff's Department, no Sheriff's Deputy has been disciplined for the incidents surrounding McAllister's incarceration.[3]

ON 28 JUNE 1969, police raided the Stonewall Inn, a popular gay bar in the West Village in New York City. What happened next has been described and written about in countless articles and books.[4] In the history of the modern lesbian, gay, bisexual and transgender (LGBT) rights movement in the United States, the Stonewall riots, an act of defiance against police abuse and repression, is often cited as its defining moment. Black and Puerto Rican transgender women, "butch" lesbians, and homeless street youth were among those who led the rioting, which lasted several days. The police action that precipitated the historical event was by no means unusual—police raids of gay bars were commonplace at the time. What was remarkable was the sustained and intense organized response by the LGBT community to the police action that galvanized a movement and captured the imagination of generations of LGBT activists.

Since Stonewall, significant progress has been made by the LGBT movement in the U.S. in confronting human rights abuses perpetrated by law enforcement. As the LGBT movement has grown in strength across the country,

---

[1] Restraint chair – a metal-framed chair in which prisoners are immobilized in four-point restraints securing both arms and legs, with a strap across the chest.

[2] "Transgendered Woman Raped in Sacramento County Jail Files Claim," The National Transgender Advocacy Organization, 19 December 2002, available at: http://www.tgcrossroads.org/news/archive.asp?aid=537; Cosmo Garvin, "What Is She Doing in a Men's Jail?," The Newsreview.com, February 13, 2003; available at: http://www.newsreview.com/issues/sacto/2003-02-13/cover.asp.

[3] Ramon Coronado, *Sacramento Bee*, 25 December 2002; National Transgender Advocacy Coalition Press Release, http://www.ntac.org.; email to Amnesty International from Dean Johansson, former attorney for Kelly McAllister, on 29 June 2004. Telephone call to Amnesty International from Dani Williams, current attorney for Kelly McAllister, on 4 August 2005.

[4] Paul Geitner, "Two Decades Since Riots Spawned Gay Rights Movement," The Associated Press, Domestic News, 23 June 1989.

the LGBT community has become more capable of holding local police departments accountable for their treatment of LGBT people. Passage of anti-discrimination legislation at the local level in some jurisdictions has greatly facilitated this progress. Increasingly, police forces across the country provide some level of sensitivity training for working with the LGBT community. Despite this progress, the findings of this report clearly indicate that the problem of police misconduct persists. AI has documented serious patterns of police misconduct and brutality aimed at LGBT people, including abuses that amount to torture and ill treatment.

AI's findings strongly indicate that police abuse and the forms it takes are often specific to the different aspects of the victim's identity, such as sexual orientation,[5] race, gender[6] or gender identity,[7] age or economic status. Identities are complex, multi-layered, and intersectional, such that a person may be targeted for human rights violations based on a composite of identities that the person seems to represent. For example, a lesbian woman who is black may not only be a target of police abuse because of her sexual orientation but also because she is a woman of color. The targeting of lesbian, gay, bisexual and transgender people for discriminatory enforcement of laws and their treatment in the hands of police needs to be understood within the larger context of identity-based discrimination, and the interplay between different forms of discrimination—such as racism, sexism, homophobia[8] and transphobia[9]—that create the conditions in which human rights abuses are perpetuated.

Much of Amnesty International's research has clearly demonstrated that discrimination, the systematic denial of rights to certain people, is a grave human rights abuse and often can lead to further human rights abuses.[10] Institutionalized discrimination dehumanizes its victim, who is deemed to be someone who can be treated inhumanely. Institutionalized discrimination feeds impunity, denies justice and can incite violence against targeted people or groups. Discriminatory practices and policies have tremendous consequences for targeted groups not only in terms of the nature of their ill-treatment by government agents or society at large, but also in terms of their access to redress and equal protection under the law. Discrimination also often leads to a lack of official action, such as investigations into alleged abuses, which further reinforces impunity.

This report confirms that in the U.S., LGBT people continue to be targeted for human rights abuses by the police based on their real or perceived sexual orientation or gender identity. Furthermore, the report shows that within the LGBT community, transgender individuals, people of color, youth, immigrant and homeless individuals, and sex workers experience a heightened risk of police abuse and misconduct. Reports to AI indicate that individuals from these populations within the LGBT community are targeted on the basis of identity and are more likely to experience negative interactions with police. Transgender people, particularly low-income transgender people of color, experience some of the most egregious cases of police brutality reported to AI. AI's findings suggest that police tend to target individuals who do not conform to gender stereotypes that govern "appropriate" masculine and feminine behavior. Race plays an important factor in determining the likelihood of an LGBT person being targeted for police abuse, indicating that such abuses likely stem from racism as well as homophobia and transphobia. These findings are consistent with research by AI and other organizations, indicating a correlation in general between race and the likelihood of a person experiencing human rights abuses at the hands of police in the U.S.[11] This report also finds that young LGBT people are more likely to experience human rights abuses by police than LGBT people in general. Transgender youth and youth of color are particularly likely to be targeted for abuse. A number of factors seem to

---

[5] Sexual Orientation: refers to the direction of an individual's sexual/emotional attraction, whether to individuals of a different sex (heterosexual), same-sex (homosexual) or both sexes (bisexual).

[6] Gender - refers to a social construction of femininity or masculinity that varies in time and place and is constructed through learned, rather than innate, behavior.

[7] Gender identity - refers to a person's deeply felt sense of identification of their gender, in relation to the social construction of masculinity or femininity. A person may have a male or female gender identity, with the physiological characteristics of the same or different sex. Gender identity is different from sexual orientation.

[8] Homophobia – used in this report to describe prejudice against lesbians, gay men and bisexual people.

[9] Transphobia – used in this report to describe prejudice against transgender people.

[10] See: *Crimes of hate, conspiracy of silence: Torture and ill-treatment based on sexual identity* (AI Index: ACT 40/016/2001), June 2001.

[11] See *Race, Rights and Police Brutality* (AMR 51/147/1999), 1 September 1999; *Rights for All*, (AMR 51/035/1998), 1 October 1998.

contribute to this, including the high number of LGBT homeless youth. It is estimated that in some cities in the U.S. up to 40 percent of homeless youth are gay, lesbian, bisexual or transgender.[12]

AI's research has revealed that law enforcement officers profile LGBT individuals, in particular gender variant individuals[13] and LGBT individuals of color, as criminal in a number of different contexts, and selectively enforce laws relating to "morals regulations,"[14] bars and social gatherings, demonstrations and "quality of life."[15] Transgender individuals in particular report being profiled as suspicious or as criminals while going about everyday business such as shopping for groceries, waiting for the bus, or walking their dogs.

AI received reports of LGBT individuals being targeted for sexual, physical or verbal abuse in many different situations and contexts. Reports of sexual and physical abuse by law enforcement officers against LGBT individuals are often accompanied by homophobic and transphobic slurs, and in some instances verbal abuse escalates to physical or sexual abuse. Information received by AI suggests that verbal abuse against LGBT individuals is frequently sexualized, in particular against lesbians and transgender individuals. The failure of authorities to tackle issues such as homophobia and transphobia in police forces creates a climate in which such violations can proliferate.

AI has received reports of cruel, inhuman and degrading treatment of LGBT individuals during arrests, searches and detention in police precinct holding cells. AI heard reports of officers searching transgender and gender variant individuals in order to determine their "true" gender. AI also heard allegations of misconduct and abuse of LGBT individuals in holding cells and detention centers, including the inappropriate placement of LGBT individuals in situations that compromise their safety. In particular, transgender individuals are often placed in holding cells according to their genitally determined sex, rather than their gender identity or expression,[16] placing them at greater risk of verbal, physical and sexual abuse at the hands of other detainees.

AI is concerned that U.S. authorities are failing to act with due diligence to prevent and investigate crimes against LGBT people. The U.S. continues to experience serious patterns of non-state actor violence against those who are perceived to be LGBT. Additionally, violence against LGBT people is often motivated by other forms of discrimination based on race, ethnicity and economic status – factors that also affect the victim's access to justice. Most of the U.S. police departments surveyed do provide some form of LGBT training, something AI welcomes. However, many police departments do not have well-developed policies and do not train their officers adequately on how to respond appropriately to crimes committed against LGBT individuals. Reports to AI indicate a pattern of police failing to respond or responding inappropriately to "hate crimes,"[17] domestic violence, and other crimes against LGBT individuals, particularly crimes against LGBT individuals of color, immigrants, and other marginalized individuals.[18] Reportedly, gay men and "masculine appearing" women may be perceived by some law enforcement officers as not requiring or deserving protection from violence.[19] LGBT victims of crimes told AI that police officers seem

---

12 Ryan C. and Futterman D., "Social and developmental challenges for lesbian, gay, and bisexual youth," SIECUS Report 2001; Cochran BN, Stewart AJ, Ginzler JA, Cauce AM, "Challenges faced by homeless sexual minorities: comparison of gay, lesbian, bisexual, and transgender homeless adolescents with their heterosexual counterparts," *American Journal of Public Health* 92.5, 2002, pp. 773-776; "Streetwork Project Study," Victim Services/Traveler's Aid, cited by The Ali Forney Center, Housing for Homeless LGBT Youth, 1991.

13 Gender Variant Individuals - used in this report to describe individuals who transgress social "norms" regarding "gender appropriate" conduct and presentation whether or not they identify with the gender associated with their sex assigned at birth. Gender variant individuals can be heterosexual, lesbian, gay, bisexual or transgender.

14 Morals regulations: regulations used to prohibit public sexual expression or conduct, including offenses such as lewd conduct and public lewdness and other behavior seen as offending public morals.

15 Quality of life policing: Quality of life policing is the term popularly applied to a law-enforcement strategy that seeks to maintain public order by aggressively enforcing laws against minor offenses, for example, public drunkenness, loitering, vandalism, littering or public urination.

16 Gender Expression - Refers to things like clothing and behavior that manifest a person's sense of oneself as male or female. This can include dress, posture, hairstyle, jewelry, vocal inflection, speech patterns, and social interactions.

17 Hate crimes: Used in this report to describe crimes that are motivated by discrimination on grounds such as race, sexual orientation or gender identity or expression. Over past decades, the problem of violence motivated by discrimination in the US has resulted in the introduction of the "hate crimes" legislation. This legislation may make a criminal act motivated by discrimination a distinct crime in the criminal code, or it enhances penalties for a crime when it is motivated by discrimination. [See Hate Crimes]

18 AI interviews with Patti Buffington, Executive Director, Genesis House, Chicago, 26 February 2004; New Immigrant Community Empowerment (NICE) and Council of Pakistan Organization (COPO), 9 March 2004; Julia Garcia, La Opportunidad, Los Angeles, 30 October 2003.

19 AI interview with C. Nicole Mason, Executive Director, National Women's Alliance, Washington, D.C., 10 October 2003.

uncomfortable interacting with them, and perform only a cursory investigation in order to exit as quickly as possible.[20] AI also received a number of reports suggesting that officers responding to crimes against LGBT individuals often focus their attention on the victim's sexual orientation, gender identity or expression, at times explicitly or implicitly blaming the victims for what happened to them.[21] According to reports to AI, police frequently respond according to transphobic, homophobic, racist or class-based stereotypes and assumptions, rather than performing a proper assessment of the situation. This may mean, for example, that when officers respond to a call for assistance in an LGBT domestic violence incident, transgender survivors, immigrant survivors and survivors of color may be arrested.[22]

AI believes that training on LGBT issues is essential, and while the majority of police departments in AI's study reported providing some form of training, 28 percent of police departments responding to AI's survey reported that they do not provide any training on LGBT issues.[23] It is important to note that the police departments surveyed in this study are in the largest city in every state and are more likely than smaller departments to develop training. Thus the problem may be wider than indicated by AI's survey.

AI has found that lack of effective systems of accountability for law enforcement officers committing abuses continues to be a persistent and widespread problem. Reports to AI suggest that many individuals do not come forward with complaints about police officer conduct, including LGBT individuals. AI received a number of complaints of hostility or attempts to dissuade people from making complaints at police stations. AI also heard several accounts of retaliation against LGBT individuals who reported police misconduct. Activists and individual police officers brought up the need for diligent supervision and commitment from leadership in order to achieve effective reform and any lasting change. Internal oversight bodies frequently are not trained in handling complaints pertaining to LGBT individuals, sex workers, youth and other marginalized communities. In many cases, complaints are ruled "unfounded" since no corroborating evidence is found. This is particularly problematic for marginalized communities that are less likely to be believed by investigators, and that may not have witnesses to support their accounts. In the event that an officer is found to be culpable for misconduct, disciplinary decisions are often inadequate and there is little consistency from case to case. Reports indicate that a low number of officers are suspended or fired, even for serious abuses. Among existing external or independent review boards, AI's findings indicate a lack of training and expertise in LGBT issues, raising concerns about their ability to respond to and investigate complaints made by this population. External review boards frequently are also limited by inadequate funds, staff and access to information, and have been criticized for failing to perform sufficient outreach.

---

[20] AI interviews with Andy Thayer, CABN, Chicago, 15 September 2003; Rashawn Lusk, Client of the Rafael Center, Chicago; Annette Lamoreaux, ACLU – Texas, Houston, 1 December 2003; Julia Garcia, La Opportunidad, Los Angeles, 30 October 2003; Anonymous LGBT Service Provider, Los Angeles, 27 October 2003; Marshall Wong, Human Rights Commission - Hate Crime Reporting Unit, Los Angeles, 27 January 2004; Anonymous, APICHA Outreach Workers, New York City, 30 March 2004; Mark Reyes, Bronx Lesbian and Gay Health Consortium, New York City, 11 March 2004; New York Anti-Violence Project Administration, New York City, 23 February 2004; Al Thurk, San Antonio, 2 March 2004; M'Bwende Anderson, NYAC, Washington, D.C., 16 March 2004; 26 February 2004; telephone interview with Robbyn Stewart, New York City, 21 January 2004.

[21] AI interviews with George Unger, Los Angeles chapter, Parents and Friends of Lesbians and Gays, 3 October 2003; Rick Garcia, Executive Director, Equality Illinois, Chicago, 14 November 2003; Dan Biggs and Karen S., Chicago Recovery Alliance, Chicago, 27 February 2004; Miranda Stevens, TYRA, Chicago, 25 February 2004; Matt Pulling and Susan Holt, STOP Partner Abuse/Domestic Violence Program, Los Angeles, 30 September 2003; Jih-Fei Cheng, APICHA, New York City, 8 March 2004; Basil Lucas, Hate Crimes Coordinator and Director of Police Relations, NYG&LAVP, New York City, 23 February 2004; Hank, Esperanza Center – Community Meeting, San Antonio, 4 December 2003; Rick Gipprich, San Antonio Rape Crisis Center, San Antonio, 2 December 2003; GiGi Thomas and Cyndee Clay, HIPS, Washington, D.C., 20 November 2003; Jessica Xavier, Transgender Activist, Washington, D.C., 24 March 2004.

[22] AI interviews with Gelsys Rubio, Director, Latino Counseling Services, Chicago, 25 February 2004; LGBT Rights Advocate, Chicago, 12 November 2003; Lora Branch, Director, City of Chicago Department of Public Health, Chicago, 26 February 2004; Ujima Moore, Amassi, 29 January 2004; Matthew Pulling and Susan Holt, STOP Partner Abuse/Domestic Violence Program of the Los Angeles Gay and Lesbian Center, 30 September 2003; Staff of Jeff Griffith Center, Los Angeles Gay and Lesbian Center, 29 January 2004; New York Anti-Violence Project, 23 February 2004; The Triangle Foundation, Detroit, 19 March 2004; C. Nicole Mason, Executive Director, National Women's Alliance, Washington, D.C., 10 October 2003.

[23] Twenty-eight percent of police departments (eight out of 29) responding to AI's survey.

2

NATIONAL AND INTERNATIONAL LAWS AND STANDARDS*

IT IS IMPORTANT TO UNDERSTAND the issue of police misconduct and brutality within the larger context of the need to recognize the human rights of LGBT people. The United States, like many other countries, has a long history of both criminalizing same-sex sexual conduct and failing to protect LGBT people against discrimination on the basis of their sexual orientation or gender identity.

Criminalization and failing to protect LGBT people from discrimination inherently deny LGBT people access to their full human rights and create a climate in which LGBT people are more likely to face human rights abuses whether in detention, on the street or in the home. Pervasive discrimination and lack of legal recognition means that LGBT people are consistently subjected to discrimination and frequently denied their economic, social and cultural rights; the right to access to the most basic areas of daily life, such as employment, housing and health services.

The emergence of a strong LGBT rights movement has been successful in pushing forward greater recognition of the rights of LGBT people in the last three decades. As of March 2005, 16 states and the District of Columbia protect workers against discrimination based on sexual orientation in both the public and private sectors, and an additional 11 states prohibit sexual orientation discrimination against state employees.[25] At least 285 cities, counties and government organizations in the US provide some level of protection against discrimination based on sexual orientation.[26] A number of jurisdictions, including six states,[27] the District of Columbia[28] and 67 cities and counties have laws prohibiting discrimination on the basis of gender identity.[29] It should be noted, however, that many of these non-discrimination laws do not apply to employment in the private sector.[30] An AI examination of municipal ordinances in the largest city in each of the 50 states revealed that, of the 41 of these cities that had enacted local human rights ordinances against discrimination in basic areas of life like employment, housing and public accommodations, 26 cities provided protection from discrimination on the basis of sexual orientation,[31] and 14 included gender identity as a prohibited ground for discrimination.[32]

---

* For a more detailed overview of international and domestic law see Appendix B. See also: Amnesty International, *The Human Rights of Lesbian, Gay, Bisexual and Transgender People: A Primer to working with the United Nations Treaty Monitoring Bodies and the Special Procedures of the United Nations Commission on Human Rights,* 1 March 2005, AI Index IOR 40/004/2005.

[25] Human Rights Campaign, "The State of the Workplace: For Lesbian, Gay, Bisexual and Transgender Americans, 2004," 2005, available at: www.hrc.org.

[26] Id.

[27] California, Illinois, Maine, Minnesota, New Mexico, and Rhode Island. See www.transgenderlaw.org

[28] Human Rights Campaign, "The State of the Workplace: For Lesbian, Gay, Bisexual and Transgender Americans, 2004," 2005, available at: www.hrc.org.

[29] Id.

[30] Of the 285 cities and counties with non-discrimination protections, only 152 of them extend to employment in the private sector as well. Human Rights Campaign, "The State of the Workplace: For Lesbian, Gay, Bisexual and Transgender Americans, 2003," 2004, available at: www.hrc.org.

[31] Phoenix, AZ; Los Angeles, CA; Denver, CO; Wilmington, DE; Atlanta, GA; Honolulu , HI; Chicago, IL; Des Moines, IA; Lexington-Fayette, KY; New Orleans, LA; Portland, ME; Baltimore, MD; Boston, MA; Detroit, MI; Minneapolis, MN; Kansas City, MO; Albuquerque, NM; New York, NY; Columbus, OH; Portland, OR; Philadelphia, PA; Providence, RI; Houston, TX; Seattle, WA; Charleston, WV; Milwaukee, WI.

[32] Los Angeles, CA; Denver, CO; Atlanta, GA; Chicago, IL; Lexington-Fayette, KY; New Orleans, LA; Baltimore, MD; Boston, MA; Minneapolis, MN; New York, NY; Portland, OR; Philadelphia, PA; Houston, TX; Seattle, WA.

Progress on the federal level for non-discrimination based on sexual orientation or gender identity has been extremely slow. Neither the United States Constitution nor current federal legislation explicitly provides protection from discrimination against lesbian, gay, bisexual or transgender individuals. The United States Congress has yet to pass the Employment Non-Discrimination Act (ENDA), which was first introduced in 1994. The United States Supreme Court, on the other hand, has moved further away from its reasoning in previous decisions regarding "sodomy" statutes in the last decade. In 2003, the US Supreme Court found unconstitutional all remaining criminal "sodomy" statutes in the US.[33] Despite these gains, the US has fallen behind many other countries in the legal recognition of the basic human rights of LGBT people.[34]

INTERNATIONAL LAW

The international community has adopted international human rights laws and standards that govern the conduct of states.[35] For example, the International Covenant on Civil and Political Rights (ICCPR), to which the US is a party, is the principal international treaty setting out fundamental civil and political rights, including the right to freedom from arbitrary arrest and detention, and torture, cruel, inhuman or degrading treatment.[36] The US is also a party to the Convention Against Torture and Other Cruel, Inhuman and Degrading Treatment or Punishment and to the International Convention on the Elimination of All Forms of Racial Discrimination. (Please refer to Appendix B for a full discussion on international law and standards.)

The LGBT community has struggled to realize the basic rights provided for in existing standards. Everyone, regardless of sexual orientation or gender identity or expression, is guaranteed the fullest enjoyment of civil, political, social, economic and cultural rights under international law.[37] Lesbian, gay, bisexual and transgender individuals, like all other persons, are entitled to equality before the law. International law guarantees all persons the rights to life,[38] to privacy,[39] to health,[40] to liberty of movement,[41] and to freedom of expression[42] and association,[43] as well as

---

33   Lawrence v. Texas, 539 U.S. 558 (26 June 2003).

34   Many Western European countries have laws that provide for protection from discrimination in addition to recognizing same-sex partnerships. Some, like the Netherlands and Belgium, recognize same-sex marriage. Countries such as South Africa, Fiji, Ecuador and Portugal have constitutional bans on discrimination based on sexual orientation. See www.ilga.org.

35   If the US has ratified human rights treaties, it is legally bound to comply with them. If the US has signed but not ratified a treaty it is obliged to refrain from acts that would defeat the object or purpose of that treaty. Many human rights requirements are contained in standards which have been adopted by consensus by the international community, but which are not in the form of treaties. Although these standards do not technically have the legal power of treaties, they have authoritative value and persuasive force of having been adopted by political bodies such as the UN General Assembly. [See Appendix B for more information.]

36   Articles 9 and 7, International Covenant on Civil and Political Rights,G.A. res. 2200A (XXI), 21 U.N. GAOR Supp. (No. 16) at 52, U.N. Doc. A/6316 (1966), 999 U.N.T.S. 171, entered into force Mar. 23, 1976. The US ratified the ICCPR in 1992.

37   International bodies have made statements specifically noting the human rights of lesbians and gays. Paul Hunt, Special Rapporteur on the right of everyone to the enjoyment of the highest attainable standard of physical and mental health, notes in his report to the 60th session of the Commission of Human Rights, "...the Special Rapporteur has no doubt that the correct understanding of fundamental human rights principles, as well as existing human rights norms, leads ineluctably to the recognition of sexual rights as human rights. Sexual rights include the right of all persons to express their sexual orientation, with due regard for the well-being and rights of others, without fear of persecution, denial of liberty or social interference." E/CN.4/2004/49, 16 February 2004, para.54.

38   Art. 3, Universal Declaration of Human Rights, G.A. res. 217A (III), U.N. Doc A/810 at 71 (1948); Art 6(1), International Covenant on Civil and Political Rights, G.A. res. 2200A (XXI), 21 U.N. GAOR Supp. (No. 16) at 52, U.N. Doc. A/6316 (1966), 999 U.N.T.S. 171, entered into force 23 March 1976.

39   Art. 12, Universal Declaration of Human Rights, G.A. res. 217A (III), U.N. Doc A/810 at 71 (1948); Art. 17(1), International Covenant on Civil and Political Rights, G.A. res. 2200A (XXI), 21 U.N. GAOR Supp. (No. 16) at 52, U.N. Doc. A/6316 (1966), 999 U.N.T.S. 171, entered into force 23 March 1976.

40   Art. 12(1), International Covenant on Economic, Social and Cultural Rights, G.A. res. 2200A (XXI), 21 U.N.GAOR Supp. (No. 16) at 49, U.N. Doc. A/6316 (1966), 993 U.N.T.S. 3, entered into force 3 January 1976.

41   Art. 13(1), Universal Declaration of Human Rights, G.A. res. 217A (III), U.N. Doc A/810 at 71 (1948).

42   Art. 19, Universal Declaration of Human Rights, G.A. res. 217A (III), U.N. Doc A/810 at 71 (1948); Art. 19(2), International Covenant on Civil and Political Rights, G.A. res. 2200A (XXI), 21 U.N. GAOR Supp. (No. 16) at 52, U.N. Doc. A/6316 (1966), 999 U.N.T.S. 171, entered into force 23 March 1976.

43   Art. 20(1), Universal Declaration of Human Rights, G.A. res. 217A (III), U.N. Doc A/810 at 71 (1948); Art. 22(1), International Covenant on Civil and Political Rights, G.A. res. 2200A (XXI), 21 U.N. GAOR Supp. (No. 16) at 52, U.N. Doc. A/6316 (1966), 999 U.N.T.S. 171, entered into force 23 March 1976.

freedom from arbitrary arrest and detention,[44] and from torture, cruel, inhuman or degrading treatment and punishment.[45] The UN Human Rights Committee has urged states not only to repeal laws criminalizing same-sex sexual conduct but also to enshrine the prohibition of discrimination based on sexual orientation into their constitutions or other fundamental laws.[46] It has further noted that reference to "sex" in the non-discrimination clauses of the ICCPR should be taken to include "sexual orientation," thereby affirming that the rights set out in the ICCPR cannot be denied to any individual because of their sexual orientation.[47]

The ICCPR requires that anyone deprived of his or her liberty be treated with humanity and with respect for the inherent dignity of the human person.[48] Under the terms of UN Declarations on policing, law enforcement officials should treat victims with compassion and respect for their dignity,[49] and should not inflict, instigate or tolerate any act of torture or other cruel, inhuman or degrading treatment or punishment.[50] Police should receive training to sensitize them to the needs of victims.[51] States must act with due diligence to ensure that all parts of the population are protected equally[52] and, in protecting and serving the community, police should not unlawfully discriminate on the basis of race, gender, religion, language, color, political opinion, national origin, property, birth or other status.[53] Effective mechanisms must be established to ensure the internal discipline and supervision of law enforcement officials[54] and investigations into violations should be prompt, competent, thorough and impartial.[55] When violations of human rights have occurred, all parts of the population should have equal access to remedies.[56]

---

[44] Art. 9, Universal Declaration of Human Rights, G.A. res. 217A (III), U.N. Doc A/810 at 71 (1948); Art. 9(1), International Covenant on Civil and Political Rights, G.A. res. 2200A (XXI), 21 U.N. GAOR Supp. (No. 16) at 52, U.N. Doc. A/6316 (1966), 999 U.N.T.S. 171, *entered into force* 23 March 1976.

[45] Art. 5, Universal Declaration of Human Rights, G.A. res. 217A (III), U.N. Doc A/810 at 71 (1948); Art. 7, International Covenant on Civil and Political Rights, G.A. res. 2200A (XXI), 21 U.N. GAOR Supp. (No. 16) at 52, U.N. Doc. A/6316 (1966), 999 U.N.T.S. 171, *entered into force* 23 March 1976.

[46] See for example, Human Rights Committee, *Concluding Observations: Poland*, 29/07/99 (UN Doc. CCPR/C/79/Add.110), para.23, 29 July 1999.

[47] Human Rights Committee, *Toonen v. Australia* (Views on Communication, No 488/1992, adopted 31 March 1994).

[48] Art. 10, International Covenant on Civil and Political Rights, G.A. res. 2200A (XXI), 21 U.N. GAOR Supp. (No. 16) at 52, U.N. Doc. A/6316 (1966), 999 U.N.T.S. 171, *entered into force* 23 March 1976.

[49] Declaration of Basic Principles of Justice for Victims of Crime and Abuse of Power, G.A. res. 40/34, annex, 40 U.N. GAOR Supp. (No. 53) at 214, U.N. Doc. A/40/53 (1985).

[50] U.N. Code of Conduct for Law Enforcement Officials, G.A. res. 34/169, annex, 34 U.N. GAOR Supp. (No. 46) at 186, U.N. Doc. A/34/46 (1979).

[51] General Assembly Resolution 40/34 of 29 November 1985.

[52] UN Code of Conduct for Law Enforcement Officials, G.A. res. 34/169, annex, 34 U.N. GAOR Supp. (No. 46) at 186, U.N. Doc. A/34/46 (1979), article 2.

[53] UDHR, article 2; ICCPR, articles 2 and 3; ICERD, articles 2 and 5; Code of Conduct, articles 1 and 2.

[54] UN Code of Conduct for Law Enforcement Officials, G.A. res. 34/169, annex, 34 U.N. GAOR Supp. (No. 46) at 186, U.N. Doc. A/34/46 (1979), preambular paragraph 8(d) and articles 7 and 8; Principles on Force & Firearms, principles 22-26.

[55] Principle 6, Declaration of Basic Principles of Justice for Victims of Crime and Abuse of Power, G.A. 40/34, annex, 40 U.N. GAOR Supp. (No. 53) at 214, U.N. Doc. A/40/53 (1985);; Principle 9, Principles on the Effective Prevention and Investigation of Extra-Legal, Arbitrary and Summary Executions, E.S.C. res. 1989/65, annex, 1989 U.N. ESCOR Supp. (No. 1) at 52, U.N. Doc. E/1989/89 (1989);; Article 13, Declaration on the Protection of All Persons from Enforced Disappearances, G.A. res. 47/133, 47 U.N. GAOR Supp. (No. 49) at 207, U.N. Doc. A/47/49 (1992). Adopted by General Assembly resolution 47/133 of 18 December 1992.

[56] Principles 4 and 8, Declaration of Basic Principles of Justice for Victims of Crime and Abuse of Power, G.A. 40/34, annex, 40 U.N. GAOR Supp. (No. 53) at 214, U.N. Doc. A/40/53 (1985).

3

SCOPE AND METHODOLOGY

WHILE THIS REPORT provides a national overview of the continuing problems of police misconduct and brutality as they impact LGBT communities in the US, the research for this report has primarily focused on four US cities – Chicago, Illinois; Los Angeles, California; New York, New York; and San Antonio, Texas. It is important to underscore that these cities were not selected because they represent the worst examples of police misconduct and brutality against LGBT people or because they are the cities which have necessarily come the furthest in protecting LGBT people from such abuses. Instead, these cities were chosen to enable us to look at very different and geographically diverse sets of communities. Additionally, these cities were chosen because each also has a well-documented history of police brutality and misconduct in general as well as specifically targeted toward the LGBT community. Each of these cities has also taken at least some steps in attempting to address these human rights abuses. This allows us to examine the progress that has been made as well as the challenges that remain.

Furthermore, in each city there is at least some limited local capacity to document abuses by the police in which LGBT people are specifically targeted. This report finds that the capacity to document abuses against LGBT people in the US remains extremely limited, which results in little or no ability to accurately assess this problem in most communities in the US. Even in these four cities, to greater and lesser degrees, the documentation capacity that currently exists is inadequate to accurately assess the full degree of the problem.

AI is greatly indebted to a myriad of local LGBT and police monitoring groups as well as many other organizations and individuals who have generously shared with us their own documentation and contacts. Without their support we could not have undertaken this project.

AI has obtained data for this report from a wide range of sources in order to collect information on a national as well as local level. These included surveys, interviews in the selected cities, and research of statutes, ordinances and media reports from across the US. AI was unable to independently verify all the details of some of the cases cited in this report; however, the abuses described are consistent with a pattern found across jurisdictions.

SURVEYS

On 7 November 2003, AI sent out a detailed questionnaire to law enforcement agencies across the US about their interactions with LGBT individuals, training policies, responses to incidents involving LGBT individuals and detention procedures. Surveys were sent to the police department in the largest city in each of the 50 states, the District of Columbia and San Antonio (a city studied for the report but not the largest city in Texas). AI sent a follow-up letter to unresponsive police departments on 4 December 2003 and made follow-up telephone calls to departments that had still not responded during December 2003 and January 2004.

- Of the 52 surveys sent to the Chief of Police of each selected police department, AI received 29 completed surveys. Each of the four target city police departments completed the survey, with the exception of the New York City Police Department (NYPD). However, since the NYPD afforded AI access to its administration and many of its officers, AI was able to obtain answers for many of the questions asked in the survey and this information is included in the survey results.

On 3 December 2003, AI sent out an additional survey to 52 internal affairs divisions of the above police departments on the process for filing a complaint with the departments' internal oversight bodies; policies and statistics, if any, on complaints against police officers involving LGBT individuals; and the implementation of early warning systems to identify officers who are prone to commit abuse or misconduct. AI sent a follow-up letter to unresponsive internal affairs divisions on 31 December 2003 and made follow-up telephone calls to divisions that still had not responded during January 2004.

- From the 52 surveys sent out to the heads of the internal affairs divisions, AI received 11 completed surveys. Out of the four target cities selected for the report, only the San Antonio Police Department's Internal Affairs Bureau completed the survey. There was no response from Chicago, Los Angeles or New York City.

On 8 December 2003, AI sent out surveys on the oversight of complaints as well as data collection procedures and policies for complaints made by lesbian, gay, bisexual, or transgender individuals to each of the 24 Civilian Complaint Review Boards that exist in the largest city of each of the 50 states and the District of Columbia. AI sent a follow-up letter to unresponsive Civilian Complaint Review Boards on January 5, 2004 and made follow-up telephone calls to boards that had still not responded during January and February 2004.

- From these 24 surveys sent to the director of each Review Board, AI received nine completed surveys. Two Review Boards indicated that they were unable to complete the survey: one because it only reviews closed cases where any identifying information is redacted, and the other because its commission does not actually serve as a public oversight committee and therefore does not gather the information sought by Amnesty International. Out of the four cities selected for the report whose city has a civilian oversight body, only New York City's Civilian Complaint Review Board returned a completed survey. Chicago's oversight body failed to send a response and San Antonio does not have an outside oversight body for its police department.[57]

INTERVIEWS

AI conducted over 170 interviews in the four selected cities along with additional interviews in Philadelphia, Pennsylvania; Washington, D.C.; Houston, Texas; and San Francisco, California.[58] The target cities were chosen based on the population size, the presence of LGBT activists or advocacy groups within the city, previous work done in the city on police brutality issues, and the history of police brutality in the city, as well as trying to cover the four major areas of the country – Northeast, Midwest, South and West. The organization met with lesbian, gay, bisexual, or transgender activists and advocacy organizations as well as with police brutality activists, police watchdog organizations, youth outreach organizations, immigration advocacy groups, sex work activists and advocacy groups, civil rights organizations and local community activists.[59] AI also collected over 200 testimonials through a confidential online survey requesting testimony from LGBT individuals about their interactions with police; AI conducted follow-up interviews by telephone or email in relation to testimonies received through this survey that are included in this report. AI also reviewed surveys conducted by local organizations on interactions with police occurring both in New York City and Chicago.

The organization also met with law enforcement officials in New York City, Chicago, San Antonio and Los Angeles in order to discuss their policies governing interactions with the LGBT community as well as to present issues uncovered from meetings with activist, advocate and community groups. (Please see Appendix C for a full list of all official meetings.)

A number of individuals spoke to AI on the condition of anonymity and some individuals requested that the location where the alleged incident took place not be disclosed; however, names and locations are on file with AIUSA.

---

[57] The mission of the Los Angeles Office of Independent Review (OIR) is to monitor the Los Angeles County Sheriff's Department (LASD). OIR replied that it performs its role not through the direct intake and investigation of complaints, but rather through complete access to, review of, and recommendations about internal misconduct investigations undertaken by the LASD.

[58] AI conducted interviews in Los Angeles (29 September-6 October 2003, 27 October-3 November 2003 and 26-30 January 2004); San Antonio (14-17 October 2003 and 1-5 December 2003); Chicago (15-19 September 2003, 10-14 November 2003 and 23-27 February 2004); and New York (1 March-9 April 2004).

[59] In documenting patterns of abuse and misconduct, AI cites to an illustrative but not exhaustive list of interviews conducted.

OTHER SOURCES

Amnesty International tracked incidents that were documented in the media through routine state-by-state media searches. The researchers documented cases of hate crimes committed against LGBT individuals and incidents of police brutality committed against LGBT individuals, and followed documented media accounts of police responses to same-sex domestic violence calls and hate crimes by members of the public targeting LGBT individuals along with cases and investigations of police misconduct.

The organization also documented and tracked current and pending legislation relating the inclusion of sexual orientation and gender identity and expression in state and federal anti-discrimination and/or hate crime laws; federal immigration legislation or policies that could have an adverse affect on LGBT individuals who are also immigrants; and the inclusion, in city and municipal ordinances, of sexual orientation and gender identity and expression in the local anti-discrimination or hate crime ordinances.[60]

For the purpose of this study, AI refers to young LGBT people as individuals under the age of 21. AI has used a wide range of terminology in this report (please refer to the glossary in Appendix A). It should be noted that in matters of gender and sexuality, the terms people use and identify with can vary widely from culture to culture. In this report the phrase "lesbian, gay, bisexual or transgender (LGBT)"is used because they are the English terms most commonly used in the international human rights discourse. However, this is in no way intended to ignore the diversity of other terms and identities, nor to deny the cultural connotations attached to these terms.

While AI conducted outreach within LGBT communities (as detailed above), relatively few cases of police misconduct and abuse against lesbians and transgender men were documented. AI believes that this is in part due to the challenges of documenting violence in such cases.

Violence against women is characteristically underreported because women are ashamed or fear skepticism and disbelief. Virtually every culture in the world contains forms of violence against women that are nearly invisible because this violence is seen as "normal." Even in countries where laws criminalize violence against women, tolerance of violence may be found at all levels of society. Moreover, women and men whose sexuality and gender expression and/or identities do not conform to social and cultural norms of "appropriate" femininity or masculinity are targeted for stigma, discrimination and violence. As the UN Special Rapporteur on Violence against Women has affirmed, women who choose options other than heterosexuality may be targeted for violence for doing so.[61] Violence against lesbians is part of a spectrum of violence to which women can be subjected if they depart from accepted codes of sexual behavior. Often the gender discrimination that women face is combined with other forms of discrimination: the prevalence of sexism and homophobia in societies puts lesbians at grave risk of abuse in the home and in the community. These factors also pose challenges to women in reporting violence against them.

Lesbians, transgender men and women who are perceived as too masculine fear reporting abuse and violence as all too often they are seen as responsible for the violence committed against them and that the violence is seen as a "punishment" for their lack of conformity. Women whose sexuality or gender identity or expression already makes them "suspect" experience threats in relation to reporting, including the threat of further abuse or violence, which causes them to "go underground", not report or fail to give the "whole story". Many women also fear breaches of confidentiality by police, judges, prosecutors and/or other service providers. This may be particularly threatening to women who have sex with other women or women whose gender expression is masculine, who fear that information about their experiences and identities will be leaked or otherwise not protected. As a result, they fear extortion, blackmail or public repudiation.

---

[60] AI surveyed legislation in each of the 50 states and the District of Columbia as well as the largest city by population in each of the 50 states along with the four target cities.

[61] Radhika Coomaraswamy, "1997 Report of the Special Rapporteur on Violence Against Women," United Nations, E/CN.4/1997/47, 12 February 1997, paragraph 8.

It should also be noted that relatively few cases of violence and abuse of bisexual women and men were reported. Bisexuals are often targeted because of same-sex sexual activity or when they are with someone of the same sex, and as such they are perceived as being lesbian or gay, whether they identify that way or not. Moreover, lack of acceptance of bisexuals from within LGBT communities may also cause bisexual women and men to fear a lack of support from within the LGBT community as well as disinterest from external communities.

The challenges of documenting violence against lesbians, transgender men and bisexuals, which leads to the invisibility of these human rights violations, warrant further study and are beyond the scope of this report.[62]

---

[62] See: Submission by the International Gay and Lesbian Human Rights Commission, member of the SG Study on Violence Against Women Task Force, *Sexual Orientation, Gender Expression and Violence Against Women*, Expert Group Meeting: "Violence Against Women: a statistical overview, challenges and gaps in data collection and methodology and approaches for overcoming them" 11-15 April 2005, Geneva, Switzerland.

4

PROFILING AND SELECTIVE ENFORCEMENT

IN VARIOUS COUNTRIES ACROSS THE WORLD, AI has found that homophobia and transphobia towards LGBT people often motivate other abuses. Politically motivated allegations of same-sex sexual conduct have been used to suppress criticism, shut down organizing and silence political opponents.[63] In the US, for example, "sodomy" is no longer a crime since the 2003 Supreme Court decision in *Lawrence*,[64] but many states do not currently afford LGBT individuals full protection from discrimination (see international and domestic law – Appendix B). Furthermore, AI has found that while certain laws may not be discriminatory on their face, they are open to discriminatory application. AI believes that some laws are particularly prone to discriminatory enforcement—for example vague statutes that do not clearly define prohibited behavior and allow for significant discretion on the part of law enforcement officers. As police officers make decisions about who to stop, question or detain, discrimination may come into play and may determine both the initiation and outcome of interactions.

Profiling or discriminatory enforcement of laws governing arrest and detention constitutes arbitrary arrest or detention in violation of the provisions of the Universal Declaration of Human Rights (UDHR) and the ICCPR regarding non-discrimination, deprivation of liberty and equality before the law. Profiling and selective enforcement can affect individuals in virtually every sphere of their daily lives and often has an impact that goes far beyond the initial incident. For example, in a study on racial profiling in the US released in 2004, AI found that the practice of racial profiling leaves its victims feeling humiliated, depressed, helpless and angry, and furthermore reinforces residential segregation, creates fear and mistrust, and engenders reluctance in reporting crimes and cooperating with police officers.[65] AI heard similar reports from LGBT communities and individuals who have experienced profiling or selective enforcement based on their sexual orientation or gender identity or expression, as well as race, age or other status leading to arbitrary detention.

AI's research has revealed that law enforcement "profile" LGBT individuals, in particular transgender and gender variant individuals and LGBT individuals of color, as potential criminals in a number of different contexts, and selectively enforce "morals regulations," statutes and regulations governing bars and social gatherings, demonstrations and quality of life statutes. Transgender women, in particular transgender women of color, for example, have been profiled as criminal suspects while going about everyday business. Such practices contravene a number of major international human rights treaties, covenants and declarations that the US has ratified: the United Nations Charter,[66] the UDHR,[67] the ICCPR[68] and the International Convention on the Elimination of All Forms of Racial Discrimination (ICERD).[69]

---

[63] For example, Malaysian opposition figure Anwar Ibrahim was imprisoned because of politically-motivated "sodomy" charges. See *Malaysia: Double injustice heaped on Anwar Ibrahim*, 18 April 2003 (AI index: ASA 28/015/2003). Ibrahim was freed on 2 September 2004 after Malaysia's highest court overturned his 15-year sentence.

[64] Lawrence v. Texas, 539 U.S. 558 (26 June 2003).

[65] "Threat and Humiliation: Racial Profiling, Domestic Security and Human Rights in the United States," Amnesty International USA, September 2004.

[66] Art. 1, Para 3, U.N. Charter, June 26, 1945, 59 Stat. 1031, T.S. 993, 3 Bevans 1153, *entered into force* Oct. 24, 1945.

[67] Art. 2, Universal Declaration of Human Rights, G.A. Res. 217 A (III), U.N. GAOR, 3d Sess., U.N. Doc. A/810 (1984).

[68] Art. 2(1), International Covenant on Civil and Political Rights, adopted by the General Assembly 19 December 1966, *entered into force* 23 March 1976, ratified by the United States in 1992, 999 U.N.T.S. 171.

[69] Art. 2, International Convention on the Elimination of All Forms of Racial Discrimination, adopted by the General Assembly 21 December 1965, *entered into force* 4 January 1969, ratified by the United States in 1994, 660 U.N.T.S. 195 (1966).

The most common contexts and forms of profiling and selective enforcement targeting LGBT individuals found by AI are described below.

4.1

POLICING GENDER: PROFILING OF TRANSGENDER INDIVIDUALS

On 15 January 2004, a Latina transgender woman went to the Silver Dollar Bar in San Antonio. Bar security officers came in and asked her to step outside, where police officers accused her of stealing some money from another patron at the bar. An officer reportedly said, "People like you are bad," "People like you make the world a bad place," and "Shut up, fag." She denied the charges and offered that officers could search her purse. Three police officers and two detectives surrounded her. One of the officers started to search her while the others stood watching. "The officer rolled down my skirt so that my belly was exposed and my pubic hair. I said, 'Look sir, my private part is out.' He told me to shut the fuck up. He told me to turn around. He then did the same thing behind – rolled down my skirt and exposed my butt. The Silver Dollar Bar is right on the side of the road, so anyone driving past could see. He then lifted my blouse and exposed one of my breasts. He wanted to see if I had a bra on – I didn't." She told AI, "I didn't ask to be searched by a female officer. I've tried that before – they don't care. To them we're all men, but we're not." She was then handcuffed. When she tried to tell the officer that the handcuffs were too tight, he reportedly said, "You should have thought of that before you committed a crime" and told her to "shut the fuck up." She was then pushed into the back of the police car, scraping the skin on her foot; the foot was reportedly bleeding. Shortly after, she was told to get "the fuck out." She said that she was not leaving until she got their badge numbers and was told, "Just shut the fuck up and get out of here." One of the officers gave his number but said it so fast that she couldn't get it. The others would not give her their badge numbers. She was not charged with any crime. She told AI, "I know to be respectful to police officers, but I'm tired of the way they are treating us."[70]

THIS SECTION WILL EXAMINE POLICE PROFILING or selective enforcement of laws and ordinances against LGBT individuals, particularly transgender individuals, on the basis of their perceived transgression of social "norms" regarding "gender appropriate" conduct and presentation.

AI received a number of reports that law enforcement officers treat an individual's deviance from stereotypical gender "norms" as grounds for suspicion. While lesbians, gay men and transgender and bisexual people may be profiled or targeted for selective enforcement of regulations for the same reason – because they are all considered "gender outlaws" – the context as well as the ways and means in which such a violation manifests itself can vary enormously. According to some advocates, the quality of police interactions can be affected by how visible an individual's perceived gender variance is. Advocates also emphasize that stereotypes about gender may be compounded by presumptions of criminality based on race, age or socioeconomic status.[71] For transgender individuals, reports indicate that harassment is more severe the less a transgender woman or man "passes" as a woman or man, which in turn can be a function of her or his socioeconomic status and the extent to which she or he wants or can afford hormones and sex reassignment surgery.[72]

Reports indicate that failure to adhere to gender expectations contributes to arbitrary arrest and detention of transgender and gender variant people. AI has heard reports of widespread profiling of transgender women as sex workers, inappropriate and selective targeting of transgender and gender variant individuals to produce identification and "prove" their gender identity; and selective "policing" of the use of bathrooms designated as male or female. Other forms of misconduct and abuse reportedly include inappropriate and sometimes abusive behavior when identification is produced and does not match an individual's gender expression; deliberate and humiliating improper pronoun use; inappropriate searches to determine an individual's genitally determined sex **(see Detention and Searches)**; as well as verbal, physical and sometimes sexual abuse.

---

[70] Telephone interview with Anonymous, 21 January 2004.

[71] AI interview with Martha Matthews, Former Staff Attorney, and Sharon Murphy, Chapter Coordinator, ACLU of Southern California, 3 October 2003.

[72] AI interviews with Anonymous Transgender Service Provider, Los Angeles, 2 October 2003; Shirley Bushnell, Van Ness Recovery House - Prevention Division, 1 October 2003.

4.1.1

LAW ENFORCEMENT TRAINING AND POLICIES

A 61-year-old white transgender woman and her business partner, who is also a transgender woman, were detained for questioning by plainclothes officers in Burbank, California in 2000. When the officer asked whether they had drugs or weapons in the car, the woman reportedly told the officer "No, I am a pre-op transsexual and have prescription drugs in the car." The officer's response was reportedly, "What the hell does that mean … are you a he or a she?" She told AI, "I stopped volunteering information at that point as I felt I was in a no-win situation." Following a search they were told they could leave. The women asked the officers to identify themselves but they reportedly refused to do so. She attempted to file a complaint and secure an apology on five occasions and was eventually told that the police department did not believe her version of events and they were supporting the officers. During one of her attempts to make a complaint at the station, she spoke with a sympathetic female lieutenant watch commander who reportedly said that the men in the department were uncomfortable with her transsexuality and that they had refused a transgender sensitivity training when the opportunity was presented to them.[73] AI contacted Burbank Police Department and an official told AI that the department provides cultural awareness training, but that there was no specific component regarding transgender issues.[74]

AI IS CONCERNED by the lack of transgender-specific policies, procedures and training for law enforcement personnel, especially in light of the findings detailed below and throughout this report. Out of the 29 police departments responding to AI's survey, 21 (72 percent) report having no policy regarding interactions with transgender people, only five (17 percent) reported having any policy and three (10 percent) failed to provide a response.

- **Chicago:** The Chicago Police Department reports that it has no specific policy for interacting with transgender individuals.

- **Los Angeles:** The Los Angeles Police Department (LAPD) reports that it does have a specific policy governing interactions with transgender individuals.

- **New York:** It is unclear whether or not the NYPD has a specific policy that governs interactions with transgender individuals, but it appears to have guidelines for practice.[75]

- **San Antonio:** San Antonio Police Department reported that it does not have specific policies or practices governing interactions with transgender individuals. Police officials in San Antonio also indicated to AI that there is "nothing specific" in the training program on transgender issues.[76]

AI urges authorities to develop transgender-specific policies and procedures and to ensure that issues relating to interactions with transgender individuals and communities are incorporated into police training as a matter of urgency.

---

[73] Emails and telephone conversations with a transgender woman in Burbank, CA, 23 February 2004, 7 March 2005 and 10 March 2005.

[74] AI telephone conversation with Burbank Police Department, 30 March 2005.

[75] In interviews between AI and various NYPD officials it was reported that the NYPD does have some form of practice regarding interactions with transgender individuals. For the purposes of this report, AI has included the NYPD in the survey results as answering that the department does have a practice governing interactions with transgender individuals, even though NYPD did not formally respond to AI's written survey.

[76] AI interview with Chief Albert Ortiz and Dep. Chief Jeffrey Page, SAPD, 4 December 2003.

4.1.2
PROFILING TRANSGENDER WOMEN AS SEX WORKERS

"They used to arrest transgender women for wearing women's clothing; now they arrest transgender women for loitering with intent to solicit. There is still so much work ahead of us, doing sensitivity trainings for law enforcement and the criminal justice system."

Vivianna Hernandez, Los Angeles Gay and Lesbian Center[77]

"The police assume we are on the street to do sex work. Why else would a transgender be on the street? Lots of transgender people are academics and have college degrees, but they are totally ignorant of it."

Transgender woman speaking to Amnesty International at the Asian Pacific AIDS Intervention Team Community Forum Meeting, 29 January 2004

"No tenemos el derecho a vivir." (We don't have the right to live.)

Julia Garcia, La Opportunidad, Los Angeles[78]

AI HAS FOUND A STRONG PATTERN of police unfairly profiling transgender women as sex workers.[79] AI received reports of such practices in Chicago, Los Angeles, New York and San Antonio, as well as in Washington, DC; Philadelphia, Pennsylvania; San Francisco, California; and Houston, Texas.[80] Transgender individuals are often the subject of intense police scrutiny and AI heard many reports of transgender women being stopped by police and questioned about their reason for being on the street and where they were going, often under the pretext of policing sex work, even when those stopped were engaging in routine daily activities such as walking a dog or going to a local shop.[81] AI attended a meeting in Los Angeles between Bienestar's Transgeneros Unidos support group and officials of the Hollywood-Wilcox Division of the LAPD, where a number of the predominantly Latina participants recounted instances of profiling as sex workers by officers while they were engaged in activities such as hailing a cab or walking down the street.[82] In 2001, 50 transgender women affiliated with the Transgeneros Unidos (Transgender People United) program of Bienestar, a full-service community organization working with Los Angeles' Latino/a LGBT communities, demonstrated against profiling as sex workers and ongoing harassment by officers in front of the Hollywood-Wilcox Precinct of the LAPD. Since that time, the Captain of the division has met regularly with Transgeneros Unidos to discuss ongoing concerns.

---

[77] AI interview with Vivianna Hernandez, Los Angeles Gay and Lesbian Center, Anti-Violence Project, 31 March 2005; email from Vivianna Hernandez, Los Angeles Gay and Lesbian Center, Anti-Violence Project, 26 April 2005.

[78] AI interview with Julia Garcia, La Opportunidad, 30 October 2003.

[79] Sex work is a criminal offense in the United States, however, prostitution is legal in those counties of the state of Nevada with populations lower than 400,000 people. Source: NRS § 244.345 (8) (2004). Pervasive discrimination and lack of legal recognition means that LGBT people are consistently subjected to some of the harshest forms of discrimination and denied their economic, social and cultural rights including the right to access to the most basic areas of daily life, such as employment, housing and health services. Those within the LGBT community facing severe socioeconomic marginalization may commit offenses, such as sex work and theft, in order to survive life on the street.

[80] AI interviews with Shirley Bushnell, Van Ness Recovery House Prevention Division, Los Angeles, 2 October 2003; Martha Matthews, former staff attorney, ACLU Foundation of Southern California, Los Angeles, 3 October 2003; Anonymous Transgender Service Provider, Los Angeles, 2 October 2003; GLASS focus group, Los Angeles, 31 October 2003; Carrie Davis, Gender Identity Project, New York, 3 February 2004; Vanessa Edwards Foster, Local and National Transgender Activist, Houston, 30 November 2003.

[81] AI interviews with Andy Kim, Chicago Coalition for the Homeless, Chicago, 14 November 2003; Rashawn Lusk, Client of the Rafael Center, Chicago, 18 February 2004; GLASS focus group, Los Angeles, 28 January 2004; Martha Matthews, former staff attorney, ACLU Foundation of Southern California, Los Angeles, 3 October 2003; Ujima Moore, Amassi, Los Angeles, 29 January 2004; Anonymous, Client of Streetworks, New York City, 5 March 2004; Anonymous, ACT UP monthly meeting, New York City, 3 March 2004; Erica, Member of FIERCE!, New York City, 2 March 2004; Donna, Client of Positive Health Project – Transgender Tuesday Group, 24 February 2004; Anonymous, Response to FIERCE! Survey on Police Harassment in the West Village, New York City; Anonymous, Response to FIERCE! Survey on Police Harassment in the West Village, New York City; David Ewell, Executive Director, San Antonio AIDS Foundation, San Antonio, 5 December 2003; Christie Lee Littleton, San Antonio Gay and Lesbian Center, 16 October 2003; Vanessa Edwards Foster, Local and National Transgender Activist, Houston, 30 November 2003.

[82] AI interview with Transgeneros Unidos meeting, Los Angeles, 28 October 2003.

Police officials made comments to AI that appear to suggest that there is a commonly held assumption that transgender individuals are sex workers. For example, one LAPD Captain stated, "There's a small percent of transgenders in prostitution" at a community meeting,[83] however, he later told AI that 80 percent of the transgender community is involved in sex work, because of "sexual addiction" or because they are engaging in "survival sex."[84] An official at the 6th Precinct in Manhattan, New York, told AI that there are no prostitutes arrested in the 6th Precinct who are *not* transgender.[85]

AI is concerned that subjective and prejudiced perceptions of transgender women as sex workers often play a significant role in officers' decisions to stop and arrest transgender women. Community-based organizations and individuals reported that profiling of transgender women as sex workers by law enforcement officers frequently leads to arbitrary arrest and detention.[86] For example, an advocate in Chicago told AI that officers see transgender women as easy targets when they need to meet their allotted "arrest quota."[87] Reports to AI from a number of advocates indicate a pattern of selective enforcement of solicitation ordinances against transgender people of color, immigrants and homeless youth.[88] One New York attorney reported that 80 percent of transgender women of color he works with have experienced police harassment or false arrest based on unfounded suspicions of engagement in sex work.[89]

- **Los Angeles:** In 2003, a transgender woman reported that she was arrested for solicitation when she was walking her dog.[90]

- **New York:** An African American transgender woman told AI that she was leaving a meeting at the Gay and Lesbian Center in the West Village when she was stopped by a white male officer for "prostitution" while walking down Christopher Street. The officer allegedly took her bag, emptied out the contents and threatened to hit her with his stick if he saw her again.[91]

- **San Antonio:** A white transgender woman reportedly worked for a motel, where her shift ended at 3 a.m. She was reportedly stopped by SAPD about four or five separate times on her way home after her night shift on the assumption that she was a sex worker. Eventually, her employers had to contact SAPD and explain that she needed to walk home in the early hours of the morning after her shift ended. She is not harassed anymore.[92]

Such profiling and arrests appear to primarily take place under vague laws allowing for significant discretion on the part of individual police officers, such as those creating offenses of "loitering with intent to solicit," "public lewdness" or "disorderly conduct." Similarly, the National Coalition of Anti-Violence Programs (NCAVP) has found that that police frequently target transgender people under cover of vice law enforcement or so-called "quality of life" campaigns.[93] AI and other organizations are concerned that vaguely worded regulations lend themselves to

83   AI interview with Transgeneros Unidos meeting, Los Angeles, 28 October 2003.

84   AI interview with Captain Downing, Hollywood-Wilcox Division, LAPD, 26 January 2004.

85   AI interview with Inspector Fitzgerald, Captain Hanley and Deputy Chief Gerrish, NYPD 6th Precinct, New York City, 15 March 2004.

86   AI interviews with Gelsys Rubio of Latino Counseling Services and Heather Bradley of Night Ministry, Lakeview Coalition, Chicago, 12 November 2004; GLASS Focus Group, Los Angeles, 24 January 2004; Dean Spade, Sylvia Rivera Law Project, New York City, 19 February 2004; Vanessa Edwards Foster, National and Local Transgender Rights Activist, Houston, 30 November 2003.

87   AI interview with Lora Branch, Director, City of Chicago Department of Public Health, Chicago, 26 February 2004.

88   AI interviews with Miranda Stevens, TYRA, Chicago, 25 February 2004; RL, Client, Rafael Center, Chicago, 26 February 2004; Heather Bradley, Night Ministry, Chicago, 25 February 2004; Horizons Youth Drop In, Chicago, 13 November 2003; Martha Matthews, former staff attorney, ACLU Foundation of Southern California, Los Angeles, 3 October 2003; GLASS Mobile Unit, Los Angeles, 29 October 2003; GLASS focus group, Los Angeles, 31October 2003; Jesse Ehrensaft-Hawley, FIERCE!, New York City, 22 January 2004; Carrie Davis, Gender Identity Project, New York City, 3 February 2004. In 1996 San Francisco Task Force on Prostitution found that the San Francisco Police Department selectively enforced laws against the most visible sex workers – those working on the street – and the most vulnerable, including African American, transgender and immigrant women. "The San Francisco Task Force on Prostitution: Final Report," BAYSWAN, March 1996. See also: O'Leary Claudine and Olivia Howard, "The Prostitution of Women and Girls in Metropolitan Chicago: The Preliminary Prevalence Report," 23 May 2001.

89   AI interview with Dean Spade, Sylvia Rivera Law Project, New York City, 19 February 2004.

90   AI interview with Anonymous Transgender Service Provider, Los Angeles, 2 October 2003.

91   AI interview with transgender woman, Positive Health Project, New York City, 24 February 2004.

92   As reported during AI interview with Christie Lee Littleton, transgender advocate, Gay and Lesbian Center of San Antonio, 16 October 2003.

93   "Anti-Lesbian, Gay, Bisexual and Transgender Violence in 2002," National Coalition of Anti-Violence Programs, 2003 Preliminary Edition, 26.

discriminatory application since these laws and regulations leave almost entirely to an officer's judgment not only the determination of suspicion, but also the definition of offending conduct.

In Chicago, Los Angeles and New York, organizations reported that possession of two or three condoms was used by police officers in a discriminatory manner as evidence to justify the arrest of transgender women perceived to be engaged in sex work. AI has heard from outreach workers that many of their clients are therefore reluctant to take condoms or safe sex kits.[94] AI also heard of police harassment and arrest of transgender as well as LGBT outreach workers in Chicago, Los Angeles and New York.[95]

- **New York:** A transgender youth of color was reportedly doing outreach in 2001. She had a bag of sex kits with flyers to hand out. The police approached her and reportedly arrested her for prostitution.[96]

AI is concerned by reports that many transgender individuals will not challenge charges because to plead "not guilty" may mean spending time in detention before trial.[97] Many transgender people are fearful of spending time in detention because they are often at heightened risk of torture and ill-treatment at the hands of both guards and other inmates. (See **Searches and Detention** section.) Furthermore, transgender individuals express fear of the criminal justice system due to pervasive discrimination against transgender people, even in securing legal counsel. For example, AI heard one report of a lawyer who was unwilling to represent a transgender woman until she "found God."[98]

Although AI did not receive the same level of reports on this issue from gay or lesbian individuals, AI also heard reports that LGB individuals, particularly young gay men of color in Chicago's Lakeview district and in Los Angeles, are profiled on the basis of their gender identity or expression and assumed to be sex workers.[99]

- **Chicago:** In February 2004, a Latino and two African American young gay men met at a taco stand. They were stopped by two officers who told them, "You fucking faggots, put your hands on the car." When one of the young men did not have his identification papers on him, one of the officers said, "You're out here selling your ass, but no one is going to buy it." Reportedly, the officer said, "I'll find a reason to arrest you."[100]

In response to AI's concerns, police officials in New York, San Antonio and Los Angeles told AI that officers stop and question individuals under suspicion of soliciting only when their conduct somehow objectively indicates that they are engaging in such transactions. The NYPD told AI that officers' determinations of whether an individual is engaged in sex work are based on observation and consideration of the time of day, location and conduct of individuals, such as waving down cars. According to NYPD officials, "We identify by watching to see if they approach numerous cars, are dressed provocatively, and so on." Chief Ortiz of SAPD indicated to AI, "We can stop and talk to anyone at any time. If we see someone waiting for a bus … and they are still there an hour later, then we are going to

94 AI interviews with Lakeview Coalition - Gelsys Rubio, Latino Counseling Services and Heather Bradley, Night Ministry, Chicago, 12 November 2003; Patti Buffington, Executive Director of Genesis House, Chicago, 26 February 2004; RL, Client, Rafael Center, Chicago, 18 February 2004; Angel Fabian, Director of Community Organizing and Health Education, Clinica Romero, Los Angeles, 30 October 2003; Jesse Ehrensaft-Hawley, Director, FIERCE!, New York City, 22 January 2004; Anya Mukaraji-Connolly, Peter Cicchino Youth Project, Urban Justice Center, New York City, 16 January 2004; Michelle Sosa, Positive Health Project – Tuesday Transgender Group, New York City, 24 February 2004; Justine Sullivan, Streetworks, New York City, 5 March 2004.

95 AI interviews with Lora Branch, Director, City of Chicago Department of Public Health, Chicago, 26 February 2004; Angel Fabian, Clinica Romero, Los Angeles, 30 October 2003; Peter Cicchino Project, Urban Justice Center, New York City, 16 January 2004; Positive Health Project, Chicago, 24 February 2004; Anonymous member, FIERCE! New York, 22 January 2004.

96 AI interview with Anonymous member, FIERCE!, New York City, 2 March 2004.

97 One advocate told AI, "If you protest your arrest, you have to stay longer." AI interviews with Streetworks, New York City, 5 March 2004; Stephen Edwards, Attorney, New York City, 17 February 2004; Dean Spade, Sylvia Rivera Law Project, New York City, 19 February 2004.

98 As reported in an AI interview with Dean Spade, Attorney, Sylvia Rivera Law Project, New York City, 19 February 2004.

99 AI interviews with Karen Stanczykiewicz, Chicago Recovery Alliance, Chicago, 27 February 2004; Bill Streep, Rafael Center, Staff Meeting, Chicago, 14 November 2003; LGBT Rights Advocate, Chicago, 12 November 2003; Gelsys Rubio, Latino Counseling Services and Heather Bradley, Night Ministry, Lakeview Coalition, Chicago, 12 November 2003; Rick Garcia, Executive Director, Equality Illinois, Chicago, 14 November 2003; Raul, Alex, Antonio and Jose, Horizons Youth Drop In, Chicago, 19 February 2004; Heather Bradley, Night Ministry, Chicago, 25 February 2004; Lora Branch, City of Chicago Department of Health, Chicago, 18 February 2004. Patrick Mangto, Ohana House, Los Angeles, 26 March 2004.

100 AI interview with Horizons Youth Drop-In, Chicago, 19 February 2004.

ask."[101] Captain Downing of the Hollywood-Wilcox division of the LAPD emphasized that police stops based solely on an individual's attire or location are unjustified, and that the law requires that individuals be engaged in conduct which objectively evidences an intent to solicit, such as flagging down cars and speaking with drivers. Nevertheless, he also stated that individuals' "mannerisms" and possession of condoms are used as evidence of intent to solicit.[102] Furthermore, one of the officers present at the meeting between LAPD and Transgeneros Unidos noted that in his experience, transgender women dress in a way designed to be "noticed," thereby inevitably attracting police attention. AI remains concerned that subjective and prejudiced perceptions of transgender women as sex workers often play a significant role in officers' decisions to stop and arrest transgender women.

Targeting of LGBT individuals because of their gender identity and/or race violates their right to freedom from discrimination under the ICCPR, the Convention against Torture and the International Convention on the Elimination of Racial Discrimination.

4.1.3

IDENTIFICATION

AS PART OF EXPRESSING their chosen identity, transgender individuals frequently change their names to reflect their gender. The European Court of Human Rights has ruled that prohibiting transsexual people from adopting a change of name or changing their civil status was contrary to Article 8 of the European Convention on Human Rights, which protects an individual's right to privacy.[103] However, transgender individuals in the US often experience difficulties in changing or obtaining identification documents that match their gender identities. Individuals who are transitioning, undocumented immigrants, homeless people or those who do not meet the requirements for altering the gender on their identification because, for example, they cannot afford hormones or cannot afford or do not wish to undergo sex reassignment surgery, may not be able to obtain identification consistent with their gender expression.[104] Accordingly, a common fear expressed to AI by transgender individuals and communities is being stopped by a police officer and being asked for identification.[105] AI heard a number of reports of transgender individuals being stopped and asked for identification, in some cases apparently to establish simply whether an individual is male or female.[106]

AI's findings indicate that when transgender or gender variant individuals produce identification to officers that does not match their gender expression, individuals are regarded as fraudulent or deceitful, creating a heightened risk of abuse and harassment.[107] Advocates contend that officers assume the identification is fraudulent in such instances and, in some cases, reportedly have confiscated transgender women's identification, believing it to be "void."[108]

- **Los Angeles:** A Latina transgender woman was reportedly arrested for providing false information to a police

---

[101] AI interview with Chief Ortiz, San Antonio Police Department, 4 December 2003.

[102] Transgeneros Unidos meeting, Los Angeles, 28 October 2003.

[103] *Christine Goodwin v. The United Kingdom* (28957/95) [2002] ECHR 583 (11 July 2002).

[104] AI interview with Shirley Bushnell, Van Ness Recovery House - Prevention Division, 1 October 2003.

[105] There are various state and federal documents that record a person's name and gender, such as drivers' licenses, birth certificates, Social Security records, passports and immigration documents. Procedures for changing all of these documents are different, vary from state to state, are often complex and can be expensive. Although some states only require a letter from a health professional saying the person is intending to transition from one sex to the other, other states require genital surgeries before changing the gender. See: *In the Matter of Robert Henry McIntyre*, 715 A.2d 400 (Pa. 1998) and *The Matter of Eck* 584 A.2d 859 (N.J. Super. 1991). Some transgender people are fearful that changing the gender on their immigration documents may reduce their chances of becoming a citizen. Lisa Mottet and John M. Ohle, "Transitioning Our Shelters: A Guide to Making Homeless Shelters Safe for Transgender People," National Gay and Lesbian Task Force Policy Institute, National Coalition for the Homeless, 2003.

[106] AI interviews with Dean Spade, Sylvia Rivera Law Project, New York City, 19 February 2004; Shirley Bushnell, Van Ness Recovery House - Prevention Division, Los Angeles, 2 October 2003.

[107] AI interviews with Shirley Bushnell, Van Ness Recovery House - Prevention Division, 1 October 2003; Vivianna Hernandez, LAGLC-AVP, Los Angeles, 26 March 2004; Rick Garcia, Executive Director, Equality Illinois, Chicago, 14 November 2003; Anya Mukarji-Connolly, Peter Cicchino Youth Project, Urban Justice Center, New York City, 16 January 2004; Anonymous, Streetworks, New York City, 5 March 2004; Vanessa Edwards Foster, National and Local Transgender Activist, Houston, 30 November 2003.

[108] AI interview with Shirley Bushnell, Van Ness Recovery House - Prevention Division, 1 October 2003.

officer when she presented a driver's license identifying her gender as female. While the charges were subsequently dropped, as a result of her arrest she was found to be in violation of a previously imposed probation order and was incarcerated for 30 days.[109]

Reports to AI indicate that when police officers interact with transgender individuals, they often use inappropriate pronouns or an individual's prior male or female name. In some instances this may be reflective of a failure to understand adequately the need of transgender people to express their gender identity, and therefore a product of inadequate training. However, AI also heard reports of officers deliberately using a name or pronoun that does not match an individual's gender expression in order to humiliate.[110]

- **Los Angeles:** Despite the existence of an LAPD policy requiring officers to address transgender individuals as they present themselves,[111] officers reportedly frequently insist on using male pronouns when addressing transgender women, calling them "sir," and telling them, "I have to call you by your legal name."[112]

- **Washington, DC:** In December 2002 a transgender woman called the police after her boyfriend reportedly started choking her. When the police saw her ID they started using masculine pronouns and calling her "mister" and "he."[113]

One of many issues that a transgender policy should cover is how to address a transgender individual; some police departments already include this in their policies. For example, a representative from the San Francisco Police Department told AI that the San Francisco Police Department has developed a policy whereby officers are required to address transgender individuals by either the name on their identification or the name they regularly use if they have not had their identification corrected to reflect gender identity.[114] According to Los Angeles Police Department's response to AI's survey, its policy requires officers to address transgender persons as they present themselves. Police officials in New York also indicated to AI that individuals will be addressed according to how they present themselves, but that there is no written policy on the use of pronouns. Reportedly, officers are "trained to interact with how people want to be addressed."[115]

AI believes that officers should be required to address transgender individuals by either the name on their identification or the name they regularly use if they have not had their identification corrected to reflect gender identity. In investigative circumstances an officer may respectfully ask gender- and name-related questions. Once those questions have been answered an officer must refer to an individual by the name he or she regularly uses.

---

[109] AI interview with Vivianna Hernandez, LAGLC-AVP, Los Angeles, 26 March 2004.

[110] AI interview with Shirley Bushnell, Van Ness Recovery House – Prevention Division, Los Angeles, 1 October 2003; Stephen Edwards, Attorney, New York City, 17 February 2004; Pauline Park, NYAGRA, New York City, 11 February 2004; Anthony, Client of Gay Men's Health Crisis, New York City, 19 March 2004; Carl Siciliano, Executive Director, Ali Forney Center, New York City, 13 February 2004; Margaux Delotte-Bennett, SMYAL, Washington, D.C., 20 November 2003; GiGi Thomas, Program Assistant, HIPS, Washington, D.C., 20 November 2003.

[111] LAPD response to AI survey, 11 December 2003.

[112] AI interviews with Captain Downing, Hollywood-Wilcox Division, LAPD, Los Angeles, 26 January 2004; Shirley Bushnell, 1 October 2003; Sheriff Baca, Linda Castro and Jeffrey Prang, LASD, Los Angeles, 29 January 2004; Anonymous Transgender Service Provider, 2 October 2003.

[113] AI interview with GiGi Thomas, Program Assistant, and Cyndee Clay, Executive Director, HIPS, 20 November 2003.

[114] In investigative circumstances an officer may respectfully ask gender- and name-related questions. Once those questions have been answered, however, the officer must refer to individuals by the name he or she regularly uses. "San Francisco Police Department standards for interactions with the transgender communities: Stops and Searches 12/22/03." AI heard reports, however, that in some instances officers in San Francisco do not adhere to these procedures. AI interview with Chris Daly, Staff Attorney of the Transgender Law Center, San Francisco, 27 October 2003.

[115] AI interview with Commissioner James Fyfe, Detective Kevin Zatariski, with other NYPD administration officials, NYPD, New York City, 24 March 2004.

4.1.4
POLICING BATHROOM USE

Dean Spade, a transgender man, was arrested in 2002 by a Port Authority police officer while using the men's room at Grand Central station, New York. "I entered a restroom, a cop followed me into the restroom and asked me to show ID. I explained that I was in the right restroom." When two friends came to his assistance, the officer detained them and, finally, arrested all three of them. "The cop was really being aggressive," Spade said. "We tried to leave and he pushed us against the wall ... We spent 23 hours in jail and ultimately the charges were dropped because there was no legal basis for our arrests."

Interview with Dean Spade, 29 September 2004

REPORTS TO AI OF POLICE MISCONDUCT directed towards transgender and gender variant communities also included the "policing" of bathroom use. The majority of public bathrooms are designated male or female, even though there may be no laws codifying these social conventions.[116] Therefore, access to them can result in transgender individuals being subjected to arrest, harassment or abuse by officers who use their own perceptions of gender identity or expression to determine who should or should not be allowed into a particular bathroom. Transgender individuals report fear of being stopped or questioned by other people who are using the bathroom, private security guards or police, who may be called to arrest a transgender person for using the "wrong" toilet.[117] AI has heard reports in Los Angeles, New York and San Antonio that police have demanded identification from transgender people when they have attempted to use public bathrooms.[118] Bathroom access issues become more of an issue with intersecting identities—people of color, homeless and young people are already under higher scrutiny.

Organizations representing transgender people recommend gender-neutral bathrooms and point out that transgender and gender variant individuals must be afforded access to safe and dignified bathroom facilities.[119] Transgender individuals should not be arrested or detained solely for using a bathroom appropriate to their gender identity or expression.

---

[116] AI has not been able to conduct extensive research on the existence of laws or ordinances governing bathroom use.

[117] See Shannon Minter and Christopher Daley, "Trans Realities: A Legal Needs Assessment of San Francisco's Transgender Communities," 2003

[118] AI interviews with Dean Spade, Sylvia Rivera Law Project, New York City, 19 February 2004; Julius, Member of FIERCE!, New York City, 2 March 2004; Carla, Member of Positive Health Project – Tuesday Transgender Group, New York City, 24 February 2004; Esperanza Community Meeting, San Antonio, 4 December 2003. See also: Duncan Osborne, "Trans Activists Charge Harassment: Police selectively requiring ID at public bathrooms at Christopher St. riverfront," *Gay City News*, 27 June-3 July 2003.

[119] San Francisco City has a regulation which states that individuals have the right to use the bathroom that is consistent with their gender identity, and the Human Rights Commission strongly urges that all places of public accommodation and employment provide a gender-neutral bathroom option. http://www.ci.sf.ca.us/site/sfhumanrights_page.asp?id=6274

4.1.5

MORALS ENFORCEMENT: POLICING PUBLIC SPACE

"When officers are working in areas where people have sex in their cars, if it's a man and a woman or even two women, the officers usually check to make sure there is not a serious crime occurring (such as rape) and then send them on their way. The parties are told to take it to a hotel or take it home. However, if there are two men consensually involved in the car, officers arrest them more often than not. This is discriminatory enforcement."

AI interview with LASD Sergeant Don Mueller, 27 January 2004

"When a police officer sees a [heterosexual] couple making love, they are left alone on most occasions, but if gays are involved, they [police] are on them."

Andrew Thomas, Attorney in San Antonio[120]

R. Boevingloh, a 60-year-old white gay man, was in a park in St Louis, Missouri in June 2001 and reports that he was wearing dark sunglasses, walking with a cane in one hand and a soft drink in the other, when he greeted an undercover policeman as they passed each other. Mr. Boevingloh immediately was handcuffed, put in a police car and subsequently charged with lewd conduct. At trial, the undercover policeman testified that Mr. Boevingloh had rubbed his crotch area and made prolonged eye contact with the officer. He was placed on two years probation. He told AI, "I did nothing wrong, did not 'cruise' anyone, did not expose myself, did not hurt anyone and was targeted simply for being a gay male in a city park … Nothing is more unfair than singling out a group and making them criminal when they are not."

Email to Amnesty International from R. Boevingloh, 23 February 2004

A San Antonio Park Ranger testified in a trial against a gay man charged with a lewd conduct offense that he had arrested at least 500 gay men and no women. He also reportedly said he "wanted to rid the park of gays."[121]

IN THE CONTEXT OF THIS REPORT AI uses the term "morals regulations" to refer to regulations used to prohibit public sexual expression or conduct, including offenses such as lewd conduct and public lewdness and other behavior seen as offending public morals. AI acknowledges that people have a reasonable expectation to enjoy public spaces without individuals engaging in sexual relations in such spaces. Such regulations, however, are often vaguely worded so as to allow for significant discretion on the part of law enforcement officers, and AI has found that gay men are disproportionately affected by discriminatory enforcement of "moral regulations."[122]

AI's findings indicate that the vagueness of morals regulations lead to arbitrary arrest and detention of gay men because of the discretion granted to officers in determining what is considered "offensive," rendering the enforcement of such regulations prone to homophobia, racism and sexism. The arbitrary arrests and detentions that may result from the use of such vague statutes or regulations are human rights abuses under both the UDHR and the ICCPR. Reports indicate a pattern of officers engaging in unlawful entrapment techniques, soliciting and inviting prohibited conduct, as part of undercover operations. AI has received reports of discriminatory application of morals regulations against gay men of color. AI has also received several reports of verbal and physical abuse by officers, in particular during undercover operations. AI believes that the discriminatory aspects of targeted lewd conduct operations create an atmosphere conducive to abuse, and foster a climate of impunity. Many individuals are unlikely to

---

[120] Interview with Andrew Thomas, Lawyer, San Antonio, 4 December 2003.

[121] Matt Lum, "Where is the Outrage? Recent Allegations Uncover History of Abuse in San Antonio," The Texas Triangle, posted 2 August 2001.

[122] In Los Angeles, between August 2000 and July 2001, of 649 arrests under Section 647(a), 88 percent were of men; excluding arrests involving sex work, 99 percent were of men. Remarks of Jon Davidson, Senior Counsel, Lambda Legal Defense and Education Fund, 24 January 2002, at a meeting with Los Angeles City Attorney Rocky Delgadillo; "Petition for an Independent Investigation of LAPD Lewd Conduct Arrest Practices," Gay and Lesbian Action Alliance, 11 April 2000. AI interview with Andrew Thomas, Lawyer, San Antonio, 4 December 2003. The California Supreme Court has repeatedly noted that California Penal Code Section 647(a), which prohibits "lewd conduct," has been selectively enforced against gay men. In the case of a gay man who reportedly "solicited an undercover police officer to perform an act of oral copulation" the California Supreme Court noted that the nature of conduct criminalized by California Penal Code Section 647(a) makes it susceptible to discriminatory enforcement: Pryor v. Municipal Court, 25 Cal.3d 238, 252, n.8 (1979). In an effort to stem discriminatory enforcement practices, the California Supreme Court stipulated that, for a person to be convicted, the prohibited conduct must occur in the presence of another person or persons who may be offended by it: People v. Rylaarsdam, 130 Cal. App.3d Supp. (1982). *See also:* People v. Superior Court *(Caswell)*, 46 Cal.3d 381, 401, n.10 (1988); Baluyut v. Superior Court, 12 Cal.4th 826, 830-31 (1996).

challenge false charges for fear of repercussions if their sexual orientation is revealed, contributing to the impunity with which misconduct and abuse may take place. Advocates in some cities have also raised concerns that police enforce morals statutes based on complaints from the public that are kept open indefinitely, i.e., enforcement may take place on the basis of complaints that were made months or even years ago.

AI received reports of targeted enforcement of "morals regulations" disproportionately against gay men in all four cities studied by AI, as well as in several other cities across the US including Detroit, Michigan; Columbus, Ohio; and Denver, Colorado.[123] In San Antonio it is reported that over 900 gay men were arrested in targeted sting operations from 1999 to 2001.[124] Lambda Legal Defense and Education Fund (LAMBDA) allege that the LAPD targets gay men with discriminatory law enforcement tactics and selectively enforces lewd conduct laws; they report that the number of arrests of gay men for lewd conduct in Los Angeles was between 1,800 and 2,000 per year, during 1997 to 1999.[125] The California Supreme Court has noted that California Penal Code Section 647(a), which prohibits lewd conduct, has been selectively enforced against gay men. In the case of a gay man who reportedly "solicited an undercover police officer to perform an act of oral copulation" the California Supreme Court noted that the nature of conduct criminalized by California Penal Code Section 647(a) makes it susceptible to discriminatory enforcement.[126] In LA, between August 2000 and July 2001, of 649 arrests under Section 647(a), 88 percent were of men; excluding arrests involving sex work, 99 percent were of men.[127] In Modesto, California, the county court reportedly dismissed lewd conduct charges when a defendant's attorney found that there had been no lewd conduct charges filed against heterosexuals in Modesto over a three-year period.[128] Statewide in California in 2003, 97.7 percent of those arrested for felony lewd conduct were men.[129]

[123] AI interviews with: LGBT Rights Advocate, Chicago, 12 November 2003; Ricci Levy, Jeff Montgommery, and Judy Guerin, Woodhull Foundation, New York City, 18 March 2004; Martha Matthews, former staff attorney, and Sharon Murphy, chapter coordinator, ACLU, Los Angeles, 3 October 2003; Ken Miele, Attorney, Los Angeles, 30 October 2003; Gloria McCauley, BRAVO, Columbus, 1 July 2002; Jeffery Montgomery, Executive Director of the Triangle Foundation, Detroit, 19 March 2004; Dede de Percin, Executive Director, Denver AVP, Denver, 9 April 2002. See also: NCAVP received reports of 65 cases of entrapment in connection with lewd conduct statutes in 2003: *Anti-Lesbian, Gay, Bisexual, and Transgender Violence in 2003*, National Coalition of Anti-Violence Programs, 2004; *The Pulse, A Health Assessment of the Lesbian, Gay, Bisexual, And Transgender (LGBT) Community in the Kansas City, Missouri, Bi-State Metropolitan Area*, The Lesbian and Gay Community Center of Kansas City and the Kansas City, Missouri Health Department, 3 April 2004, p. 74. "Meeting to Address Perceived Harassment; Activists, Police Differ On Reasons for Crackdown," *Sun-Sentinel*, 10 November 2003.

[124] AI interviews with Tino Romero, Martin Herrera, Gay and Lesbian Center, San Antonio, 16 October 2003; LGBT Rights and Policing Activist, San Antonio, 4 December 2001. *See also:* Matt Lum, "Where is the Outrage? Recent Allegations Uncover History of Abuse in San Antonio," The Texas Triangle, posted 2 August 2001, http://www.texastriangle.com/archive/943/coverstory.htm.

[125] Jon W. Davidson, LAMBDA Legal, Community Forum on Police Enforcement, "Statistics and History," 24 January 2000. AI interviews with Ken Miele, Los Angeles, 30 October 2003; Martha Matthews, former staff attorney, ACLU, Los Angeles, 3 October 2003. LAMBDA reportedly sought the release of lewd conduct arrest records from the LAPD for three years, but the LAPD resisted making such records public. LAMBDA's first Public Records Act request, filed on 3 July 1997, was turned down by the interim Police Chief, who said the department lacked the resources to comply with the query. Reportedly, in May 1998, police officials ordered their vice units to undertake an extensive internal examination of the arrest records. When it heard of the internal review, LAMBDA revived its PRA claim. LAPD again claimed insufficient staffing to produce the records, and for the first time claimed that the papers were exempt from disclosure. "Lambda Back in Court for LAPD Lewd Conduct Arrest Records: Documents sought to establish that police still purposely target gay men," LAMBDA Press Release, 20 January 2000.

[126] Pryor v. Municipal Court, 25 Cal.3d 238, 252, n.8 (1979). In an effort to stem discriminatory enforcement practices, the California Supreme Court stipulated that, for a person to be convicted, the prohibited conduct must occur in the presence of another person or persons who may be offended by it: People v. Rylaarsdam, 130 Cal. App.3d Supp. (1982). *See also:* People v. Superior Court (Caswell), 46 Cal.3d 381, 401, n.10 (1988); Baluyut v. Superior Court, 12 Cal.4th 826, 830-31 (1996).

[127] Remarks of Jon Davidson, Senior Counsel, LAMBDA Legal Defense and Education Fund, 24 January 2002, at a meeting with Los Angeles City Attorney Rocky Delgadillo; "Petition for an Independent Investigation of LAPD Lewd Conduct Arrest Practices," Gay and Lesbian Action Alliance, 11 April 2000; AI interview with Andrew Thomas, Lawyer, San Antonio, 4 December 2003.

[128] Michael G. Mooney, "Gay Sex Decoy Rejected," *Modesto Bee*, A1, 13 June 1998.

[129] California Attorney General, at http://caag.state.ca.us/cjsc/statisticsdatatabs/dtabsarrests.htm.

4.1.5.1

VAGUE LAWS AND TARGETED UNDERCOVER ENFORCEMENT OF MORALS REGULATIONS

The Triangle Foundation received reports in Detroit, Michigan, that State Troopers assigned to undercover operations referred to the activity as "bag a fag".[130]

A 38-year-old gay Latino man was in Griffith Park, Los Angeles when someone followed him. He reports that the individual made sexually suggestive motions to him three times. He then exposed his genitals to the individual, an undercover police officer. He reports that the officer's face became "full of hate," so he started running. He fell to the ground and the officer caught up with him, and reportedly punched him repeatedly while yelling, "Don't you run away from me, you motherfucker. You fucking fag." The man was arrested and taken to the medical ward of the jail, where he reportedly received treatment for his injuries from the fall and subsequent beating.[131]

Brian Miller was approached by an undercover police officer in West Hollywood, Los Angeles, who was making sexual advances. Miller reportedly refused suggestions made by the officer to engage in sexual relations, but was arrested by three officers for lewd conduct. Miller spent eight hours in jail and lost his job. He was released without any charges being filed against him. Miller reportedly said, "I was arrested for being gay."[132]

AS NOTED, MOST MORAL REGULATION ENFORCEMENT focuses on statutes such as "lewd conduct," "public obscenity" or "public indecency." Many, if not all, jurisdictions in the United States recognize public lewdness or indecency as a statutory offense. Some statutes prohibiting lewdness or indecency prohibit specific sexual acts or "lewd or indecent conduct" generally in "a public place," "in public" or "in public view," while under other statutes it is enough that the act is intentional and offensive to one or more persons present and as such it is not necessary that the act be committed in a public place.[133] Again, this can lead to arbitrary arrests and detentions of individuals based on an officer's "subjective" view of lewd conduct and, if applied selectively, would be in violation of both the UDHR and the ICCPR.

AI and other organizations including ACLU, LAMBDA and the Detroit Triangle Foundation are concerned that vaguely worded regulations lend themselves to discriminatory application since these laws and regulations leave almost entirely to an officer's judgment the definition of offending conduct.[134] The statutes thereby create a discretionary decision-making power regarding what is considered "immoral" or "offensive" behavior, and may be prone to abuse on the basis of homophobia, racism or sexism. Reports to AI indicate that morals regulations are prejudicially applied to gay people while no such action is taken against heterosexual persons engaging in similar activity. For example, acts that heterosexual couples can openly engage in, such as kissing, may be regarded as "offensive" when engaged in by gay couples.

---

[130] Interview with Crystal Witt, Triangle Foundation, Detroit, 19 March 2004. Such operations were reportedly ongoing from 1995 to 2004. Email to AI from Sean Kosofsky, Director of Policy, Triangle Foundation, Detroit, 6 August 2005. See also, Rudy Serra, "'Bag a Fag' Operations in Michigan, Police Misconduct, Entrapment and Crimes Against Gay Men," Triangle Foundation, 3 May 2000, available at: http://www.tri.org/tripdfs/bagfag.pdf.

[131] LACLC Anti-Violence Project, Hate Crime Incident Report Form, Los Angeles, 10 September 1999.

[132] Tony Ortega, "Gay Dismay: The Sheriff's Department Transfers Two Deputies Involved in 'Unauthorized' Undercover Arrests," *New Times Los Angeles* (California), 2 November 2000.

[133] Wharton's Criminal Law (15th ed.) § § 307, 308. See also: 50 Am Jurisprudence 2d, Lewdness, Indecency, and Obscenity § 1.

[134] The Michigan Chapter of the American Civil Liberties Union (ACLU) and the Triangle Foundation sued the Detroit Police Department in federal court for the discriminatory application of the city's "annoying person" and solicitation ordinances to gay men gathering at the city's Rouge Park, and achieved a $170,000 settlement as well as the revision of the two ordinances: Darren A. Nichols, "Detroit Settles Lawsuit Over Police Sting on Gays," *Detroit News*, 16 May 2002, 02D; LAMBDA challenged inappropriate and discriminatory applications of the California Penal Code section 647(a), California's lewd conduct in Los Angeles. *LAMBDA Legal Defense and Education Fund v. Los Angeles Police Department.*; Myron D. Quon, "Selective Enforcement of Lewd Conduct Laws: Police Targeting of Gay Men in Los Angeles," Lambda Legal, 1 June 1997.

- **Detroit, Michigan:** The city of Detroit settled a lawsuit filed by the ACLU of Michigan and several men who alleged police used vague city ordinances to unfairly entrap them at Rouge Park. Officers enticed and arrested about 500 men during the sting operation, then impounded their cars. Officers used the vaguely worded "annoying persons" ordinances to ticket the men, many of whom were simply talking with other men or flirting. The men's vehicles were also impounded, and they were forced to either pay $900 to reclaim the vehicles or contest the ticket in court.[135]

- **Massachusetts:** Following a lawsuit filed by Gay and Lesbian Advocates and Defenders on behalf of a gay man harassed by Massachusetts State Troopers, the State Police issued new guidelines in March 2001 specifying that "socializing and expressions of affection" are not considered sexual conduct, and that public sexual conduct is not illegal unless there is a "substantial risk" that the conduct will be observed by a casual passerby.[136]

In a number of cities, law enforcement agencies utilize targeted undercover operations as a primary means of enforcing of morals regulations.[137] Undercover officers patrol areas known to be frequented by gay men and invite sexual or lewd conduct by their words or behavior. These actions have been questioned by organizations such as LAMBDA Legal Education and Defense Fund, who point out that the requirement in many lewd conduct statutes that a third party be "offended" may not be met when no other person was present apart from the undercover officer who by his actions solicited or encouraged the conduct.[138]

- **Los Angeles:** California Penal Code Section 647(a) prohibits "lewd or dissolute conduct in any public place or in any place open to the public or exposed to public view."[139] Over the past decades, advocates and courts alike have criticized the LAPD's enforcement of public morals regulations as discriminatory, arbitrary and abusive with respect to gay men.[140] Discriminatory enforcement of such regulations in Los Angeles still appears to persist;[141] for example, LAPD's enforcement activities are reportedly concentrated in areas where gay men are thought to congregate. AI heard reports that LAPD enforcement efforts were stepped up during the weekend of West Hollywood's LGBT Pride festival in 2003, resulting in arrests of over 40 men over the weekend, despite the fact that West Hollywood is technically outside the jurisdiction of the LAPD.[142]

---

[135] Darren A. Nichols, "Detroit Settles Lawsuit Over Police Sting on Gays," *Detroit News*, 16 May 2002.

[136] Andrea Estes, "New Rules Alter Line Drawn on Public Sex," *Boston Globe*, 2 March 2001. See also General Order in investigating sexual activity in public spaces by the Massachusetts State Police, copy of Order available at: http://www.glad.org/GLAD_Cases/generalorder.shtml.

[137] For example, in Los Angeles, San Antonio and Columbus, Ohio. Jeb Phillips, "Men Still Cruising at Park; Crackdown on sex in Gahanna woods hasn't fazed many," *Columbus Dispatch*, 18 October 2002, 01B.

[138] See for example: Myro Dean Quon, WRO Staff Attorney, "Selective Enforcement of Lewd Conduct Laws: Police Targeting of Gay Men in Los Angeles," 1 June 1997; "LAMBDA Back in Court for LAPD Lewd Conduct Arrest Records: Documents sought to establish that police still purposely target gay men," 20 January 2000; *LAMBDA Legal Defense and Education Fund v. Los Angeles Police Department*, press release available at: http://cache.lambdalegal.org/cgi-bin/iowa/cases/record?record=135. In Roanoke, Virginia, Circuit Court juries acquitted gay men charged with soliciting undercover police officers for oral sex in two separate cases, after hearing arguments that the undercover officers had been the ones who had pursued the topic of sex during their conversations in the park: Laurence Hammack, "Charges dropped in 2 park sex cases; Decision made after 2 other defendants acquitted," *Roanoke Times*, 24 September 1999.

[139] Cal. Pen. Code § 647 (2005)

[140] The California Supreme Court has repeatedly noted that California Penal Code Section 647(a), which prohibits "lewd conduct," has been selectively enforced against gay men. In the case of a gay man who reportedly "solicited an undercover police officer to perform an act of oral copulation" the California Supreme Court noted that the nature of conduct criminalized by California Penal Code Section 647(a) makes it susceptible to discriminatory enforcement: Pryor v. Municipal Court, 25 Cal.3d 238, 252, n.8 (1979). In an effort to stem discriminatory enforcement practices, the California Supreme Court stipulated that, for a person to be convicted, the prohibited conduct must occur in the presence of another person or persons who may be offended by it: People v. Rylaarsdam, 130 Cal. App.3d Supp. (1982). *See also:* People v. Superior Court *(Caswell)*, 46 Cal.3d 381, 401, n.10 (1988); Baluyut v. Superior Court, 12 Cal.4th 826, 830-31 (1996).

[141] Lambda reviewed arrest reports from March and April 2001, finding 10 cases where individuals were arrested although the reports show that no person was present other than an undercover officer, who solicited or encouraged the conduct. Letter from City Attorney James K. Hahn to LAMBDA Legal Defense and Education Fund, Inc., 3 May 2001; AI interview with Martha Matthews, former staff attorney, and Sharon Murphy, chapter coordinator, ACLU of Southern California, 3 October 2003. Remarks of Jon Davidson, LAMBDA Legal Defense and Education Fund, 24 January 2002, at a meeting with Los Angeles City Attorney Rocky Delgadillo; Petition for an Independent Commission on Selective and Prejudicial Enforcement Practices, Gay and Lesbian Action Alliance, 5 May 1998; Letter Brief to California Supreme Court in Tucker v. Municipal Court, Supreme Court No. S080680, LAMBDA Legal Defense and Education Fund, 16 August 1999.

[142] AI community meeting, 26 January 2004.

Reports involving park or transit police have also alleged such abuse, raising concerns of lack of training, supervision and accountability for officers charged with policing activities prone to misconduct, but without the experience or training of formal police departments.

- **New York:** On 18 November 2004, a federal jury awarded a gay man $1.1 million after finding that his rights had been violated during an arrest for public lewdness in a New York Port Authority bathroom, and that the Port Authority had a policy of making such arrests. According to Alejandro Martinez, he was on his way to work when he entered the men's room and a man he later learned was an officer flirted with him. "He looked at me," Martinez said. "He gave me a smile." Martinez reportedly ignored him and went to the urinal. When Martinez went to wash his hands the man stood between him and the sinks, so he quickly left. The man reportedly followed him outside, called him back and said, "You know you are under arrest." Another plainclothes officer said, "Wow, look how fast you got the first one," and the first officer responded, "Yeah, I did a good trap," according to Martinez. When he objected, Martinez said the first officer clenched his fist in front of his face and said, "You calling me a liar? You want me to break your teeth?" Later, as he was being processed, Martinez said he heard another officer refer to him and the six other men arrested on that morning as "faggots" and "queers." When one of the men arrested complained, an officer reportedly said, "I can't do anything about that. I've got a quota to fill." Martinez also reported that he was held for 18 hours and endured homophobic abuse and threats of violence from the police. In September 2000, Martinez was acquitted of the public lewdness charge in a state trial.[143]

- **San Antonio:** Reports to AI indicate a pattern of officers engaging in entrapment techniques, soliciting and inviting prohibited conduct. Several advocates expressed concern to AI about practices whereby officers entice gay men into sex acts, then arrest them on charges of indecent exposure. LGBT advocates have been raising their concerns about undercover activities for several years.[144] Undercover operations were suspended while SAPD conducted a review, however, they were reinstated in March 2003. Following the review, the Chief of San Antonio Park Police, Steven W. Baum, was asked to implement recommendations arising from the findings. Recommendations included no longer using the same five officers for covert operations, but instead having 20 officers volunteer for the assignment. Reportedly, SAPD provided video and audio surveillance equipment and trained the Park Police on how to conduct the operations. According to the chief, the Park Police now conduct stings in areas frequented by lesbians as well as heterosexuals, and no longer focus only on gay men, as in past operations. Nevertheless, data provided by the Park Police appears to suggest that gay men continue to be targeted and arrested—43 cases involving single men were recorded, compared with only eight heterosexual couples through the year up to November 2003.[145] According to park rangers, most arrests occur after rangers run across a man displaying his genitals or masturbating.[146] The Chief of San Antonio Park Police maintains that officers are not "enticing or provoking behavior—we are being accosted."[147] In documentation, analyzed by AI, of previous arrests made during sting operations, however, accounts were given of rangers using words and body language to give the impression that they wanted sex.[148]

In addition to the use of so-called "morals regulations," AI is concerned that even though "sodomy" laws have been struck down following *Lawrence*, such statutes are reportedly still utilized against LGBT individuals in some areas. For example in Virginia, a judge recently sentenced a man to six months in prison reportedly for "solicitation

---

[143] Duncan Osborne, "Cops' Entrapment Scheme Busted," *Gay City News*, Vol. 3, Issue 348, 25 November-1 December 2004. Available at: http://gaycitynews.com/gcn_348/copsentrapmentscheme.html.

[144] For example, The Gay and Lesbian Community Center of San Antonio met with Parks and Recreation officials in November 1999 and asked them to suspend covert operations. (Gip Plaster, "Travel Warning Issued to Gay Men About San Antonio," 6 January 2000, available at: http://www.baybs.com/news/2000/01/06/NationalNews/Travel.Warning.Issued.To.Gay.Men.About.San.Antonio-35414.shtml). The Center also raised concerns with the US Justice Department and asked officials to investigate claims of misconduct and civil rights violations against gay men. The Justice Department reportedly asked San Antonio Parks and Recreations Department to conduct an investigation.

[145] San Antonio Park Police, Covert Operations Unit, Monthly Activity Report, November 2003.

[146] Debbie Nathan, "'Homo Patrol': Are San Antonio Rangers the Real Perverts in the Park?" *San Antonio Current* online, 27 January-4 February 2000.

[147] AI interview with Chief Steven W. Baum, San Antonio Park Police, 4 December 2003.

[148] Gay and Lesbian Community Center of San Antonio, Police Entrapment Reports, (1999-2001).

of sodomy" after he was arrested for propositioning an undercover officer in a public restroom.[149] Furthermore, it has been reported in New York that 296 arrests between 1981 and 2001 were made under New York State's law against consensual "sodomy," although the law had been declared unconstitutional in 1980.[150] Arbitrary arrest and detention is prohibited under international law.[151]

AI is concerned about reports from advocates alleging that arrests are frequently based on misrepresentation of events by undercover police officers, who often are the only witnesses to the alleged offense. Allegations have been made that police officers in Los Angeles "embellish or fictionalize aspects of a police report to justify the arrest" in such cases.[152] Advocates also charge that the standard language used in police reports is rarely amended to reflect the individual circumstances of the incident, raising concerns about their veracity. In Detroit and Los Angeles, advocates with access to a representative number of arrest reports have noted that the reports bore a remarkable similarity. AI reviewed several reports in San Antonio and observed the same pattern.

AI is also concerned by reports in Chicago, Los Angeles, New York, Washington D.C. and Detroit that indicate police target locations where Latino, African American and/or South Asian, as well as immigrant individuals, are reported to congregate for lewd conduct enforcement.[153] In Los Angeles, 54 percent of arrests made between August 1999 and July 2001 were of men of color (41 percent Latino and 11 percent African American).[154] Targeting an individual on this basis of his or her race and/or sexual orientation violates the right to be free from discrimination under international law and standards.[155]

- **Los Angeles:** "On the afternoon of Thursday, June 10, 1999, I accompanied [a defense attorney] on some discovery defense work with regard to a particular case… As we approached the site and parked, I noticed a middle-aged Latino man walking towards the bathroom. We … walked toward the bathrooms. The walk to the bathroom took less than one minute. Upon entering the bathroom, I observed a tall Caucasian man … the Latino who previously walked into the bathroom was in one of the bathroom stalls. I began assisting in taking measurements and notes, and observed the Latino man exit the bathroom stall and walk past us. The Caucasian man stopped the Latino man, identified himself as a police officer and told the Latino man that he was under arrest for lewd conduct … At no time did I see the Latino man engage in any wrongful or lewd conduct."[156]

Discriminatory policing of morals regulations has a potentially severe impact on LGBT immigrants, who could face deportation as a consequence of a conviction, since a felony charge is a deportable offense, and charges considered moral turpitude negatively impact immigration proceedings.[157] Furthermore, policing of parks and other public

149 Adrian Brune, "VA Man Sentenced for Sodomy Solicitation," The WashingtonBlade.com, 20 February 2004, available at: http://www.washblade.com/2004/2-20/news/localnews/sentanced.cfm. See also: Justin Bergman, "Anti-Sodomy Code Challenged/ Convict's Case Cites High Court Ruling Abolishing Texas Law," The Associated Press, *Richmond Times Dispatch* (Virginia), 14 July 2004. Other reports include a man who was reportedly charged and jailed under a repealed "importuning law" in Ohio: Eric Resnick, "Man jailed for breaking law that wasn't in effect," *Gay People's Chronicle*, 19 September 2003.

150 The text of the law had remained in penal code books that police officers use to decide what charges to bring against a defendant, and was not removed before 2000 after intense lobbying by the Empire State Pride Agenda and others. Officials claimed that most of these charges would have been changed to "public lewdness" but declined to check District Attorney records. Duncan Osborne, "Sodomy Busts Continue Years After Law Nixed," *Gay City News*, 14-20 March 2003.

151 International Covenant on Civil and Political Rights, G.A. res. 2200A (XXI), 21 U.N. GAOR Supp. (No. 16) at 52, U.N. Doc. A/6316 (1966), 999 U.N.T.S. 171, *entered into force* 23 March 1976.

152 Petition for an Independent Investigation of LAPD Lewd Conduct Arrest Practices, Gay and Lesbian Action Alliance, 11 April 2000.

153 AI interviews with Jeffrey King, In the Meantime Men, 2 October 2003; Martha Matthews, former staff attorney, and Sharon Murphy, chapter coordinator, ACLU of Southern California, 3 October 2003; Association of Latin Men for Action (ALMA), Chicago, 16 September 2003; Pradeep Singla, Attorney, New York, 19 February 2004; Audre Lorde Project, New York, 10 March 2004; Sean Kosofsky, Triangle Foundation, Detroit, 19 March 2004.

154 Remarks of Jon Davidson, Senior Counsel, LAMBDA Legal Defense and Education Fund, 24 January 2000 at LGBT community forum on police enforcement.

155 Art. 2, International Convention on the Elimination of All Forms of Racial Discrimination, 660 U.N.T.S. 195, *entered into force* Jan. 4, 1969; Art. 2, International Covenant on Civil and Political Rights, G.A. res. 2200A (XXI), 21 U.N. GAOR Supp. (No. 16) at 52, U.N. Doc. A/6316 (1966), 999 U.N.T.S. 171, *entered into force* Mar. 23, 1976.

156 Statement of Jeffrey Scroger, UCLA law student, submitted with the Gay and Lesbian Action Alliance, Petition for an Independent Investigation of LAPD Lewd Conduct Arrest Practices, 11 April 2000.

157 ACLU of Southern California, Los Angeles, September 2003.

areas particularly affects individuals with limited financial means and individuals who are not "out" to their families or neighbors, since these are often the only spaces where they are able to meet and socialize.[158]

AI believes that the discriminatory aspects of targeted lewd conduct operations create an atmosphere conducive to misconduct and abuse. AI is concerned by reports of ill-treatment in connection with undercover operations.[159]

- **San Antonio:** Two men in San Antonio were reportedly beaten when they were arrested for lewd conduct. Allegedly one man was kicked, beaten and punched. The other man ran into the woods and waited for the police to leave; when he came back for his car, police patrolling the area saw him and he was reportedly also beaten.[160]

Police officials told AI that targeted enforcement of morals statutes is in response to community complaints.[161] However, in Los Angeles both the Christopher Commission[162] and advocates have challenged the LAPD's reliance on public complaints as justification for the enforcement of Section 647(a), noting that arrests are rarely based on current complaints by members of the public.[163] Comments to AI by LAPD officials suggest that complaints may be kept open indefinitely.[164] In San Antonio, officials told AI "most of this work is complaint driven" and if "complaints come in often enough, we have to deal with it."[165] However, AI received reports from advocates that such complaints are often vague and homophobic in nature, and may not specifically relate to sexual activity but rather to the presence of gay men in parks.[166] The Supreme Court of California upheld an appeals court determination that lewd conduct charges in the town of Mountain View were the result of discriminatory enforcement against gay men. The trial court had examined police records for a two-year period and determined that "the officers' method of operation was designed to ferret out homosexuals ... without any relationship to the alleged problems at that location for which the citizen complaint had been initially lodged."[167] Under the UN Code of Conduct for Law Enforcement Agencies, states must act to ensure that all parts of the population are protected equally.[168] To ensure greater transparency around morals enforcement, AI calls upon authorities to release the number and nature of complaints.

> "The biggest problem we are having from the standpoint of wrongfully charged defendants is that 95 percent of them are so embarrassed by the charge, either indecent exposure, lewd behavior or assault [sexual] on an officer, they are afraid to fight."
>
> Andrew Thomas, Civil Attorney, San Antonio, Texas[169]

---

158 AI interview with Members of Anonymous LGBT Youth Program, Los Angeles, 29 January 2004.

159 Los Angeles Gay and Lesbian Center, Hate Crime Incident Report; AI interview with Andrew Thomas, Attorney, San Antonio, 4 December 2003; Anti-Violence Project, Los Angeles, 10 September 1999.

160 AI interview with Andrew Thomas, Attorney, San Antonio, 4 December 2003.

161 AI interviews with Captain Downing, Hollywood-Wilcox Station, LAPD, 26 January 2004; Chief Albert Ortiz, San Antonio Police Department, 4 December 2003.

162 The Christopher Commission is an independent commission chaired by attorney Warren Christopher that investigated the LAPD after Rodney King was beaten severely by the LAPD on 3 March 1991. The commission investigated the structure of the LAPD, including recruitment, training practices, internal disciplinary action and its citizen complaint system.

163 AI interview with Jim Lafferty, National Lawyers Guild, Los Angeles, 30 October 2003; remarks of Jon Davidson, Senior Counsel, LAMBDA Legal Defense and Education Fund, 24 January 2000 at LGBT community forum on police enforcement; remarks of Jon Davidson, LAMBDA Legal Defense and Education Fund, 24 January 2002, at a meeting with Los Angeles City Attorney Rocky Delgadillo; letter from LAMBDA Legal Defense and Education Fund, Inc. to LAPD Commander Willie L. Pannell, 2 April 2001; letter brief to California Supreme Court in *Tucker v. Municipal Court*, Supreme Court No. S080680, LAMBDA Legal Defense Education Fund, 16 August 1999.

164 AI interview with Captain Downing, Hollywood-Wilcox Station, LAPD, 26 January 2004 (citizen complaints "can stay open as long as the problem exists.")

165 AI interview with Chief Albert Ortiz, San Antonio Police Department, San Antonio, 4 December 2003.

166 AI interview with Andrew Thomas, Lawyer, San Antonio, 4 December 2003.

167 Baluyut v. Superior Court, 911 P.2d 1 (Cal. 2000)

168 Art. 2, UN Code of Conduct for Law Enforcement Officials, G.A. res. 34/169, annex, 34 U.N. GAOR Supp. (No. 46) at 186, U.N. Doc. A/34/46 (1979).

169 AI interview with Andrew Thomas, Lawyer, San Antonio, 4 December 2003.

> "I think the overall thing is that this was a policy that took advantage of the humiliation of being arrested for public lewdness … They counted on the fact that people were so humiliated that they would accept a guilty plea."
>
> Michael L. Spiegel, Attorney representing gay man charged with public lewdness in New York[170]

The discriminatory and selective enforcement aspects of targeted lewd conduct operations not only create an atmosphere conducive to abuse, but also foster a climate of impunity. Officers are often able to act, secure in the knowledge that their behavior will not be investigated thoroughly or indeed at all. AI is concerned that many individuals charged under morals regulations may not challenge an officer's version of events, questionable entrapment techniques or abuse as they are silenced out of fear of their sexual orientation being revealed, public embarrassment, loss of employment or immigration repercussions.[171] Furthermore, many of those arrested are unable to afford the costs of mounting a defense.[172] This exacerbates the climate of impunity. As a result, individuals may be wrongfully convicted of a criminal offense, carrying potentially significant consequences.[173]

Police reportedly fuel stigmatization of gay men in some locations by releasing information to the media, leading to televised arrests or local papers printing the names of those arrested under such statutes.[174] The stigmatization of gay men in San Antonio is further demonstrated by the media's coverage of the arrests of gay men in sting operations, often, allegedly, after having been tipped off by law enforcement. A local TV station aired a news segment entitled "Perverts in the Park," showing men being led out of the bathrooms after being arrested for indecent exposure, believed by advocates to have fueled undercover efforts and further complaints from citizens. Such disclosure may be in contravention of Article 4 of the Code of Conduct for Law Enforcement Officials, which stipulates that law enforcement must respect privacy and confidentiality.

- **San Antonio:** Benny Hogan was arrested as part of a sting operation by the San Antonio Police Department. Soon after, his name appeared in a local media account of the park arrests. Three days after the article appeared, Hogan went into his garage and hanged himself. His family filed a civil lawsuit against *San Antonio Express-News*. The *Express-News* has since ceased printing the names of those arrested for indecent exposure.[175]

The new Park Commissioner in San Antonio told AI that he has taken steps so that the media are not alerted to where arrests are being made, although he indicated that sometimes the media are waiting at the jail and are always focused on gay men.[176]

However, according to some advocates, these operations do little to curb sexual activity at the targeted locations regardless of whether the media is alerted to the arrests or not. Instead, several US organizations advocate the use of alternative methods such as posting warning signs, additional lighting, writing tickets, and patrols by uniformed police, arguing this will curtail sexual activity without resorting to humiliating and abusive practices.[177] In some

---

[170] Duncan Osborne, "Cops' Entrapment Scheme Busted," *Gay City News*, Vol. 3, Issue 348, 25 November-1 December 2004. Available at: http://gaycitynews.com/gcn_348/copsentrapmentscheme.html.

[171] Advocates in San Antonio report that employers and media are promptly notified of arrests, especially if they are of someone notable. AI interview with Andrew Thomas, Attorney, San Antonio, 4 December 2003.

[172] AI interviews with Martha Matthews, former staff attorney, and Sharon Murphy, chapter coordinator, ACLU of Southern California, 3 October 2003; Ken Miele, Esq., 30 October 2003.

[173] Individuals labeled "sex offenders" are required to register with law enforcement agencies, and the label may impact a person's ability to adopt or foster a child. Low-income individuals are adversely impacted if their cars are impounded, which can be costly and may mean difficulty in meeting job requirements, particularly in many areas of the US with underdeveloped public transportation systems. Advocates also note that convictions can result in loss of the ability to adopt a child, loss of employment and professional licenses as well as deportation. Martha Matthews, former staff attorney, and Sharon Murphy, Chapter coordinator, ACLU, Los Angeles, 3 October 2003.

[174] AI has heard reports of publishing of names in San Antonio, TX; East Hampton, NY; Ottawa, IL; Tupelo, MS; and Lathrop, CA. TV coverage has reportedly taken place in San Antonio, TX and Jefferson County, MO; New Orleans, LA; Roseville, MN; Providence, RI; and Milwaukee, WV. Following such public humiliation, arrestees have reportedly committed suicide in San Antonio and Providence.

[175] AI interview with Rick Gipprich, San Antonio Rape Crisis Center, San Antonio, 2 December 2003; Yvonne, PFLAG, San Antonio, 4 December 2003; LGBT Rights and Policing Activist, San Antonio, 15 October 2003.

[176] AI interview with Chief Steven Baum, San Antonio Park Police, 4 December 2003.

[177] AI interview with Martha Matthews, former staff attorney, and Sharon Murphy, chapter coordinator, ACLU, Los Angeles, 3 October 2003; see also Doug Caruso, "Coalition Offers Ways to Combat Public Sex," *Columbus Dispatch*, 6 August 2001, 1C.

cities, organizations have emphasized dialogue between the police and affected communities, focusing on providing training and education as well as a commitment from the police to investigate allegations of misconduct.[178] For instance, the City of West Hollywood does not allow enforcement of Section 647(a) within its jurisdiction, while the Los Angeles County Sheriff's Department has reportedly ceased undercover enforcement operations throughout the county due to a lack of resources.[179]

4.1.6
POLICE RAIDS OF LGBT GATHERINGS

AT THE TIME OF THE STONEWALL RIOTS in New York in 1969, police raids of bars and nightclubs frequented by LGBT individuals were a regular occurrence in cities across the United States. For example in the late 1960s, nightly raids on gay bars in Los Angeles—particularly in the Silver Lake district—were reported, leading to a number of arrests and allegations of police brutality.[180] Although raids of gay bars are no longer as widespread,[181] reports indicate continued police targeting of venues where LGBT people socialize. According to the NCAVP, between 1999 and 2003, police raids have been reported in New York, Massachusetts, Michigan, Minnesota, San Francisco, Chicago, Detroit, Houston and St Louis.[182]

Reports to AI indicate that LGBT bars and establishments in traditionally "gay neighborhoods" in some cities are largely allowed to operate without interference by police. AI has heard, however, reports of police targeting LGBT bars catering to transgender individuals and communities of color, particularly in areas outside traditionally gay neighborhoods.[183] Reportedly, police raids in several locations have been attributed to enforcement of administrative codes, such as health department violations; however, advocates charge that such enforcement would not ordinarily be undertaken primarily by police, and that these violations are merely a pretext for harassment and intimidation of bar owners and patrons.[184]

AI is concerned about reports of verbal and physical abuse as well as inhumane and degrading treatment of LGBT individuals during raids. Some raids have reportedly involved high numbers of officers and excessive force against individuals. For example,

- **Fresno, California:** A gay nightclub filed a lawsuit in January 2003, alleging that Fresno police continually harassed the establishment's members and employees. Police officers allegedly made homophobic comments, including comments "about homosexuals being wrong under God's law," during raids of the club.[185]

---

178 AI interviews with Heather Bradley, Night Ministry, Chicago, 24 February 2004; Carmen Vazquez, Deputy Executive Director, Empire State Pride Agenda, New York City, 8 April 2004; Mark Reyes, Bronx Lesbian and Gay Health Resource Consortium, New York City, 11 March 2004. See also Tom Bailey, Jr., "Police, Gay Leaders Meet in Spirit of Cooperation After Public Sex Arrests," *The Commercial Appeal* (Memphis), 3 March 2001.

179 AI interviews with Captain Long, LASD West Hollywood Station, 29 January 2004; Sheriff Baca, Linda Castro and Jeff Prang, 29 January 2004.

180 Len Evans, "Gay Chronicles: California," available at: http://www.geocities.com/gueroperro/Chron1-Calif-page.htm.

181 Karen Matthews, "Three Decades After Riot, Gays and Lesbians Take Stock of Progress," *Associated Press*, 26 June 1999.

182 Note: only 11 to 13 cities across the U.S. report to the National Coalition of AVP. See further: Anti-Lesbian Gay Bisexual and Transgender Violence: A Report of the National Coalition of Anti-Violence Programs 1999, 2000, 2001, 2002, 2003.

183 AI interview with Staff of Anonymous LGBT Service Providers, Los Angeles, 28 October 2003.

184 For example, uniformed or vice officers are reported to enter LGBT bars or parties, ostensibly to check fire code, licensing or health department violations. AI has heard such reports in Los Angeles, California; Chicago, Illinois; and New York City. AI interviews with Julio Rodriguez, President and Executive Director, ALMA, Chicago, 24 February 2004; Yves Michel Fontaine, GMHC, New York, 19 March 2004; APICHA, Outreach Workers, New York, 30 March 2004; Ricci Levy, Executive Director, Woodhull Foundation, 18 March 2004; Martha Mathews and Sharon Murphy, ACLU, Los Angeles, 3 October 2003.

185 Michael Baker, "Nightclub Files Suit, Alleges Harassment," *Fresno Bee*, 10 January 2003.

- **Highland Park, Michigan:** In the early hours of 2 March 2003, police reportedly raided The Power Plant, a popular gay after-hours club, arresting the club owner and several hundred patrons. The club operator was arrested on several charges, including operating an illegal establishment and selling alcohol without a liquor license. Three hundred fifty misdemeanor citations for illegal trespass were issued to the club's patrons, and more than 150 cars were impounded and towed from the scene. Reportedly, 50 to 100 officers stormed the premises dressed in black clothing and using laser sights, causing panic among patrons. Patrons were bound with their hands behind their back and forced to lay face-down on the concrete floor, in some cases for more than eight hours. Reports indicate that those arrested were not permitted to use the bathroom and several were forced to relieve themselves where they lay. Some reported being kicked in the head and back, slammed into walls and verbally abused. Reportedly, officers were heard saying, "Those fags in there make me sick." The Wayne County Sheriff's Department claimed they were acting on complaints from neighbors and were acting in response to concerns of public safety.[186]

- **New York:** On 16 November 2003, a Pinoy[187] transgender man reported attending a fundraising event in Brooklyn, New York. The fundraising event was attended by many LGBT people of color. Police officers reportedly saw four individuals standing outside the event drinking alcoholic beverages in public, a misdemeanor offense. The transgender activist reportedly took photographs of two undercover officers. Two officers allegedly grabbed him, pushed him down on the trunk of the car, kicked his legs apart and repeatedly hit his head against the trunk, then handcuffed him. According to witnesses, the police began indiscriminately spraying people with mace (a type of pepper spray), punching people, beating them with billy-clubs and dragging them along the sidewalk. The transgender man reported witnessing a "queer"[188] Latino man in a fetal position on the ground being kicked by four officers. He also reported seeing police pull a black woman by her hair to the ground and beat her with their batons. According to the organization holding the event, at least 20 people suffered injuries in the course of the incident, including blunt trauma, lacerations, contusions and lower back spasms. One person reportedly required medical treatment for a hematoma on his right frontal skull caused by a severe blow to the head. Eight people were reportedly arrested but all charges against them were later dismissed at trial. AI understands that a civil lawsuit against NYPD is now pending.

AI believes the types of treatment alleged constitute torture or cruel, inhuman or degrading treatment in contravention of international standards,[189] and further violates standards requiring that law enforcement officials respect and protect human dignity and maintain and uphold the human rights of all persons.[190] Law enforcement officials also must use force only when strictly necessary and only after non-violent means are attempted first, with any use of force proportional to the lawful objectives and with restraint.[191] Furthermore, selective targeting of individuals based on their sexual orientation, gender identity or expression, or race violates international standards under ICERD and the ICCPR that prohibit discrimination.

---

186 Letter to Chief of Staff Don Cox, Wayne County Sheriff's Department, from Jeffrey Montgomery, Executive Director, Triangle Foundation, 11 March 2003; AI interview with Sean Kosofsky, Director of Policy, and Crystal Witt, Victim Advocate, Triangle Foundation; Detroit, 19 March 2004.

187 An American of Filipino descent. The term is used as a form of ethnic pride.

188 Queer: as used in the US context of identity politics, is an umbrella term for a range of sexual orientations and gender identities that include lesbian, gay, bisexual and transgender.

189 Article 16(1), Convention Against Torture and Other Cruel, Inhuman and Degrading Treatment or Punishment, G.A. res. 39/46 [Annex 39 U.N. GAOR Supp. (No. 51) at 197, U.N. Doc. A/39/51 (1984)] *entered into force* 26 June 1987.

190 Article 2, Code of Conduct for Law Enforcement Officials, G.A. Res. 34/169, (17 December 1979).

191 International Human Rights Standards for Law Enforcement, A Pocket Book on Human Rights for the Police, available at: http://www.unhchr.ch/html/menu6/2/pocketbook.pdf.

4.1.7

DEMONSTRATIONS: TARGETING OF LGBT DEMONSTRATORS AND ACTIVISTS

AI HAS HEARD REPORTS indicating that law enforcement officers have targeted for abuse and arrest protestors at demonstrations on LGBT issues, as well as LGBT contingents or participants in more general protests. One advocate in New York told AI, "There is a tendency to separate queer activists from the others."[192]

Increasingly, across the United States law enforcement agencies are employing a range of tactics aimed at controlling crowds at large gatherings and demonstrations. AI has previously raised concerns that such tactics have resulted in serious human rights abuses.[193] Furthermore, the security measures instituted after the September 11 attacks, including the 2001 USA Patriot Act, reportedly have further had a chilling effect on the right to protest.[194] In New York City, advocates claimed that the creation of an NYPD Counter Terrorism Bureau had increased police powers to investigate political activity, and resulted in greater law enforcement presence and severely aggressive policing tactics at demonstrations. AI has received reports that law enforcement personnel have selectively targeted LGBT contingents and activists at demonstrations; employed excessive force at LGBT demonstrations and rallies; used homophobic and transphobic slurs; and arbitrarily detained and searched individuals.

- **New York:** In March 2003, NYPD officers reportedly verbally and physically abused members of "Irish Queers," who had erected a platform on which to protest the exclusion of LGBT individuals in the annual parade to mark St Patrick's Day. J.F. Mulligan was reportedly slapped across the face by an officer who shoved Mulligan's face against the metal grating of a partition inside the police van. Mulligan claims that at the precinct he heard another officer say, "Little faggots all over the place today." Another member, Emmaia Gelman, reported that she was grabbed by officers who pulled her onto the roof of a police truck where they were stationed, and one officer laid her down so that her head hung over the side, while clamping down on her neck with his boot. She alleges that she was then handcuffed and dragged headfirst off the police vehicle.[195]

Advocates reported to AI that transgender and gender variant demonstrators tend to be selectively targeted by police.

- **San Antonio:** After refusing to show her ID at a political demonstration on 30 October 2003, a lesbian woman was arrested. Officers allegedly pulled her to the ground and kneed her in the back. She reported bruises across the front of her chest from the pavement, and scratches and bruising on her back. At the police station, she reports that officers pulled up profiles on their computer and repeatedly asked her, "Are you this man? No, you can't be, you're too ugly." Eventually, when the officers saw her ID, they housed her with the women.[196]

- **San Francisco:** At a demonstration that took place in 2003, most of the transgender activists who were detained were reportedly subjected to strip and cavity searches while reportedly very few of the other detainees were searched.[197]

---

[192] AI interview with Jennifer Flynn, New York City AIDS Housing Network, 3 March 2004.

[193] Letter to Oakland Police Department, 14 April 2003, Ref.: AMR 51/056/2003; letter to Chicago Police Department, 28 March 2003, Ref.: AMR 51/036/2003; letter to Jeb Bush, Ref.: AMR 51/160/2003. Furthermore, the security measures instituted after the September 11 attacks, including the 2001 USA Patriot Act, have reportedly further had a chilling effect on the right to protest. See: *Civil Rights Concerns in the Metropolitan Washington, D.C. Area in the Aftermath of the September 11th, 2001 Tragedies*, Chapter 4: National Crises, Civil Rights and Civil Liberties: A Historical Review, available at www.usccr.gov/pubs/sac/dc0603/ch4.htm.

[194] The 2001 Patriot Act created a broad definition of "domestic terrorism". The law defines "domestic terrorism" as acts committed in the United States "dangerous to human life that are a violation of the criminal laws," if the US government determines that they "appear to be intended" to "influence the policy of a government by intimidation or coercion," or "to intimidate or coerce a civilian population." See: http://www.amnestyusa.org/waronterror/patriotact/

[195] Mick Meenan, "Two Grassroots Busts on St. Pat's – On Fifth Avenue, Activists Faced Swift Arrest; In Park Slope Accommodation Reached," *Gay City News*, 27 March 2003.

[196] AI interview, Esperanza Center Community Meeting, 4 December 2003.

[197] AI interview with Dylan Vade, Transgender Law Center, San Francisco, 23 October 2003.

- **San Francisco:** In another incident, an activist reported to AI that she witnessed the harassment of a transgender man during an anti-war demonstration in March 2003. She reported that she was detained with the transgender protestor and a large group of other demonstrators in a covered parking lot for about 10 hours before being transferred to the county jail, where they were again detained outside in the cold because the facility was full. She told AI that police officers wanted to subject the transgender activist to a "medical test" to prove that he was biologically female for placement purposes. She alleges that she overheard one female officer interrogate the transgender activist in front of a crowd of people and say to him, "Just answer me: Do you have a penis or a vagina?" She described the whole event as "truly horrible" and dehumanizing.[198]

AI is concerned at reports that LGBT demonstrators were detained and denied medication despite carrying necessary prescriptions and identification. AI heard reports of transgender individuals and LGBT people of color being detained for longer than other protestors before being released following an arrest at a demonstration.

- **New York:** Activists in New York reported that when Operation Homeland Resistance conducted civil disobedience in New York City in May 2003, a number of LGBT activists were arrested. According to organizers, "a higher percentage of women, the majority people of color, and the majority of queer people were detained overnight while others were released only after six hours." The last person reportedly released from police detention several days later was a black lesbian.[199]

- **Miami, Florida:** A white transgender woman was arrested at a protest in 2003 and detained in the general men's population. She was reportedly in possession of hormones and other medications, which were accompanied by a prescription, but according to her attorney, she was denied access to her medications for the three days she was detained. She related to her attorney that she was strip-searched "extra times" because she was transgender and was verbally harassed by law enforcement personnel. Her attorney also raised concerns that she was housed with the male population. She has reportedly been charged with a felony violation for possession of a controlled substance—allegedly for being in possession of prescription medication without a prescription.[200]

The right of peaceful assembly is a basic human right.[201] The Basic Principles on the Use of Force and Firearms by Law Enforcement Officials stipulate that, when dispersing assemblies, force must be avoided, or, where that is not possible, it is minimally used.[202] Furthermore, international standards prohibit arbitrary arrest and detention and require that law enforcement officials protect the health of persons in their custody.[203]

---

[198] Emails from Livi Yoshioka-Maxwell to AIUSA, 18 February 2004 and 22 April 2005. Email from AIUSA to Livi Yoshioka-Maxwell, 22 April 2005.

[199] Press Release: "Operation Homeland Resistance Closes Out Week One of Civil Disobedience Actions: Protesters Vow to Escalate 'Homeland Resistance,'" 8 May 2003. AI interview with Rickke Mananzala, New York City, 23 March 2004.

[200] As reported during AI interview with Dean Spade, Attorney, Sylvia Rivera Law Project, New York City, 19 February 2004.

[201] Art. 21 and Art. 22(1) International Covenant on Civil and Political Rights, G.A. res. 2200A (XXI), 21 U.N. GAOR Supp. (No. 16) at 52, U.N. Doc. A/6316 (1966), 999 U.N.T.S. 171, *entered into force* 23 March 1976. See also Art. 20 of the Universal Declaration of Human Rights, G.A. res. 217A (III), U.N. Doc A/810 at 71 (1948).

[202] Basic Principles on the Use of Force and Firearms by Law Enforcement Officials, Eighth U.N. Congress on the Prevention of Crime and the Treatment of Offenders, principles 12, 13.

[203] See: Art. 9, ICCPR, G.A. res. 2200A (XXI), 21 U.N. GAOR Supp. (No. 16) at 52, U.N. Doc. A/6316 (1966), 999 U.N.T.S. 171, *entered into force* Mar. 23, 1976; and Article 6, Code of Conduct for Law Enforcement Officials, G.A. res. 34/169, annex, 34 U.N. GAOR Supp. (No. 46) at 186, UN Doc. A/34/46 (1979).

4.2

"QUALITY OF LIFE" ENFORCEMENT AND GENTRIFICATION

"[How] do we ensure that age or skin color or national origin or harmless mannerisms will not also become the basis for distinguishing the undesirable from the desirable? We can offer no wholly satisfactory answer to this important question. We are not confident that there is a satisfactory answer except to hope that by their selection, training and supervision, the police will be inculcated with a clear sense of the outer limit of their discretionary authority."

James Q. Wilson and George L. Kelling, "Broken Windows"[204]

"Quality of life ordinances make it much easier for the local police force to criminalize, harass and arrest LGBT and people of color."

Testimony of Trishala Deb, program coordinator of the Audre Lorde Project[205]

"Being black and being trans gives the police the right to do what they want. I was sitting on a stoop trying to find something in my bag. An officer from the 10th Precinct asked me for my ID and then gave me a ticket for disorderly conduct. The officer told me that if he saw me in the area again, he would arrest me. I told him that he'd better get used to seeing me because I worked in offices nearby. When it went to court the summons was dismissed—thankfully, I have a good lawyer."

AI telephone interview with transgender woman, 26 February 2004

"ZERO TOLERANCE" AND "QUALITY OF LIFE" POLICING is a law-enforcement strategy that seeks to create public order by aggressively enforcing laws against minor offenses; for example, public drunkenness, loitering, vandalism, littering or public urination.[206] This method of policing is premised on a theory, which asserts that minor social disorder, if left unattended, causes serious crime. Leading the way for other police departments both nationally and internationally, New York City began implementing a "quality of life" initiative in 1993. While the approach has been credited with a reduction in the city's crime rate,[207] the increased arrest rates for minor offences, largely involving people of color, have also reportedly led to an increase in complaints of police abuse and misconduct, giving rise to several high profile police brutality cases.[208] NYPD officials told AI that "quality of life" enforcement remains an important aspect of police activity, and is a priority in precincts such as the 6th precinct.[209] Furthermore, a number of "quality of life" provisions have been successfully challenged in domestic courts on the grounds that they are overly vague and afford too much discretion to the police or on the basis of selective enforcement.[210]

---

[204] James Q. Wilson & George L. Kelling, "Broken Windows," *The Atlantic Monthly*, March 1982, at 29.

[205] Testimony of Trishala Deb from AIUSA Racial Profiling Hearings, Judson Memorial Church, 3 October 2004.

[206] Bernard E Harcourt, "Reflecting on the Subject: A critique of the social influence conception of deterrence, the broken windows theory, and order maintenance policing New York-style," *Michigan Law Review*, November 1998.

[207] Peter A. Barta, "Giuliani, Broken Windows, and the Right to Beg," 6 Geo. J. Poverty Law & Pol'y, 165. Some observers also argue that these practices did not truly cause the reduced crime rates. Andrew Karmen, *New York Murder Mystery: The True Story Behind the Crime Crash of the 1990s*, at 13-24 (2000); Brandon Garrett, "Remedying Racial Profiling," 33 Colum. Human Rights L. Rev. 41.

[208] A study by the Legal Aid Society found that 85 percent of drug arrests under Operation Condor involved people of color. Richard Goldstein, "Street Hassle," *Village Voice*, 30 April 2002. The organization estimated that as many as a third of the arrests were for offenses like trespassing, "farebeating," peddling or drinking in public. Kevin Flynn, "Shooting Raises Scrutiny of Police Antidrug Tactics," *The New York Times*, 25 March 2000. Eliot Spitzer, Attorney General of the State of New York, Civil Rights Bureau, New York City, New York. "The New York City Police Department's 'Stop & Frisk' Practices: A Report to the People of the State of New York," 1 December 1999; "Police Practices and Civil Rights in New York City," U.S. Commission on Civil Rights Report, August 2000. Jeffrey Rosen, "Zero Tolerance: When Good Policing Goes Bad," *The Washington Post*, 23 April 2000. McArdle, A., & Erzen, T., Eds., *Zero Tolerance: Quality of Life and the New Police Brutality in New York City*. New York: New York University Press (2001).

[209] AI interview with Deputy Inspector Kevin Fitzgerald, 6th Precinct, New York City, 15 March 2004.

[210] City of Chicago v. Morales, 527 U.S. 41 (1999); State v. Burnett, 755 N.E.2d 857 (Ohio 2001) cert. denied, 122 S. Ct. 1790 (2002); Johnson v. City of Cincinnati, No. 00-4477 (6th Cir. 2002).

Reports to Amnesty International in all four cities studied indicate a pattern of discriminatory enforcement of "zero tolerance" and "quality of life" regulations against members of LGBT communities, in particular transgender individuals, LGBT people of color, LGBT youth, homeless and poor individuals, and those engaged or perceived to be engaged in sex work. LGBT individuals may initially be targeted under "quality of life" regulations on the basis of their race, ethnicity, age or socio-economic status, and in many cases it is difficult to gauge whether they were also targeted on the basis of their sexual orientation or gender identity. While a person may initially be targeted based on their race, for example, the risk of police abuse may increase when the person's sexual orientation or gender identity becomes apparent.[211]

4.2.1
DISCRIMINATORY ENFORCEMENT OF "QUALITY OF LIFE" ORDINANCES

"If there is a group of queer youth of color hanging out in front of the subway station on Christopher Street the police will tell them they are loitering, but if it's a group of white tourists blocking the subway entrance they don't say anything."

Gabriel Martinez, FIERCE!, New York [212]

"They see homeless people on the street as committing a crime—but if they cannot get a shelter, what are you going to do?"

Outreach Worker, Gay and Lesbian Adolescent Social Services, Los Angeles [213]

AI IS CONCERNED that some "quality of life" ordinances give rise to discriminatory application and misconduct by police. "Quality of life" regulations such as loitering, disorderly conduct and noise violations are frequently vague, thereby affording individual police officers considerable discretion when enforcing such regulations. Such statutes are prone to abuse by individual officers who may be motivated by their own prejudice or acting on complaints from members of the public motivated by homophobia, transphobia and racism. "Quality of life" regulations that are not vague, such as those criminalizing the consumption of alcohol, storage of belongings, and urination in public spaces also tend to be discriminatorily applied towards certain communities. One advocate noted, "The police cannot possibly prosecute all minor offenders with equal force ... Instead of genuine zero tolerance, the police must inevitably exercise discretion about where to focus their limited resources."[214] Reports to AI suggest that policing of such ordinances have mostly impacted those who stand at the intersection of identities, and that there are significant racial, age-related and socioeconomic disparities in the manner in which these regulations are policed.

AI found a pattern in each of the cities studied that LGBT individuals of color are disproportionately targeted for enforcement of "quality of life" ordinances. For example, AI heard reports that LGBT people of color in some instances are perceived to be "out of place" in areas identified as predominantly white LGBT communities, based on stereotypes about the racial makeup of the LGBT community.[215]

AI also notes that young LGBT people have very few spaces to socialize and congregate, as many may not be able to be "out" at home and they do not have access to age-restricted, fee-paying venues. LGBT youth will therefore often tend to congregate in LGBT-friendly areas where they feel safe. AI has received a number of reports indicating that young LGBT people are subjected to police misconduct, harassment and abuse in the context of policing "quality

---

[211] AI interviews with Malaika Parker, Director, Bay Area Police Watch, San Francisco, 27 October 2002; Dean Spade, Sylvia Rivera Law Project, 19 February 2004; Staff of Anonymous LGBT Service Providers, Los Angeles, 27 October 2003.

[212] Quoted in Sascha Brodsky, "Fierce Kids: Village group advocates for queer and homeless youths," *Gay City News*, issue No. 4, 21-27 June 2002, available at: http://www.gaycitynews.com/GCN4/FierceKids.html.

[213] AI interview with Outreach Worker, Gay and Lesbian Adolescent Social Services, Los Angeles, October 2003.

[214] Jeffrey Rosen, "Zero Tolerance: When Good Policing Goes Bad," *The Washington Post*, 23 April 2000; Jeffrey Rosen, "Why Patrick Dorismond Didn't Have to Die," *The New Republic*, 10 April 2000.

[215] AI interviews with Lora Branch, City of Chicago Department of Public Health, Chicago, 26 February 2004; Streetworks Youth Drop-In Notes, New York, 5 March 2004; Jesse Ehrensaft-Hawley, FIERCE!, 22 January 2004; FIERCE! surveys conducted in 2002, in which respondents reported that officers regularly verbally abuse LGBT youth of color using homophobic and transphobic slurs, and tell them "move on," "we don't want you here," "go away," and "if you don't leave, we'll arrest you."

of life" regulations curbing activities such as "loitering" or "unreasonable" noise. Reports indicate that transgender youth and LGBT youth of color in particular have been targeted through selective enforcement of "quality of life" provisions, in some cases while conducting outreach for non-governmental organizations.[216] AI has heard reports suggesting that law enforcement personnel have profiled young LGBT individuals of color as gang members.[217] In Los Angeles, for example, Latina lesbians are reportedly profiled by police as gang members based on gender variant appearance, behavior and attire, such as wearing baggy pants.[218]

- **Chicago:** A young African American gay outreach worker was waiting at a bus stop in December 2003 when Chicago police officers allegedly arrested him for loitering with the intent to solicit, despite providing identification and corroborating information from the organization he represents. He was reportedly detained in a downtown precinct for two days.[219]

- **San Antonio:** Monique, a 17-year-old Hispanic lesbian, told AI that she was with three "straight" friends when park police in Breckenridge Park stopped her in 2003. Officers asked her for her ID and threatened to arrest her. One officer reportedly said, "I could put you in jail for not having your ID." Monique told AI, "I dress kind of weird. More tomboyish so the police look at me more. They keep asking me questions like 'Where do you live?' 'What are you doing out so late?' My 'straight' friends don't get asked even if they are the one driving. They ask me all the questions. SAPD are not as bad as the park police."[220]

Discriminatory policing of "quality of life" regulations appears to be strong in gentrifying areas,[221] which have traditionally provided safe space for LGBT individuals. Reportedly, gentrification is frequently accompanied by increased policing of "quality of life" ordinances, as law enforcement agencies are charged with protecting the revitalized space.[222] AI heard that residents' groups in Chicago and New York reportedly have placed strong demands on law enforcement and municipal authorities to increase enforcement of "quality of life" ordinances, in some cases attempting to drive out perceived "undesirable elements" themselves.[223] AI is concerned that such pressure may foster a climate which is likely to lead to discriminatory application of the law, abuse and misconduct by the police, as they respond to demands to "clean up" the area. The Audre Lorde Project has commented that in relation to gentrification, "it becomes painfully obvious that people who do not fit into these categories (such as LGBTST[224]

---

[216] AI interviews with Sylvia Bertran and Alex Sanchez, Homies Unidos, Los Angeles, 27 January 2004; GLASS focus group discussion, Los Angeles, 29 October 2003; Q-Team, Los Angeles, 1 November 2003; Cyndee Clay and GiGi Thomas, HIPS, Washington D.C., 20 November 2003. See also: *The Impact of Juvenile Laws in California*, The Center on Juvenile and Criminal Justice, June 1998.

[217] AI interviews with Members of Anonymous LGBT Youth Program, Los Angeles, 29 January 2004; Q-Team meeting, 1 November 2003; Margaux Delotte-Bennet, Sexual Minority Assistance League, Washington, D.C., 20 November 2003.

[218] AI interview with Sylvia Beltran and Alex Sanchez, Homies Unidos, Los Angeles, 29 January 2004.

[219] AI interview with Anonymous, Chicago, February 2004.

[220] Interview with Monique, San Antonio PFLAG Meeting, San Antonio, 4 December 2003.

[221] Gentrification is a term used in land development to describe a trend whereby previously "underdeveloped" areas become "revitalized" as persons of relative affluence invest in property and begin to "upgrade" the neighborhood economically. See eg: Business Ass'n of Univ. City v. Landrieu, 660 F.2d 867, 874 n.8 (3d Cir. 1981) cited in Jon C. Dubin, "From Junkyards to Gentrification: Explicating a Right to Protective Zoning in Low-Income Communities of Color," *Minnesota Law Review*, April 1993, 77 Minn. L. Rev. 739.

[222] "No Homeless People Allowed (1994),"National Law Center on Homelessness and Poverty; Robert C. Ellickson, "Controlling Chronic Misconduct in City Spaces: Of Panhandlers, Skid Rows, and Public-Space Zoning," *Yale L. J.* 1165 (1996); Dirk Johnson, "Chicago Council Tries Anew with Anti-Gang Ordinance," *New York Times*, 22 February 2000; Steve Miletich, "Sidewalk Law Is Posted," *Seattle Post-Intelligencer*, 19 May 1994; Michael Ybarra, "Don't Ask, Don't Beg, Don't Sit," *New York Times*, 19 May 1996; AI interview with Christopher Daly, Staff Attorney, Transgender Law Center, San Francisco, 27 October 2003.

[223] Some residents and organizations, including Chicago Alternative Policing Strategy, have organized activities such as a "Midnight March," held October 2003, where residents as well as officers from the 19th and 23rd Districts marched through the neighborhood, reportedly shouting at young people perceived to be sex workers or criminals to "get out." AI received reports indicating that participants particularly focused on African American transgender youth and "equated trans folks with crime." AI interviews with Alyssa Siegel, Lakeview Coalition, Chicago, 26 February 2004; Karen Stanczykiewicz, Chicago Recovery Alliance, Chicago, 27 February 2004. In New York, a drop-in center for young LGBT youth was reportedly forced to move from the West Village in the mid-1990s under pressure from community groups. Richard Goldstein, "New Skool versus Old School in Greenwich Village," *Street Hassle*, 24-30 April 2002. AI further heard a number of reports alleging that residents in the West Village have placed demands on law enforcement and municipal authorities to increase enforcement of "quality of life" ordinances, particularly against young LGBT individuals of color, and have themselves thrown ice, hot water and even urine on them from windows. AI interview with FIERCE!, New York City, 22 January 2004.

[224] LGBTST – Lesbian, Gay, Bisexual, Two-Spirited and Transgender. The term "two-spirited" is derived from Native American languages used to describe people who displayed both male and female characteristics [see glossary].

people and people of color) are virtually powerless and are seen as having little or no value or legitimacy in the larger community."[225] AI has heard reports indicating that young LGBT people in West Hollywood, California; Chelsea and the West Village, Hudson River Piers and Times Square in New York; Lakeview in Chicago; and the Castro in San Francisco are routinely harassed, ticketed, told to move on or arrested.[226]

- **New York:** FIERCE!, a community organizing project for LGBT youth in New York City, conducted a survey of young LGBT people in the West Village and Chelsea in 2003.[227] The organization found that 59 out of 60 respondents had experienced police harassment, violence or misconduct. The majority of complaints alleged verbal abuse, harassment and threats of arrest. Of these, 15 respondents felt they were targeted on the basis of their sexual orientation, 13 on the basis of their race.

Amnesty International is concerned by reports in each of the cities studied that "quality of life" ordinances are selectively enforced against homeless individuals.[228] Those within the homeless communities who are particularly marginalized, including LGBT people, youth and individuals of color, are reportedly more likely to be targeted for selective enforcement and other police misconduct. Reports indicate that a significant number of homeless individuals are LGBT. As discussed later in Chapter 9, "Identity-Based Discrimination and Police Abuse," many members of the LGBT communities face severe economic hardship on the basis of discrimination, particularly transgender individuals, and may face additional discrimination on the basis of race, immigration status, age and gender. It is estimated that in some cities in the U.S. up to 40 percent of homeless youth are lesbian, gay, bisexual or transgender.[229] In some cities, this number may be even higher.[230] Reports also indicate that a significant proportion of the transgender community is homeless, particularly transgender persons of color and immigrants.[231] AI notes that shelters and other resources for homeless individuals do not adequately accommodate LGBT individuals, particularly transgender individuals.[232]

- **Los Angeles:** At PATH, Los Angeles' largest homeless shelter, transgender women are reportedly housed in men's dormitories, placing them at risk of abuse by other residents, and of being challenged by security officers who demand to see their genitals when they use women's bathrooms. As a result, transgender women avoid the shelter.[233]

[225] The Audre Lorde Project, *Police Brutality Against Lesbian, Gay, Bisexual, Two-Spirit and Transgender People of Color in New York City*, draft report at 23 July 2000 (on file with Amnesty International Research Department).

[226] AI interviews with Lora Branch, Director, City of Chicago Department of Public Health, Chicago, 26 February 2004; Kate Walz, Formerly of First Defense Legal Aid, Chicago, 24 February 2004; Cara Thaxton, Victim Advocacy Coordinator and Lisa Tonna, Director of Advocacy and Legislative Affairs, Horizons Community Services, Chicago, 23 February 2004; Horizons Youth Drop-In, Chicago, 13 November 2003; Karen Stanczykiewicz, Chicago Recovery Alliance, Chicago, 27 February 2004; Joey Mogul, Queer to the Left and People's Law Center, Chicago, 12 November 2003; Anonymous member of FIERCE!, New York, 2 March 2004; Kim Hawkins, Director, Peter Cicchino Youth Project, Urban Justice Center, New York, 16 January 2004; Rachel Herzig, Critical Resistance National Office, San Francisco, 23 October 2003; Carl Siciliano, Ali Forney Center, New York City, 13 February 2004; GLASS Focus Group Session, Los Angeles, 29 October 2003; Malaika Parker, Director, Bay Area Police Watch, Ella Baker Center, San Francisco, 27 October 2003.

[227] While most respondents reported harassment by NYPD officers, adverse interactions with law enforcement have also involved a number of other law enforcement agencies including the Transit Police, the Parks Police and the privately run Hudson River Trusts Police as well as other, smaller private agencies.

[228] David Rosenzweig and Eric Malnic, "Police Sweeps of Skid Row Are Curbed," *Los Angeles Times*, 3 April 2003, at A1; Carla Rivera, "LA to Pay Dozens of People Held in Skid Row Sweeps," *Los Angeles Times*, 12 June 2003, at 6. NYPD's training manual cites homelessness among listed "quality of life offenses." *NYPD, Police Students Guide: Quality of Life Policing*, 23 September 2003. "Pattern and Practice: Systemic Violations of the Civil Rights of Homeless New Yorkers by the NYPD," *Picture the Homeless*, 7 November 2002; Onofre Serna v. The City of San Antonio and Al Philipuus, 244 F. 3d 479 (5th Cir. 2001). See also: "Mean Sweeps: A Report on Anti-Homeless Laws, Litigation and Alternatives in 50 United States Cities," National Law Center on Homelessness and Poverty, s1996.

[229] Cochran BN, Stewart AJ, Ginzler JA, Cauce AM. "Challenges faced by homeless sexual minorities: Comparison of gay, lesbian, bisexual, and transgender homeless adolescents with their heterosexual counterparts," *American Journal of Public Health* 92.5 (2002), p. 773-776.

[230] Advocates estimate that one-third to one-half of the 22,000 homeless youth in New York City are gay, lesbian, bisexual or transgender. Daria Karp, "Fierce Gay Youth Confront Distressed West Village Residents," *Youth City News*, 2002, found at: http://www.jrn.columbia.edu/studentwork/children/2002/karpgay.asp.

[231] AI interviews with Carol Soebel, Los Angeles, 30 January 2004; Julia Garcia, La Opportunidad, Los Angeles, 30 October 2003. See also, Sharon Minter and Chris Daley, "Trans Realities: A Legal Needs Assessment of San Francisco's Transgender Community," National Center for Lesbian Rights and Transgender Law Center, 2003.

[232] Transitional living programs in the city specifically intended for LGBT youth account for less than 80 beds. Daria Karp, "Fierce Gay Youth Confront Distressed West Village Residents," *Youth City News*, 2002.

[233] AI meeting with community advocates, 26 January 2004.

Both homeless and young LGBT individuals, particularly individuals of color, have reported frequent identification checks by law enforcement, sometimes resulting in searches, interrogations and the issuance of tickets, as well as arrest, detention and in some instances the destruction or confiscation of identification papers.[234] In Chicago, homeless and transgender youth reported police demanding ID papers, sometimes on a daily basis, and in some instances police allegedly confiscated identification or threw it away.[235] AI is concerned by the impact that such practices could have on the homeless LGBT community and LGBT youth, particularly gender variant and transgender individuals who may not be in possession of identification matching their gender identity or expression. The selective targeting of homeless and young LGBT individuals for identification checks based on their sexual orientation, gender identity or expression, or race violates standards under ICERD, ICESCR and the ICCPR that prohibit discrimination.

---

[234] AI interviews with Heather Bradley, Night Ministry, Chicago, 27 February 2004; Members of Picture the Homeless, New York City, 16 February 2004; Patrick Markee, Senior Policy Analyst, Coalition for the Homeless, New York City, 9 February 2004; Kate Barnhart, Neutral Zone, New York, 11 February 2004.

[235] AI interviews with Heather Bradley, Night Ministry, Chicago, 25 February 2004; Lisa Tonna and Carmen Abrego, Horizons Anti-Violence Program, Chicago, 16 September 2003; Karen Stanczykiewicz, Chicago Recovery Alliance, Chicago, 27 February 2004.

5

SEXUAL, PHYSICAL AND VERBAL ABUSE

On 19 July 2000, Frederick Mason, a 31-year-old African American nurse's assistant with no criminal record, was arrested following a verbal altercation with his landlord. Mason claims that at the police station, two unidentified officers took him to an interrogation room, where he was handcuffed by the elbows and pinned to a wall. The arresting officer is alleged to have pulled down Mason's pants and sprayed blue cleaning liquid on a billy club before ramming the baton into Mason's rectum. As he raped Mason, the officer is alleged to have made remarks such as "I'm tired of you, faggot ... you sick motherfucker." A second unidentified officer is alleged to have witnessed Mason's pants being pulled down, but walked away during the assault. Witnesses have attested that Mason entered police custody in good health and when released had blood streaming from his rectum. Mason's family doctor confirmed that he had been injured in the anal area. Mason contends that he was subjected to abuse—including racist and homophobic names such as "faggot ass nigger" and "nigger fag"—from the moment he was arrested.[236] In 2002, Mason received an out-of-court settlement of $20,000.[237]

THE ALLEGED TARGETING OF LGBT INDIVIDUALS for sexual, physical or verbal abuse occurs in many different situations and contexts, as will be presented in detail below and throughout this report. Sexual, physical and verbal abuse frequently occur together. Reports of sexual and physical abuse of LGBT people by law enforcement officials often include homophobic and transphobic slurs. In some instances, verbal abuse escalates to physical or sexual abuse. Information received by AI suggests that verbal abuse of LGBT individuals is frequently sexualized, in particular toward lesbians and transgender individuals. The failure of authorities to tackle issues such as homophobia and transphobia in police forces creates a climate in which such violations can proliferate.

AI heard reports of sexual harassment and abuse of LGBT individuals in all cities studied as well as in other locations in the U.S. including Philadelphia; Washington, D.C.; Athens, Georgia; Montgomery, Alabama; and San Francisco, California. Sexual abuse and misconduct by police officers may cover a range of conduct, including rape, sexual assault, threatened sexual assault, sexual contact, as well as sexually explicit language and gestures. AI's findings also include reports that LGBT individuals have been subjected to sexual abuse or harassment while in detention, at the hands of other detainees and, in some cases, by officers.

AI received reports in Chicago; Los Angeles; New York; San Antonio; San Francisco, Sacramento and San Diego, California; Lehigh Valley, Pennsylvania; Austin, Texas; Lincoln, Rhode Island; and Connecticut of LGBT individuals being subjected to physical abuse including being kicked, slammed against walls and beaten with a baton.

AI heard numerous reports of officers being verbally abusive towards LGBT individuals with officers frequently focusing on perceived sexual orientation or gender identity or expression of individuals in a derogatory and demeaning manner. AI has heard reports from Chicago; Los Angeles; New York; San Antonio; Springfield, Illinois; Philadelphia and Lehigh Valley, Pennsylvania; San Francisco, California; and Washington, D.C. of officers using slurs including "faggot," "dyke," "freak" and "he/she." AI is concerned at such reports, noting that verbal abuse serves to dehumanize LGBT people, creating a climate of prejudice and impunity in which misconduct as well as egregious

---

[236] Amnesty International, *Allegations of Homophobic Abuse by Chicago Police Officers*, 1 June 2001 (AMR 51/027/01).

[237] Patel, Julie. "City Settles Police Brutality Lawsuit," *Chicago Sun-Times*, 17 July 2002, p 23; Frank Main, "Police Union Files Lawsuits to Discourage False Claims," *Chicago Sun-Times*, 25 February 2004.

physical or sexual abuse is more likely to take place.

Reports indicate that, in particular, LGBT individuals who do not conform to traditional gender "norms," especially in their appearance or presentation, are more likely to be singled out for verbal, physical and sexual abuse, and that transgender individuals are disproportionately targeted by law enforcement. Furthermore, incidents reported to AI indicate that homophobia, transphobia and racism often occur together in incidents of police misconduct and abuse against LGBT people of color. AI's findings further suggest that a significant proportion of reports of sexual, physical and verbal misconduct against LGBT individuals concerned people of color, mirroring general trends of police brutality in the U.S. Advocates had also raised concerns about increased profiling of immigrants of color as a result of police policies and practices adopted in the wake of 11 September 2001.[238]

Age and socioeconomic and immigration status also compound the risk of sexual, physical and verbal abuse by law enforcement. AI also received a number of reports of sexual misconduct by police against individuals perceived to be engaging in sex work, including extortion of sexual favors in exchange for leniency or protection. A Chicago advocate told AI that young LGBT individuals who engage in sex work report that officers—sometimes on duty and other times not—ask for sexual favors.[239] Officers in New York and Chicago reportedly subject LGBT youth to verbal and physical abuse.[240] Physical abuse against LGBT sex workers, particularly transgender individuals, was reported to AI in Chicago, Los Angeles, New York, San Antonio, Philadelphia and D.C.[241] AI heard reports in Chicago, Los Angeles, New York and San Antonio that officers engage in homophobic, transphobic, racist and sexist verbal abuse when communicating with particular communities, including LGBT people of color, homeless, youth, sex workers and immigrants.[242]

---

[238] AI interviews with Julio Rodriguez, President, ALMA, Chicago, 16 September 2003; Gelsys Rubio, Latino Women's Center, Chicago, 25 February 2004; Heather Bradley, Youth Outreach Minister, Night Ministry, Chicago, 25 February 2004; Nina Farina, Southwest Youth Collaborative, Chicago, 20 February 2004; Angel Fabian, Director of Community Organizing and Health Education, Clinica Romero Community Center, Los Angeles, 30 October 2003; Saurav Sarkar, Solidarity Action for Human Rights, and Namita Chad, Desis Rising Up and Moving, New York City, 9 March 2004; Glen Magpantay, Sin Yen Ling and Khin Mai Aung, AALDEF, New York City, 4 February 2004; Ben Shepherd, Activist, New York City, 6 May 2004; Yves Michael Fontaine, Clinical Coordinator, Gay Men's Health Crisis, New York City, 19 March 2004; Pradeep Singla, Attorney, New York City, 19 February 2004; Annette Lamoreaux, ACLU, Houston, 1 December 2003; Rachel Herzig, Field Organizer, and Rose Braz, National Director, Critical Resistance, San Francisco, 23 October 2003; Staff of a National Latino LGBT Organization, Washington, D.C., 19 November 2003.

[239] AI interview with Heather Bradley, Night Ministry, Chicago, 25 February 2004.

[240] AI interviews with Andy Thayer, Chicago Anti-Bashing Network, Chicago, 15 September 2003; Darren E. Bowden, Former Executive Director, First Defense Legal Aid, Chicago, 11 November 2003; Anonymous member, Horizons Youth Drop-In, Chicago, 19 February 2004; Kate Walz; First Defense Legal Aid, Chicago, 24 February 2004; Heather Bradley, Night Ministry, Chicago, 25 February 2004; Anonymous young transgender woman, Online Form, New York, 30 January 2004; Anonymous, FIERCE! Community Group Meeting, New York City, 2 March 2004.

[241] AI interviews with Ujima Moore, Amassi, Los Angeles, 29 January 2004; Rashawn Lusk, Client, Rafael Center, Chicago, 18 February 2004; Juhu Thukral, Director, Sex Workers Project; Melissa Ditmore, Network of Sex Work Projects, New York, 11 March 2004; Michelle Sosa, Positive Health Project and Michelle Sosa's Transgender Tuesday Group, New York, 24 February 2004; Clients at GLASS mobile unit, Los Angeles, 29 October 2003; Staff Member of an FtM Transgender Support Organization and Simmi Ghandi, INCITE!, Los Angeles, 28 October 2003; Julia Garcia and Antonio, La Opportunidad and Ralph Showers, Jovenes Inc., Los Angeles, 30 October 2003; Jessica Xavier, Transgender Activist, Washington, D.C., 24 March 2004; Cyndee Clay and GiGi Thomas, HIPS, Washington, D.C., 20 November 2003; Chris Daley, TGLC, San Francisco, 27 October 2003; Lee Carpenter, Center for Gay and Lesbian Civil Rights, Philadelphia, 15 March 2004.

[242] AI interviews with Heather Bradley, Night Ministry, Chicago, 25 February 2004; Ujima Moore, Amassi, Los Angeles, 29 January 2004; Dean Spade, Sylvia Rivera Law Project, New York City, 19 February 2004; Clients, GLASS Mobile Unit, Los Angeles, 29 October 2003; group interview at Horizons Youth Drop-In, Chicago, 13 November 2003; Patti Buffington, Executive Director, Genesis House, Chicago, 26 February 2004; Anonymous, New York, 26 February 2004; Michelle Sosa and Transgender Tuesday Group, Positive Health Project, New York, 24 February 2004; Denise, San Antonio AIDS Foundation, San Antonio, 5 December 2003; Rick Gipprich, San Antonio Rape Crisis Center, San Antonio, 2 December 2003; Shirley Bushnell, Van Ness Recovery House Prevention Division, Los Angeles, 1 October 2003; Anonymous, Los Angeles, 29 September 2003.

5.1

SEXUAL ABUSE

> "You'd be surprised how many policemen I had sex with. They'd say, "You do it with me, or I'm going to arrest you for prostitution." Then they'd tell me to go home and I better not tell anybody."
>
> Toni Collins, Co-Founder of D.C.'s Transgender Health Empowerment[243]
>
> "The police are not here to serve; they are here to get served… Every night I'm taken into an alley and given the choice between having sex or going to jail."[244]
>
> AI interview with Native American transgender woman in Los Angeles

AI HEARD REPORTS OF SEXUAL HARASSMENT AND ABUSE of LGBT individuals in Chicago, Los Angeles, New York and San Antonio as well as in other locations including Montgomery, Alabama; Washington, D.C.; Athens, Georgia; Philadelphia, Pennsylvania; and San Francisco, California. Reports included allegations of rape and other sexual abuse by police officers, including sexual assault, threatened sexual assault, sexual contact, as well as sexually explicit language and gestures.

AI received reports of police sexually abusing and harassing transgender individuals in Chicago, Los Angeles, New York, San Antonio, Washington, D.C., Philadelphia and San Francisco.[245]

- **Los Angeles:** A Native American transgender woman reported that in October 2003, at around 4 a.m., she was walking down Highland near the intersection with LaBrea when two LAPD officers pulled over and told her they were going to take her to jail for "prostitution." She told the officers that she was just walking, and wasn't engaged in sex work. The officers reportedly handcuffed her, put her in the patrol car and drove her to an alley off Hollywood Boulevard. According to the woman, one of the officers pulled her out of the car, still handcuffed. The officer reportedly began hitting her across the face, saying "you fucking whore, you fucking faggot," and then grabbed her by the mouth, covering it while he continued hitting her. The officer allegedly threw her down on the back of the patrol car, ripped off her miniskirt and her underwear and raped her, holding her down and grabbing her hair. The second officer is also alleged to have raped her. According to the woman, they threw her on the ground and said, "That's what you deserve," and left her there.[246] She reports that she contacted 911 but that the responding paramedics did not believe her. As the LAPD allows anonymous and third party complaints, AI contacted the LAPD to provide details on the nature of this allegation (without revealing the confidential identity of the individual concerned). LAPD indicated a willingness to investigate this allegation further; however, were unable to do so without speaking to the complainant.[247]

- **New York:** Two young, Latina transgender women report being approached and questioned by police officers in a patrol car in 2001. The officers allegedly threatened them with arrest unless they had sex with them. The women reportedly performed oral sex on the officers before being let free. They did not report the incident because of their undocumented immigration status and threats of retaliation.[248]

---

243 Toni Collins, Co-Founder of D.C.'s Transgender Health Empowerment, as quoted in Bob Moser, "Disposable People," *The Intelligence Report*, Southern Poverty Law Center, Issue 112, Winter 2003.

244 AI interview with AB, Los Angeles, 29 October 2003.

245 AI interviews with Daniel, Gay Men's Health Crisis, New York City, 19 March 2004; Client, Rafael Center, Chicago, 18 February 2004; Clients, San Antonio AIDS Foundation, San Antonio, 5 December 2003; Lee Carpenter, Center for Gay and Lesbian Civil Rights, Philadelphia, 15 March 2004. Chris Daley, Elly Kugler and Jo Hirschmann, "Walking While Transgender: Law Enforcement Harassment of San Francisco's Transgender/Transsexual Community," Ella Baker Center for Human Rights and TransAction in San Francisco, April 2000; AI interview with HIPS, Washington, D.C., 20 November 2003.

246 AI interview with Clients of GLASS Mobile Unit, Los Angeles, 29 October 2003.

247 See also: Training and Accountability, Complaint Systems below. AI heard from officials that anonymous and third party reporting poses a barrier to proper investigation. According to the Inspector General (who has the power to audit, investigate and oversee LAPD's handling of complaints of misconduct by police officers), there is a tendency to use the fact that an investigator was unable to speak with a complainant as a reason not to investigate.

248 AI interview with Daniel, Gay Men's Health Crisis, New York City, 19 March 2004.

- **Orange County, California:** A transgender advocate told AI: "About two years ago two MTF [transgender female] youth were at a club in Orange County. They were driving home when they were pulled over by the cops. The cops looked at their ID and saw M [male] on the license. They were told that they had to follow the cops and they were taken to a secluded place and asked to give the officers blow jobs."[249]

While this section concentrates on alleged misconduct by police officers, AI has also heard several reports of sexual abuse of transgender individuals held in detention. Reports indicate that transgender people are at risk of sexual violence while in detention and may be subjected to sexual harassment, sexual assault and in some instances rape. (See **Searches and Detention** section for additional information.)

- **Montgomery, Alabama:** Marissa, a white transgender lesbian woman, reports that in 2001 she was abused in jail. She told AI, "Two jailers and a state trooper made me strip in front of them while they looked on … I was made to dance around in front of them, shouting 'I've got a penis, I've got a penis!' Then they made me hold my penis in front of them and show them I could masturbate. I was then cavity searched; the anal search was excruciatingly painful, much more than any physician-directed rectal exam I ever had. I was then told to shower while one guy watched. By this time I was very, very weak, and collapsed, injuring my arm, shoulder and back …. I pleaded to see a doctor but was ignored and forced to walk to a cell carrying a mattress. The police officers and jailers constantly referred to me as 'that dick' …. Apart from the fact that I was repeatedly forced to admit I was a man, I was called 'faggot,' 'sir' and 'fucking pansy.'"[250]

AI also received reports of lesbians experiencing sexual assault and harassment at the hands of police officers.[251]

- **Athens, Georgia:** In 2004, a lesbian from Athens filed a civil lawsuit alleging that a former Gwinnett County Georgia deputy raped her because she is a lesbian. The officer is accused of forcing her into her apartment at gunpoint and raping her. The woman said the officer vowed to "teach her a lesson" and said "the world needed at least one less dyke and he was going to make sure that happened."[252] He was charged with rape, false imprisonment, aggravated assault with a deadly weapon, aggravated assault with intent to rape, and violating his oath of office. According to the Athens-Clarke County District Attorney's office, while acquitted on a number of charges, the officer was found guilty of violating his oath of office. The officer agreed to a deal whereby he received two years probation where he was to have no contact with the victim, he was banned from Athens-Clarke County, and promised not to appeal the decision.[253]

- **Los Angeles:** A young Latina lesbian was arrested with a friend for shoplifting in October 2003. As they were being transported to the station, the two women began talking about how their girlfriends were going to be angry with them for getting into trouble. The arresting officer began asking them questions such as "You guys are gay? You have a girlfriend? Where is your girlfriend at? What do you and your girlfriend do?" The officer then asked the two women to kiss, telling them he would let them go if they did so.[254]

Reports include gay men who have been raped, including with objects, and sexually abused. (See, for example, the case of Frederick Mason, above.)

- **Los Angeles:** In February 2003, police came to a 36-year-old gay Latino man's house to get him to testify against a friend who had robbed his house. When he refused to go with them, one officer reportedly shouted, "You homo

---

249 Transgender advocate speaking to AI at the Asian Pacific AIDS Intervention Team Community Forum Meeting, 29 January 2004.

250 Email from Marissa to AI, 27 February 2004; Correspondence between Marissa and AI, 26 April 2005.

251 AI interviews with Members of GLASS focus group, Los Angeles, 28 January 2004; Anonymous member of FIERCE!, New York, 22 January 2004.

252 "Alleged Rape Victim Wants Deputy Charged With a Hate Crime," The Associated Press State and Local Wires, 8 August 2003.

253 Telephone interview with Matt Carzon of the Athens-Clarke County District Attorney's office, 3 p.m., 1 November 2004; "Lesbian rape trial begins in Georgia," The Advocate, 17 March 2004, http://www.advocate.com/new_news.asp?id=11699&sd=03/17/04b.

254 AI interview with Members of GLASS focus group, 28 January 2004.

faggots, wasted our time with shit like this!" The officer pushed the Latino man against the couch and "poked him with a club from behind," simulating rape and saying, "You must be used to that."[255]

AI also heard reports of sexual abuse of young gay men in Chicago, Illinois.[256]

- **Chicago:** AI heard from young gay men and advocates in Chicago that a particular officer had taken young men to a clock tower and that, in the words of one alleged victim, he will "remove his badge, gun and belt and then beat you unless you give him a blow job, after which he'll just leave you there."[257]

- **Chicago:** In 2001, a 16-year-old gay, white, homeless boy reported that he was subjected to verbal harassment by two officers who would pull over whenever they saw him. They reportedly assumed he was a sex worker, and allegedly subjected him to homophobic comments and slurs, often with sexual undertones, such as: "You're having anal sex with everyone else, why not with us?" and "You may as well come over and do me."[258]

Under international law, the rape of a prisoner by a state official is considered to be an act of torture. Other forms of sexual abuse may be torture and are clearly violations of the internationally recognized prohibition of cruel, inhuman and degrading treatment or punishment, which governments are called upon to interpret "so as to extend the widest possible protection against abuses, whether physical or mental."[259] Sexual abuse also violates the right to be treated with respect for human dignity, and the right to privacy under international law, both enshrined in the ICCPR. Targeting of individuals because of their sexual or gender identity or expression violates not only their right against sexual abuse but also their right to be free from discrimination, which is enshrined in the ICCPR and Convention Against Torture.

---

[255] Intake Report, Los Angeles Gay and Lesbian Center Anti-Violence Project, Los Angeles, 11 February 2003; AI interview with Vivianna Hernandez, LAGLC AVP, Los Angeles, 24 February 2005.

[256] AI interview with Heather Bradley, Night Ministry, Chicago, 25 February 2004; Anonymous "A" (name on file with AIUSA), Horizons Youth Drop-In, Chicago, 26 February 2004.

[257] AI interview with Anonymous "C" (name on file with AIUSA), Horizons Youth Drop-In, 26 February 2004.

[258] As reported in AI interview with Darron E. Bowden, Former Executive Director, First Defense Legal Aid, Chicago, 11 November 2004.

[259] Explanatory footnote to Principle 6, *United Nations Body of Principles for the Protection of All Persons Under Any Form of Detention or Imprisonment*.

5.2
PHYSICAL ABUSE

On 13 August 2001, Jeremy Burke, a white transgender man, was visiting his partner. According to Burke, the Housing Authority security guard refused to let Burke in, citing a policy that residents must come down to the lobby to admit a visitor. Burke attempted to explain that his partner was ill and needed the medication he brought for her. According to Burke, the security guard shoved him into the elevator.[260] Approximately 15 minutes after he arrived at his partner's apartment, three police officers came to the door, entered the apartment and pulled Burke out of a chair, carried him into the hallway and started punching him in the face, chest and eyes. Reportedly, Burke's head was slammed into the floor and wall.[261] The police report, which consistently uses the wrong pronouns and refers to Burke as a woman, alleges that Burke attempted to strike and later to bite one of the officers, but was subdued. Burke was arrested on charges of assault, battery, resisting arrest and trespassing and was taken to the police station, where he alleges he was subjected to humiliating and transphobic verbal abuse and medical neglect.[262] Burke was vomiting bile and blood for several days after the beating and finally, after the third day, he was taken to San Francisco General Hospital where it was discovered that his kidneys were injured from the beating and that he was bleeding internally. Reportedly, his black eye and bruises were visible and documented.[263] All charges were eventually dropped except the trespassing count. On 24 July 2003, Burke filed a civil suit against the City and County of San Francisco.[264] According to his attorney, the case will be heard in November 2005.[265]

"Bias against lesbians and gays also contributes to excessive use of force. As one LAPD officer put it, 'It's easier to thump a faggot than an average joe. Who cares?' Another officer said that gay people tend to get beaten more frequently than straight people because 'they love it. They want to get hit.'"

LAPD officers, cited in the Christopher Commission Report[266]

"Law enforcement officials may use force only when strictly necessary and to the extent required for the performance of their duty."

Article 3, UN Code of Conduct for Law Enforcement Officials[267]

POLICE BRUTALITY AND USE OF EXCESSIVE FORCE has been one of the central themes of Amnesty International's work against human rights violations in the U.S. and the organization has worked on police brutality for a number of years. For example, AI has previously documented patterns of ill-treatment across the U.S., including police beatings, unjustified shootings and the use of dangerous restraint techniques to subdue suspects.[268] The Human Rights Committee, charged with monitoring the implementation of the terms of the ICCPR, has expressed concern regarding police abuse in the U.S., stating: "The Committee is concerned at the reportedly large number of persons killed,

---

[260] John Caldwell, "Trans Phobia by the Bay and in LA," GayWired.com, LA/Southern California Edition, 30 August 2002/Volume 21, Issue 09, available at www.gaywired.com/storydetail.

[261] Paras. 19 and 21, First Amended COMPLAINT *Jeremy Burke v. City and County of San Francisco, Officer Anton Collins (#142), and Officer Lee (#1057), Deputy Sheriff Veloro (#1702), Dorothy Lipkins, San Francisco Housing Authority, McCoy's Patrol Services, and/or DOES 1 through 100.* Case No. 408175 (filed 24 July 2003).

[262] David Keifer, "Transgender Sues Police," *San Francisco Examiner,* 8 August 2002.

[263] Para 25, First Amended COMPLAINT *Jeremy Burke vs. City and County of San Francisco, Officer Anton Collins (#142), and Officer Lee (#1057), Deputy Sheriff Veloro (#1702), Dorothy Lipkins, San Francisco Housing Authority, McCoy's Patrol Services, and/or DOES 1 through 100.* Case No. 408175 (filed 24 July 2003).

[264] First Amended COMPLAINT *Jeremy Burke vs. City and County of San Francisco, Officer Anton Collins (#142), and Officer Lee (#1057), Deputy Sheriff Veloro (#1702), Dorothy Lipkins, San Francisco Housing Authority, McCoy's Patrol Services, and/or DOES 1 through 100.* Case No. 408175 (filed 24 July 2003).

[265] AI interview with Waukeen McCoy, Attorney for Jeremy Burke, 12 July 2005. The first trial resulted in a hung jury but the case has been rescheduled for a retrial in November 2005.

[266] The Christopher Commission Report, Chapter 4: Racism and Bias Affecting the Use of Excessive Force, page 91, available at http://www.parc.info/reports/pdf/chistophercommision.pdf.

[267] Adopted by the UN General Assembly in 1979.

[268] See Amnesty International, *United States of America: Rights for All,* 1 October 1998 (AI Index: AMR 51/35/98).

wounded or subjected to ill-treatment by members of the police force in the purported discharge of their duties."[269]

AI received a number of reports of LGBT people being targeted for physical abuse by law enforcement officers based on their sexual orientation or gender identity or expression. In some reports, physical abuse by law enforcement was the result of excessive force employed during arrest. In others, LGBT individuals who were victims of a crime were subjected to physical abuse by responding officers. Other organizations have also reported on incidences of police violence against LGBT individuals. The National Coalition of Anti-Violence Programs documented 31 reports of physical violence against LGBT individuals by law enforcement officers in 2003.[270]

As noted above, AI found that a significant proportion of reports of physical misconduct against LGBT individuals concerned people of color, mirroring general trends of police brutality and misconduct in the U.S.[271] Few studies are available specifically regarding the incidence of physical abuse against LGBT individuals of color. However, reports to AI indicate that policing of LGBT individuals varies along gender and racial lines.

In an email to Amnesty International, a transgender woman from Pennsylvania described the following incident:

"When I came out as a transsexual, I went from a $100,000 a year job to homeless and on welfare in less than two years. In the Summer of 2000, after a disagreement over one of my welfare payments, the police arrived at the welfare office, and the next thing I knew a cop was breathing down my neck, pushing me toward the door while I tried to explain that I had an appointment. There were four officers outside. One officer got in my face with the most vile insults I could imagine; his buddy stood nearby, nightstick in hand, ready to strike. The other two watched uncomfortably nearby. I got the impression they were trying to goad me to fight or react so they could run me in. The one officer, the leader, was so vicious and abusive even his one ally seemed distressed at the mindless aggression and hate he spewed forth. The anger and hate directed at me was more intense than I could describe. I thought I was going to be killed right in front of welfare. With every push—or stab—of his billy club, I thought I would die. Finally, I collapsed. Between the pain of the blows and the mental distress, I broke down. I curled up in a fetal position on the sidewalk, crying and babbling about how I was suffering from depression and I had tried suicide and this was not a good thing to do to someone in my state of mind. I begged them to call crisis intervention. For my plea I received kicks and screams and spit. Finally, 'Go home!' he screamed at me. 'Go home and kill yourself, go home to your faggot boyfriend.' 'She is not a boy,' I retorted between desperate sobs, 'she is a woman like me.' This really pissed him off. I prepared for the next kick. But by this time, the other three cops were imploring him to stop and let me up. I guess there was one sensible cop that could smell a lawsuit in the making. 'You don't treat people like this in a public place, too many witnesses,' I heard somebody say. So they let me up—or more accurately they grabbed me and placed me on my shaky feet. Officer Testosterone was still screaming but now it was to go. He screamed at me to 'walk, just walk, faggot.' I sent letters explaining the incident to the State Attorney General, the welfare board, the Mayor and the Chief of Police, to no avail. I learned, however, that it is perfectly legal to discriminate against transsexuals in countless ways. Go figure. That is when I decided to become an activist. Abuse can be very inspiring .... I will never forget to fear the police. I will always mistrust the system. I will never expect justice or freedom again. I learned that transsexuals, no matter how excellent ... in the past are the most undervalued and discriminated people on earth. I learned that transsexuals have no credibility and few rights."

Rachel Thompson, email to Amnesty International, 23 February 2004

---

[269] Concluding observations of the Human Rights Committee: United States of America. 03/10/95, A/50/40, para. 282.

[270] *Anti-Lesbian, Gay, Bisexual and Transgender Violence in 2003*, National Coalition of Anti-Violence Programs, New York, 2004 Print Edition, 89.

[271] Evidence of racially discriminatory treatment and bias by police has also been widely documented by commissions of inquiry, in court cases, citizen complaint files and countless individual testimonies. Reported abuses include racist language, harassment, ill-treatment, unjustified stops and searches, unjustified shootings and false arrests. See *Race, Rights and Police Brutality*, 1999 (AI Index: AMR 51/147/1999); "Amnesty International USA, Police Brutality and International Human Rights in the United States: The Report on Hearings Held in Los Angeles, California, Chicago, Illinois, and Pittsburgh, Pennsylvania," Fall 1999, Kwame Dixon and Patricia E. Allard for Amnesty International USA, February 2000; see *United States of America: Rights for All*, 1 October 1998 (AI Index: AMR 51/35/98); see *United States of America: Police Brutality and Excessive Force in the New York City Police Department*, 1 June 1996 (AI Index: AMR 51/36/96). A recent year-long study conducted by AIUSA found that the unlawful use of race in police, immigration and airport security procedures has expanded since the attacks of 11 September 2001. *Threat and Humiliation: Racial Profiling, Domestic Security, and Human Rights in the United States*, Amnesty International USA, September 2004.

Allegations of police officers physically abusing transgender individuals were reported in Los Angeles, Chicago, San Antonio and New York as well as in Pennsylvania, San Francisco and Washington, D.C.[272] AI heard that transgender women of color and transgender individuals "who may not pass" are targeted for police misconduct, including physical abuse.[273] The Ella Baker Center and TransAction in San Francisco notes that some of the worst incidents of police misconduct are targeted at immigrant transgender women."[274]

- **Los Angeles:** A white transgender woman was arrested during a September 2002 sex work sting operation conducted in hotels on Sunset Boulevard in Los Angeles. Officers allegedly questioned her as to whether she had undergone sex reassignment surgery and strip-searched her in front of three officers, apparently in order to determine her genitally determined sex. She described the situation as "humiliating." During the search, one of the officers reportedly grabbed her head and slammed it into a wall with such force that the bone holding her front teeth was broken, requiring medical treatment.[275]

- **New York:** Two NYPD officers, summoned in response to a 911 request for medical assistance in the Bronx, are alleged to have attacked JaLea Lamot, a transgender woman, in November 1998. According to witnesses, police officers verbally abused her and pushed her against a wall after discovering she was a transgender woman. A large number of officers reportedly entered the apartment and family members and a visiting neighbor were beaten, maced and arrested. The family filed a civil lawsuit alleging police misconduct and received a financial settlement from the city in 2002.[276]

- **New York:** Sammy Velez, a transgender woman, reportedly snatched a purse and two officers chased her. Velez fell to the floor and was beaten and kicked by the officers. As a result her left eyeball was reportedly ruptured, and her collarbone and facial bones were fractured. The City of New York paid Velez $75,000 to settle a claim that the police used excessive force in blinding her left eye. Reportedly, the officers involved were not disciplined.[277]

- **Chicago:** An African American transgender woman reports that in December 2004, a police officer responding to a domestic dispute broke her wrist by throwing her against a wall and to the floor. In spite of her indicating that her wrist had been hurt, the officer twisted her wrists and handcuffed them behind her. As a result of a resisting arrest charge, she was taken into custody and held for two and a half days. During that time, she reports consistently asking for and being denied medical assistance. Her broken wrist was reportedly treated only after her release.[278]

Other organizations have also found that transgender individuals are targeted for physical abuse. A 2001 Los Angeles report found that 14 percent of the 244 participants in a survey of transgender women reported that they

[272] AI interviews with Lora Branch, City of Chicago Department of Public Health, Chicago, 18 February 2004; Denise, Client, San Antonio AIDS Foundation, San Antonio, 5 December 2003; Cyndee Clay and GiGi Thomas, HIPS, Washington, D.C., 20 November 2003; Malaika Parker, Bay Area Police Watch, Ella Baker Center, San Francisco, 27 October 2003.

[273] AI interviews with Miranda Stevens, TYRA, Chicago, 25 February 2004; Lisa Tonna, Director of Advocacy and Legislative Affairs, Horizons, Chicago, 23 February 2004; Ujima Moore, Amassi, Los Angeles, 29 January 2004; Dean Spade, Sylvia Rivera Law Project, New York City, 19 February 2004; Zo, Member of FIERCE!, New York City, 2 March 2004; Jesse Ehrensaft-Hawley, Director of FIERCE!, New York City, 22 January 2004; Carrie Davis, Gender Identity Project, New York City, 3 February 2004; Juhu Thukral, Director of Sex Workers Project, and Melissa Ditmore, Network of Sex Work Projects, Urban Justice Center Sex Workers Project, New York City, 11 March 2004; Vanessa Edwards Foster, National and Local Activist, Houston, 30 November 2003; conference call with Shawna Virago, Director of the Domestic Violence Project at CUAV, San Francisco, 31 July 2002; Chris Daly, Staff Attorney, Transgender Law Center, San Francisco, 27 October 2003.

[274] Chris Daley, Elly Kugler, and Jo Hirschman, *Walking While Transgender, Law Enforcement Harassment of San Francisco's Transgender/ Transsexual Community*, The Ella Baker Center for Human Rights/ TransAction, April 2000, p xii.

[275] AI interview with Advocate, Gay and Lesbian Adolescent Social Services, Los Angeles, 28 January 2004.

[276] Duncan Osborne, "City Settles Brutality Claim – Transgendered woman, family, friends awarded $360,000," Gaycitynews.com, 15 July 2002.

[277] Deborah Sontag and Dan Barry, "The Price of Brutality: A Special Report; Police Complaints Settled, Rarely Resolved," *New York Times*, 17 September 1997.

[278] AI telephone interview with Anonymous, Chicago, 7 March 2005.

had suffered physical abuse by a police officer at least once.[279] Based on data from 1995 to 1999, the National Coalition of Anti-Violence Programs reported that although anti-transgender violence accounted for only about two to four percent of all reported incidents, those incidents accounted for approximately 40 percent of the total incidents of police-initiated violence.[280]

Lesbians are also subjected to violence by law enforcement officers because of their sexuality, particularly in terms of their physical appearance.[281] Rebecca Young from the National Drug Research Institute told AI that women perceived as "masculine" are assumed to be non-compliant and to resist arrest. During a three-year study undertaken by her organization, she reports hearing that when arrested, "masculine appearing" women are generally treated with greater physical harshness and that their handcuffs are placed too tightly.[282]

- **California:** A self-described "multiracial" lesbian told AI she was physically abused by police officers on 5 May 2003 after police arrived at their home in response to an altercation involving her white partner and a contractor on their property. She told AI that although the situation was calm, the moment she told an officer that she needed to go and help her "lover" who was sick, the officer suddenly grabbed her arm forcefully from behind, forcing her arm straight back and twisting it up at the wrist, wrenching her arm "as if it was going to pull out of the socket." When the woman attempted to break free, she was thrown to the ground and reportedly held in a chokehold.[283] She told AI that one of the officers forced down her pants and exposed her buttocks. Reportedly, one of the officers also kicked her in the back, and two others hit her on the side of the face so that her head hit the pavement. She told AI that she couldn't breathe, began to black out and that she went into convulsions.[284]

- **Washington, DC:** An African American lesbian reported that in 2002, police officers "grabbed me by the neck and smashed my face into the door and my tooth chipped." She also reported that a male officer then proceeded to unbutton her trousers during a search on the street. Officers reportedly asked, "Why are you wearing boys' underwear? Are you a dyke? Do you eat pussy?"[285]

AI also heard a number of reports of physical abuse of gay men by police officers in San Antonio, New York, Los Angeles and Chicago.[286] Reports of physical abuse by law enforcement were also received from other locations, including San Francisco, California; Oakland, California; Lincoln, Rhode Island; and Connecticut,[287] including the following:

- **Chicago:** In November 2000, Jeffrey Lyons, a 39-year-old heterosexual white man, was allegedly beaten by off-

---

279 The Transgender Community Health Report 2001 interviewed 244 transgender people and found that 37 percent had been verbally abused and 14 percent had been physically abused by the police. Reback, C., Simon, P. "The Los Angeles Transgender Health Study: Community Report, 2001." Furthermore, Communities United Against Violence in San Francisco documented that police officers perpetrated nearly 50 percent of the complaints of violence motivated by discrimination they received from transgender people. Clarence Patton, "Anti-Lesbian, Gay, Bisexual and Transgender Violence in 2001, A Report of the National Coalition of Anti-Violence Programs," 2002. Reportedly, the 50 percent includes not only police officers, but also security guards: AI interview with Sergeant Thorne of the San Francisco Police Department, 15 March 2004. See also Shannon Minter and Christopher Daley, "Trans Realities: A Legal Needs Assessment of San Francisco Transgender Communities," San Francisco: National Center for Lesbian Rights and Transgender Law Center, 2003.

280 Ken Moore, "Anti-Lesbian, Gay, Bisexual and Transgender Violence in 1999," National Coalition of Anti-Violence Programs, 2000.

281 AI interviews with Joey Mogul, Queer to the Left and People's Law Center, Chicago, 12 November 2003; Joo-Hyun Kang and Rien Murray, Audre Lorde Project, New York City, 10 March 2004.

282 AI interview with Rebecca Young, National Drug Research Institute, New York City, 10 March 2004. Young, R. M., Friedman, S. R., Case, P., Asencio, M. W., & Clatts, M. "Women injection drug users who have sex with women exhibit increased HIV infection and risk behaviors." Journal of Drug Issues, 30 (3), 2000, 499-524.

283 She reports being held in a "carotid artery" chokehold.

284 Survivor 25, email to Amnesty International, 17 March 2004; and interview 1 March 2005.

285 Kara Fox, "Maryland Lesbian Alleges Metro Police Abuse in Arrest," The Washington Blade, 26 April 2002.

286 LAGLC AVP, Hate Crime Incident report, 26 March 2002; LAGLC AVP, Hate Crime Incident Report, No date given; AI interviews with Rick Garcia, Executive Director, Equality Illinois, Chicago, 13 November 2003; ACT Up Monthly Meeting, New York City, 27 March 2004; Salvador, GLASS Mobile Unit, Los Angeles, 29 October 2003.

287 Jaxon Van Derbeken and Susan Sward, "Gay slur by cops claimed in $1.25 million suit; Son of SFPD's No. 2 named in July incident," The San Francisco Chronicle, 7 December 2002; "Lawyer for Rhode Island town denies gay teen's police brutality claim," The Advocate.com, 26 June 2001; email received by AI, Connecticut incident, 27 February 2004.

STONEWALLED

duty officers when he embraced a male friend. Officers reportedly shouted anti-gay epithets, one officer yelling, "Get this through your head: You faggots will never win." Lyons suffered a fractured cheekbone, broken nose and neurological damage.[288]

- **Chicago:** In July 2000, Kentin Waits was reportedly beaten by officers while in police custody at the 19th District station, and called "fucking faggot" and "gay motherfucker."[289]

- **Los Angeles:** In 2002, two white officers arrested an Asian gay man. During the course of the arrest the officers reportedly shoved the man's face up against a wall and beat him while shouting homophobic slurs, including "butt plug" and "girlie man."[290]

- **San Antonio:** On 31 July 2001, two heterosexual, Canadian male tourists allege that they were verbally and physically abused by the San Antonio Park Police because they were perceived to be gay. They were reportedly handcuffed, beaten, bruised and dragged face-first on the concrete by Park Rangers while being called "Canadian faggots" and subjected to other homophobic slurs.[291] After this incident it was discovered that the officer involved was previously an officer in another district in Texas, and that while on duty there he was investigated several times for alleged excessive force until he was ultimately forced to resign from the department.[292]

- **Lincoln, Rhode Island:** On 29 August 2000, Jesse Ousley, a 17-year-old boy, was walking with his boyfriend and stepped into the street in front of an off-duty police officer's unmarked car. After the near-collision, Ousley reportedly "slapped" the hood of the officer's car. The officer reportedly got out of his car and started hitting Ousley. Ousley reportedly suffered two black eyes, a bloody nose, bruises and cuts, including marks on his neck where the officer allegedly tried to choke him. Ousley's boyfriend pulled the officer off and tried to walk away with Ousley. But when the officer overheard Ousley tell his boyfriend that he loved him, he reportedly attacked Ousley again, shouting, "You [expletive] faggot." Ousley was taken to a hospital for his injuries. After the family requested an investigation, the police filed charges against Ousley, charging him with assault, disorderly conduct and malicious damage 18 days after the incident. Ousley was found guilty of malicious damage for kicking the officer's car, but the two other charges were dropped. The Ousley family filed a $1 million lawsuit against the town and police department.[293] The lawsuit has reportedly been settled for an undisclosed amount and it appears that the officer involved still remains on the police force.[294]

- **Oakland, California:** A gay Latino man was arrested while driving in Oakland in 2001. As officers put him into the patrol car, one of the officers reportedly commented on his pink socks, calling them "faggot socks," and slammed the door on his ankle—he had to have his ankle in a brace.[295]

---

[288] See Amnesty International, *Allegations of Homophobic Abuse by Chicago Police Officers*, 10 February 2001 (AI Index: AMR 51/022/2001); see *Amnesty International Renews Call for Investigation into Homophobic Abuse of Chicago Police Officers*, 22 June 2001 (AI Index: AMR 51/092/2001). See also Rick Hepp, "City, Police Sued Over Beating Outside Bar," *Chicago Tribune*, 11 January 2001, at N1. AI understands that the civil suit filed by Lyons failed as he was unable to prove that the officers were acting as officers, and as such they weren't depriving him of his civil rights under color of law, as required for his Sec.1983 claim. Accordingly, the court found that the city of Chicago was not responsible for their behavior. Lyons v. Adams, 257 F.Supp.2d 1125, (N.D.Ill. 2003).

[289] Horizons Incident Reports, Chicago, 22 May 2001; Amnesty International, *AI Renews Call for Investigation into Homophobic Abuse by Chicago Police Officers*, 22 June 2001 (AI Index AMR 51/092/01); Matt O'Connor, "Gay Man Sues City Police Over Alleged Beating," *Chicago Tribune*, 1 June 2001, at N6; Steve Warmbir, "Lawsuit Accuses Cops of Abusing Gay Man," *Chicago Sun-Times*, 1 June 2001, at 14; "Gay Chicago Man Sues Police Over Beating," The Advocate.com, 2-4 June 2001, available at: http://www.advocate.com/new_news.asp?id=2475&sd=06/02/01-06/04/01.

[290] LAGLC Anti-Violence Project, Incident Report Form, 26 March 2002.

[291] Reportedly, the arresting officer falsified an email claiming to be from an eyewitness that denied that allegations made by the two Canadians. The Municipal Integrity Division of the City of San Antonio conducted an investigation that determined Officer Armando Vidales falsified an email, supposedly from an eyewitness to the arrests. The email supported the Park Rangers' version of events and claimed that the Canadians were lying. Dan Castor, "District Attorney Drops Charges Against Canadians: Park Ranger Admits Falsifying Evidence," Press Release, 4 December 2001.

[292] Matt Lum, "Where is the Outrage? Recent Allegations Uncover History of Abuse in San Antonio," Texas Triangle, posted 2 August 2001.

[293] "Lawyer for Rhode Island Town Denies Gay Teen's Police Brutality Claim," The Advocate.com, 26 June 2001, at http://www.advocate.com/new_news.asp?id=1938&sd=06/26/01; "R.I. Gay Man Sues Town Police," The Advocate.com, 20 April 2002, at http://www.advocate.com/new_news.asp?id=4003&sd=04/20/02-04/22/02; Elizabeth Gudrais, "Judge Rejects 1 Count in Suit Against Police," *Providence Journal-Bulletin*, Rhode Island, 10 November 2003.

[294] Tim Grace, "Gay Teen Settles Suit Against Cops," *The Pawtucket Times*, 29 July 2004.

[295] AI interview with Jennifer Rakowski, Communities United Against Violence, San Francisco, 23 October 2003.

AI is also concerned by reported incidents where officers have responded to victims of crime, including hate crimes, with verbal and physical violence.[296]

- **Chicago:** A gay white man called the police in Chicago because he had been attacked. Reportedly, responding police officers made homophobic comments and taunts and pushed him, shoved him and beat his head into the pavement. He did not defend himself against the blows, but was reportedly threatened with a criminal charge.[297]

The illegal and discriminatory use of force against LGBT individuals as documented in this report violates an individual's right not to be subjected to torture or to cruel, inhuman and degrading treatment, which is specified in the ICCPR and the Convention Against Torture, treaties to which the U.S. is a party.[298]

5.3
VERBAL ABUSE OF LGBT INDIVIDUALS

> "I've had cops say, "Are you just like a faggot? Do you have a dick?"
> Transgender woman participant, meeting between Transgeneros Unidos and representatives of LAPD, Los Angeles 23 October 2003.[299]

BOTH LGBT VICTIMS OF POLICE ABUSE and activists whom AI interviewed for this report stated that homophobic and transphobic verbal abuse by police was a serious problem. LGBT people who came into contact with the police were frequently subjected to verbal abuse of a homophobic or transphobic nature. Despite the serious nature of this problem, one of the challenges in assessing the full degree of the problem is that there currently exists very limited capacity to document verbal abuse by law enforcement officers against LGBT individuals. Furthermore, there may be underreporting of these abuses.[300] However, scandals involving homophobic and transphobic slurs by law enforcement have been reported in the media. For example, in the District of Columbia in 2001, police officers were found to have been sending racist, homophobic and sexist e-mails through their patrol car computer systems. Metropolitan Police Department Executive Assistant Chief Terrance Gainer reportedly observed, "There appear to be significant numbers of people who are either ignorant or racist or homophobic or a terrible combination of all three."[301]

In the following section, reports to AI of verbal abuse against transgender individuals, lesbians and gay men will be presented in more detail.

---

[296] AI interviews with Matt Pulling and Susan Holt, STOP Domestic Violence Program, Los Angeles, 30 September 2003; Rick Garcia, Executive Director, Equality Illinois, Chicago, 13 November 2003; Al Thurk, San Antonio, 2 March 2004.

[297] AI interview with an LGBT Rights Advocate from Chicago, 12 November 2003.

[298] International standards accept that there are circumstances when law enforcement officials may use force and broadly agree about the legitimate purposes and scope of the use of force. Generally, they permit use of force for specific purposes such as self-defense and the protection of other people; restrict the amount of force which can be used to the extent necessary; and prohibit the use of force as punishment. See Art. 3, Code of Conduct for Law Enforcement Officials, G.A. res. 34/169, annex, 34 U.N. GAOR Supp. (No. 46) at 186, U.N. Doc. A/34/46 (1979); Arts. 1, 4, 5, 7, 8, Basic Principles on the Use of Force and Firearms by Law Enforcement Officials, Eighth United Nations Congress on the Prevention of Crime and the Treatment of Offenders, Havana, 27 August to 7 September 1990, U.N. Doc. A/CONF.144/28/Rev.1 at 112 (1990).

[299] Transgeneros Unidos Meeting with LAPD, Captain Downing and Sgt. Diaz, Hollywood-Wilcox Division LAPD; Lt. Ruiz, LAPD Vice; Mike Jolicoeur and Christine Nielsen, LAPD Liaisons; and Amnesty International, 23 October 2003.

[300] The NCAVP collects information from a network of approximately 27 anti-violence organizations that monitor and respond to incidents of bias affecting the LGBT community. In NCAVP's report for 2003, 11 NCAVP members collected detailed information about anti-gay incidents occurring in their cities and regions, including Chicago, IL; Cleveland, OH; Colorado; Columbus, OH; Connecticut; Los Angeles, CA, Massachusetts; Minnesota; New York, NY; Pennsylvania; and San Francisco, CA. The fact that less than half of NCAVP member programs contributed to the report reflects a fundamental and ongoing capacity and resource challenge within a growing number of anti-violence organizations. See: Clarence Patton, *Anti-Lesbian, Gay, Bisexual and Transgender Violence in 2003*, National Coalition of Anti-Violence Programs, 2004.

[301] Editorial, "Uncouth Cops with Computers," *Washington Post*, 30 March 2001, A28. See also Susan Sward, Jaxon Van Derbeken, "Gay slur by cops claimed in $1.25 million suit; son of SFPD's No. 2 named in July incident," *The San Francisco Chronicle*, 7 December 2002, pg. A21.

AI heard reports of police officers verbally abusing transgender individuals in Los Angeles, Chicago, San Antonio and New York, as well as in Philadelphia and Lehigh Valley, Pennsylvania; San Francisco, California; and Washington, D.C. Reports indicate that the use of transphobic and homophobic verbal abuse and slurs, including the use of the word "faggot" and "freak," is widespread when transgender individuals interact with law enforcement officers in the United States.[302] A 2001 survey of 244 transgender women in Los Angeles found that 37 percent of respondents reported verbal abuse by a police officer on at least one occasion.[303]

AI heard a number of reports of dehumanizing and degrading verbal abuse against transgender women.[304] Advocates report that many officers have "no respect" for transgender women, make fun of them and call them "freaks."[305] In New York, AI heard of officers yelling abusive comments at transgender women including, "you're disgusting" and "get out of here." In one incident, an NYPD officer observing an African American transgender woman on the street reportedly said, "What the fuck is that?"[306] In another case, officers called a black transgender woman and her Latina friend "monsters."[307] Verbal harassment and abuse reported to AI also include deliberately humiliating transgender people by using inappropriate pronouns or an individual's prior female or male name, and questioning what a person's "real" gender is.[308]

Reportedly, officers in Los Angeles regularly drive by transgender women who have congregated and look at, ridicule and humiliate them, asking them why they are wearing women's clothes, saying "aren't you a man?"[309] Comments reported to AI in Chicago include "you're a man."[310] AI heard reports of officers in New York, Los Angeles, Chicago and D.C. referring to transgender people as "he/she/it," or "he/she."[311]

- **Philadelphia, Pennsylvania:** Finesse Kelly, an African American transgender woman, and a friend were attempting to hail a cab in the early morning hours of 4 February 2002 in Philadelphia. A police officer reportedly hurled slurs at Finesse, including "retard" and "animal," and then arrested her.[312]

---

302 AI interviews with Andy Kim, Chicago Coalition for the Homeless, Chicago, 14 November 2003; Clients of GLASS Mobile Unit, Los Angeles, 29 October 2003. Telephone interview with Robbyn Stewart, transgender woman, New York City, 21 January 2004; email from Anonymous, a transgender woman, New York City, 30 January 2004; Jennifer Rakowski, Communities United Against Violence, San Francisco, 23 October 2003.

303 Reback C, Simon P, Bemis C, & Gatson B. The Los Angeles Transgender Health Study: Community Report, Los Angeles: University of California at Los Angeles, May 2001.

304 AI interviews with Miranda Stevens, TYRA, Chicago, 25 February 2004; Horizons Youth Drop-In, Chicago, 19 February 2004.

305 AI interviews with Miranda Stevens, TYRA, Chicago, 25 February 2004; Andy Kim, Chicago Coalition for the Homeless, Chicago, 14 November 2003; Heather Bradley, Night Ministry, Chicago, 25 February 2004.

306 NYPD officer referring to a young transgender person of color, AI interview with Ali Forney Center, New York, 13 February 2004.

307 AI interview with Michelle Sosa and her Transgender Tuesday Group, Positive Health Project, 24 February 2004.

308 AI interview with Members of GLASS Focus Groups 1 & 2, Los Angeles, 28 January 2004; Shirley Bushnell, Van Ness Recovery House Prevention Division, Los Angeles, 1 October 2003; Martha Matthews , former staff attorney, and Sharon Murphy, chapter coordinator, ACLU, Los Angeles, 3 October 2003; Anonymous Client of the GLASS Mobile Unit, Los Angeles, 29 October 2003; Anonymous Client of GLASS Mobile Unit, Los Angeles, 29 October 2003; Wendell Glenn, Director of External Programs, GLASS, Los Angeles, 31 October 2003; Staff Member of an FtM Transgender Support Organization, Los Angeles, 28 October 2003; Pauline Park, New York Association for Gender Rights Advocacy, New York City, 11 February 2004; Michelle Sosa, Positive Health Project – Transgender Tuesday Group, New York City, 24 February 2004; Anonymous, New York City, 26 February 2002; Juhu Thukral, Director, Urban Justice Center Sex Workers Project, New York City, 11 March 2004; GiGi Thomas, Program Assistant, Client Advocate, and Cyndee Clay, Executive Director, HIPS, Washington, D.C., 20 November 2003; Vanessa Edwards Foster, Houston, 30 November 2003.

309 AI interview with Staff of Anonymous Transgender Service Provider, Los Angeles, 2 October 2003.

310 AI interview with Anonymous Transgender Rights Advocate (Name and organization on file with AIUSA), Chicago, 25 February 2004.

311 AI interviews with Miranda Stevens, TYRA, Chicago, 25 February 2004; Martha Matthews, former staff attorney, and Sharon Murphy, chapter coordinator, ACLU of Southern California, Los Angeles, 3 October 2003; Michelle Sosa, Positive Health Project – Transgender Tuesday Group, 24 February 2004; Margaux Delotte-Bennett, Sexual Minority Youth Assistance League, Washington, D.C., 20 November 2003.

312 In February 2004, The Police Advisory Commission found that the officer had abused his authority by insulting and then improperly arresting Finesse Kelly. The officer received a one-day suspension and sensitivity training. See: In Re: Mark Kelly, a/k/a Finesse Kelly, and Christopher Alvarez, a/k/a Deja Alvarez, City of Philadelphia Police Advisory Commission, Complaints No. 021067and 021068, 20 January 2004, pp. 3-4, available at: http://www.phila.gov/pac/OpKellyAlvarez_20Jan2004.pdf.

- **Lehigh Valley, Pennsylvania:** "When I told them my real name, Rachel, they refused to recognize that and continued to call me by my male name ... The State Troopers tried to keep their smirks and comments at a distance, but I still heard words like 'fag' and 'freak' a number of times."[313]

As noted above, reports to AI indicate that degrading comments are frequently sexualized. For example, a Native American transgender woman told AI that officers in the Hollywood area regularly call out "suck me, bitch."[314] Verbal abuse targeting transgender individuals often insinuates that transgender women are sex workers. For example, in Los Angeles, individuals and community advocates report that officers frequently call transgender women "whore," "slut" and "prostitute."[315]

AI has also heard of instances where officers have verbally abused transgender men.[316] Verbal abuse of transgender men often targets their perceived transgression of gender "norms"; in several cases officers made derogatory comments about the men's genitalia.[317] Reports to AI indicate that transgender men are less likely to be targeted for abuse on the street, but are harassed based on their gender identity if their gender identity is discovered. "A lot of officers don't think of the possibility of trans men; they feel lied to, fooled."[318]

- **New York:** A Filipino transgender man was arrested in New York in 2003. When he gave the police his ID and papers, an officer said, "I know what you are. I know your kind. I just want you to know you're never going to have a family like me, kids like me, a dog like me. And know that whatever you strap on between your legs will never be as real or as big as mine. You're going to end up like the rest of your kind: without a job, homeless and shooting up drugs." The police put him in a cell with female arrestees. Officers walked past him repeatedly, mocking his name and asking, "What is this thing?"[319]

Reports from advocates indicate that the less a transgender individual "passes,"[320] the more harassment and attention the individual receives. This means that transphobic attitudes and verbal abuse particularly affect homeless and low-income transgender women who can't afford surgery or hormones.[321] Furthermore, race or ethnicity and socioeconomic status reportedly also play an important role in the degree of police harassment suffered by transgender women.[322]

---

[313] Email from Rachel Thompson to AIUSA, 18 March 2004. Rachel Thompson is a Caucasian, transgender woman in Lehigh Valley, Pennsylvania.

[314] AI interview with Client of GLASS Mobile Unit, Los Angeles, 29 October 2003.

[315] AI interviews with Client of GLASS Mobile Unit, Los Angeles, 29 October 2003; Staff of Anonymous Transgender Service Provider, Los Angeles, 2 October 2003. On at least one occasion such conduct formed the subject of a complaint filed at Hollywood-Wilcox Precinct.

[316] AI Interview with transgender man, Drop-in group discussion, TYRA, Chicago, 25 February 2004; Dean Spade, Attorney, Sylvia Rivera Law Project, New York City, 19 February 2004; Chris Daley, Staff Attorney, Transgender Law Center, San Francisco, 27 October 2003; Catalina Sol and Dilcia Molina, La Clinica Del Pueblo, Washington, D.C., 20 November 2003.

[317] Jeremy Burke First Amended Complaint: *Burke v. CCSF,* SFSC Case No. 408175. *Jeremy Burke vs. City and County of San Francisco, Officer Anton Collins (#142), and Officer Lee (#1057), Deputy Sheriff Veloro (#1702), Dorothy Lipkins, San Francisco Housing Authority, McCoy's Patrol Services, and/or DOES 1 through 100* (filed 24 July 2003); Deposition of JEREMY BURKE. Volume I, Thursday 7 August 2003. Examination by Mr. Ackiron. Afternoon Session: Examination by Mr. Ackiron, p. 213; Deposition of JEREMY BURKE, Volume 2, Thursday 2 October 2003. Further Examination by Mr. Ackiron, p. 235-236, p. 262-268, 271; email from Livi Yoshioka-Maxwell to AIUSA, 23 February 2003; AI interview with Dean Spade, Sylvia Rivera Law Project, 19 February 2004.

[318] AI interview with Chris Daley, Staff Attorney, Transgender Law Center, San Francisco, 27 October 2003.

[319] AI interviews with Anonymous, 7 July 2005; Dean Spade, Attorney, Sylvia Rivera Law Project, 19 February 2004.

[320] "Passing" is a term used to indicate that strangers accept that the individual is a man (for transgender men), or a woman (for a transgender woman) based on appearance.

[321] AI interviews with Anonymous Transgender Service Provider, Los Angeles, 2 October 2003; Shirley Bushnell, Van Ness Recovery House Prevention Division, 1 October 2003; GiGi Thomas, Program Assistant, Client Advocate, and Cyndee Clay, Executive Director, HIPS, Washington, D.C., 20 November 2003.

[322] AI interviews with Martha Matthews, former staff attorney, and Sharon Murphy, chapter coordinator, ACLU of Southern California, 3 October 2003; Julia Garcia, La Opportunidad and Ralph Showers, Jovenes Inc., Los Angeles, 30 October 2003; Members of ACT UP Monthly Meeting, New York, 3 March 2004; Staff Member of an FtM Transgender Support Organization, and Simmi Ghandi, Los Angeles Chapter, Incite! Women of Color Against Violence, 28 October 2003.

AI received several reports of verbal abuse of lesbians, including women who were called "dyke" as an insult during interactions with law enforcement.[323] Verbal abuse of lesbians often focuses on perceived gender transgressions. In all four cities studied by AI, reports indicate that police single out lesbians who look "masculine" for verbal harassment and abuse; as one advocate noted, "Anyone who is gender variant, such as butch lesbians, is more likely to be mistreated or seen as suspect."[324] A Latina lesbian in San Antonio told AI, "Lesbians get treated real bad … especially butch women. Some cops accuse you of taking girls away from them."[325] In a study of lesbian and bisexual drug users, Rebecca Young, from the National Drug Research Institute, found a pattern of officers threatening them with physical abuse, saying, "You want to be a man, I'll treat you like one," and heard of officers calling "butch" lesbians "wanna-be man." Reports further indicate that in particular, police target "butch-identified" women of color.[326]

Reports to AI indicate that verbal harassment of lesbian women and girls is frequently of a sexual nature. Lesbians in New York reported that police officers make comments suggesting that their sexual orientation needs to be "corrected," such as, "You need a real man" or "Try me and you won't be a lesbian."[327] AI heard of officers making such comments to women they perceive to be the more "feminine" in a couple when responding to domestic violence incidents in the San Francisco Bay Area.[328]

- **Los Angeles:** A 28-year-old Latina lesbian reported that in 2001 she was pulled over by a police officer, who asked her if the rainbow sticker on her car meant that she was gay. When she responded in the affirmative, the officer began to ask her questions about her personal life, including how old she was when she first kissed a girl, whether she had ever been with a man, and whether she used sex toys. The officer then proceeded to advise the woman that her "lifestyle" wasn't a good one, but that it was a "choice" and she "could change." The woman reported that, while his conduct made her uncomfortable, she felt compelled to answer the officer's questions.[329]

AI has heard a number of reports of police officers calling gay men "faggots". The use of the term "faggot" is reportedly also used as a general, derogatory term regardless of whether an officer perceives an individual to be gay.[330] Men who do not conform to traditional gender "norms" are targeted for verbal abuse. AI heard reports from gay men and men perceived to be displaying "feminine" characteristics that officers have subjected them to comments such as "sissy" and "princess."[331] AI also heard reports in Los Angeles and New York from police officers that if a fellow officer acted in any way "effeminate" he would be called "faggot."[332]

---

[323] AI interviews with Darron E. Bowden, Former Executive Director, First Defense Legal Aid, Chicago, 11 November 2003; Simmi Ghandi, INCITE! LA, Los Angeles, 28 October 2003; Rebecca Young, National Drug Research Institute, New York City, 10 March 2004.

[324] AI interviews with Miranda Stevens and others, TYRA Drop-In, Chicago, 25 February 2004; Lisa Tonna, Director of Advocacy and Legislative Affairs, Horizons Community Services, and Jacob Mueller, Office of GLBT Concerns, University of Illinois at Chicago, Chicago, 23 February 2004; Lora Branch, Director, City of Chicago Department of Public Health, Chicago, 26 February 2004; Joey Mogul, Queer to the Left and People's Law Center, Chicago, 17 September 2003; Anonymous, GLASS Focus Group, Los Angeles, 28 January 2004; Anonymous member of FIERCE! New York City, 22 January 2004; Justine Sullivan and Jose, Streetworks, New York, 5 March 2004; Anonymous (name on file with AIUSA), San Antonio AIDS Foundation, San Antonio, 5 December 2003; meeting with San Antonio PFLAG, San Anotnio, 4 December 2003; Marcus De Maria Arana, San Francisco Human Rights Commission, San Francisco, 15 March 2004.

[325] AI interview with Anonymous (name on file with AIUSA), San Antonio AIDS Foundation, San Antonio, 5 December 2003.

[326] AI interviews with Heather Bradley, Night Ministry, Chicago, 17 February 2004; Anonymous, (name on file with AIUSA), New York City, 23 March 2003; C. Nicole Mason, National Women's Alliance, Washington, D.C., 10 October 2003.

[327] AI interviews with Members of FIERCE!, New York City, 22 January 2004 and 2 March 2004; Rebecca Young, National Drug Research Institute, New York City, 10 March 2004.

[328] AI interview with Jennifer Rakowski, CUAV, San Francisco, 23 October 2003.

[329] LAGLC AVP, Case Intake/Incident Report Form, Los Angeles, 6 January 2001.

[330] AI interviews with Joey Mogul, People's Law Office, Chicago, 12 November 2003; Anonymous Transgender Service Provider, Los Angeles, 2 October 2003; Jeffrey King, In the Meantime, Los Angeles, 2 October 2003; eight Outreach Workers, APICHA, New York City, 30 March 2004; Anthony Miranda, Latino Officers Association, New York City, 9 March 2004; Anonymous, Gay Officers Action League, New York City, 14 April 2004; Ricci Levy, Jeff Montgomery, Judy Guerin and Andrew, Woodhull Foundation, New York City, 18 March 2004; Andrew Thomas, Lawyer, San Antonio, 4 December 2003; Jennifer Rakowski, CUAV, San Francisco, 23 October 2003.

[331] AI interview with Esperanza, San Antonio, 4 December 2003; Case Intake/Incident Report Form, L.A. Gay and Lesbian Center Anti-Violence Project, 26 March 2002.

[332] AI interviews with Sgt. Don Mueller, West Hollywood Police Department, Los Angeles, 27 January 2004; Anthony Miranda, Latino Officers Association, New York City, 9 March 2004.

- **Chicago:** A 22-year-old African American gay man was walking through a park in 2003 when he was stopped by two Chicago Police Department officers. They reportedly called him a "fag," handcuffed him and threw him in their car. He was kept in jail, without charges, overnight.[333]

- **Chicago:** When a man, who does not identify as gay, reportedly did not respond immediately to a police officer's request to remove a barricade that he had placed in a parking space in front of his place of work in order to unload musical equipment, the officer allegedly became angry and slammed him against the wall and called him a "fag." The officer charged him with disorderly conduct; however, the charges were later dismissed and the man sued and won a settlement.[334]

- **New York:** A black gay man, Mr. G., was leaving a park in 2000 when a uniformed officer pointed a gun at him, saying, "If you move, I'll shoot you." After complying with the officer's request to show identification, Mr. G. was taken to a police van waiting nearby. He reports, "The police started making gay jokes, saying, 'fags' and talking negatively about black people."[336]

- **New York:** A gay white man wore a t-shirt that said, "Fight AIDS not Iraq" to an anti-war demonstration in 2003. He passed a police officer standing in front of a fire station. The officer reportedly yelled at him, "If you didn't fuck each other in the ass you wouldn't get AIDS."[337]

AI is concerned by the remarks made by the officer in the above case that would appear to conflate AIDS with sexual orientation. Gay men of color have reportedly been subjected to verbal abuse which is both racist and homophobic in nature by law enforcement officers, including in the following incidents:

- **Chicago:** A young African American gay man was standing outside a games arcade with some friends in Chicago. Police officers reportedly passed in a squad car and yelled at them to "move their ass out of the way." The officers reportedly searched the young people, and are alleged to have verbally abused the young African American, calling him "nigger faggot" and saying that "his ass is not big enough to fuck." He was charged with disorderly conduct after talking back to the officers and was taken to the station. This caused a lot of problems with his parents, as he is not out to his family, and they wanted to know what he was doing in Lakeview. The charges were dropped after an appearance in court.[338]

AI is concerned by incidents reported to AI where officers have responded to victims of crime, including hate crimes, with verbal and physical violence.[339]

Verbal abuse against LGBT individuals as documented in this report violates the prohibition under Article 7 of the ICCPR against cruel, inhuman and degrading treatment. Cruel, inhuman and degrading treatment relates "... not only to acts that cause physical pain but also to acts that cause mental suffering to the victim."[340] This is important where people may suffer psychologically or emotionally because of the homophobic, transphobic, racist verbal abuse and degrading treatment they experience at the hands of the police. Furthermore, verbal abuse violates an individual's right to be treated with dignity, as stipulated in Article 2 of the U.N. Code of Conduct for Law Enforcement Officials, which provides that law enforcement officials shall respect and protect human dignity in the performance of their duty.[341]

[333] AI interview with Rick Garcia, Executive Director, Equality Illinois, Chicago, 14 November 2003.

[334] AI interview with Joey Mogul, Attorney, People's Law Office, Chicago, 12 November 2003.

[336] Incident report, Copwatch, New York City.

[337] AI interview with Members of ACT UP monthly meeting, New York City, 3 March 2004.

[338] AI interview with anonymous client of Horizons Youth Drop-In, Chicago, 19 February 2004.

[339] AI interviews with Rick Garcia, Executive Director, Equality Illinois, Chicago, 13 November 2003; Horizon's Incident Reports, Chicago, November 2002; Matt Pulling and Susan Holt, STOP Domestic Violence Program, Los Angeles, 30 September 2003; AI Thurk, San Antonio, 2 March 2004.

[340] The Human Rights Committee's General Comment 20 on Article 7 of the ICCPR adopted by the Human Rights Committee (44th session, 1992).

[341] U.N. Code of Conduct for Law Enforcement Officials, G.A. res. 34/169, annex, 34 U.N. GAOR Supp. (No. 46) at 186, U.N. Doc. A/34/46 (1979).

6

SEARCHES AND DETENTION

AI HAS RECEIVED REPORTS OF cruel, inhuman and degrading treatment of LGBT individuals during arrest, searches and detention in police precinct holding cells. AI heard reports of officers searching transgender and gender variant individuals in order to determine their "true" gender. AI also heard allegations of misconduct and abuse of LGBT individuals in holding cells and detention centers, including the inappropriate placement of LGBT individuals in situations which compromise their safety. In particular, transgender individuals are often placed in holding cells according to their genitally determined sex rather than their gender identity or expression, placing them at greater risk of verbal, physical and sexual abuse at the hands of other detainees.

While outside the scope of this report, AI researchers also heard reports indicating systemic issues of mistreatment and abuse of LGBT individuals in long-term detention facilities, including immigration detention centers.[342] Further research is necessary into the treatment of such individuals in longer-term detention settings.

---

[342] According to a lawsuit filed against the U.S. government, Christina Madrazo, a Mexican transgender woman, was raped twice by an INS guard at the Krome Detention Center outside Miami, Florida: Alisa Solomon, "Nightmare in Miami," *Village Voice* (New York), 26 March 2002.

6.1

SEARCHES AND "GENDER CHECKS"

"Pat-down searches rarely seem to be about weapons or safety and more often seem to be about 'gender checks.' They usually involve the officer groping a person's groin and/or breasts in an effort to 'figure things out.' Some male cops are curious or fascinated about transgender women."

Chris Daley, Transgender Law Center, San Francisco, 27 October 2003

An African American transgender woman was arrested by LAPD and taken to the county jail. She told AI, "The officers wanted to see my chest. They wanted to see if I had tits or not." They reportedly came into her cell and instructed her to remove her shirt. After she complied, they left.[343]

A transgender man was arrested during a political protest in San Francisco. He showed the officer a drivers' license that identified him as legally male and he was placed in a holding pen with the other male detainees. One officer got curious about the activist's gender status and came into the cell, then reportedly pushed him around, dragged him out and belligerently accused him of having a fraudulent identification card. A second officer asked him if he had a "dick" and groped his crotch and chest to "verify his gender."[344]

AI HEARD A NUMBER OF REPORTS of illegal and inappropriate searches of transgender and gender variant individuals in Chicago, Los Angeles, New York and San Antonio, as well as Alabama and Florida.[345] Searches may take a number of different forms, from a pat "frisk" search[346] to a strip search or body cavity search. Reports to AI indicate a pattern of officers undertaking searches which involve inappropriate touching of an individual's genitalia in order to establish an transgender individual's "true" sex, i.e., genitally determined sex. Such "gender checks" may take place, for example, if an individual's identification does not match their gender presentation, or when the individual is taken to a police station and a decision has to be made about whether a gender variant or transgender person should be placed in a male or female holding cell.[347]

---

343 AI interview with Member of GLASS Focus Group, Los Angeles, 28 January 2004.

344 Chris Daley, Elly Kugler and Jo Hirschmann, "Walking While Transgender," The Ella Baker Center for Human Rights and TransAction, San Francisco, April 2000, vii, quoting an incident reported to the Community United Against Violence.

345 AI interviews with Cara Thaxton, Victim Advocacy Coordinator, Horizons, Chicago, 23 February 2004; Rashawn Lusk, Client, Rafael Center, Chicago, 18 February 2004; Precious, Member, GLASS Mobile Unit, Los Angeles, 29 October 2003; Anonymous Gay and Bisexual Service Provider, Los Angeles, 28 October 2003; Daniel, Member, Gay Men's Health Crisis, New York City, 19 March 2004; Kim Hawkins, Director, and Anya Mukarji-Connolly, Peter Cicchino Youth Project, Urban Justice Center, New York City, 16 January 2004; Anonymous transgender woman, San Antonio AIDS Foundation, San Antonio, 5 December 2003; Chris Daley, Staff Attorney, Transgender Law Center, San Francisco, 27 October 2003.

346 A search of an individual, using the hands, that does not require the individual to remove clothing.

347 Shannon Minter and Christopher Daley, *Trans Realities: A Legal Needs Assessment of San Francisco Transgender Communities*, San Francisco: National Center for Lesbian Rights and Transgender Law Center, 2003

6.1.1

POLICE POLICY AND TRAINING PROCEDURES

> "It would depend on what the officer believed at the time" and an individual "may be dressing like a female, but if I know you're male I'm going to search you."
>
> Deputy Chief Jeffrey Page, Resource Management Division of the San Antonio Police Department[348]

THE UNITED NATIONS HUMAN RIGHTS COMMITTEE has stated that to ensure protection of the dignity of a person who is being searched by a state official, a body search should only be conducted by someone of the same sex.[349] The existing standards clearly seek to establish guidelines whereby the safety and dignity of individuals in detention are safeguarded, principles that should be understood to include transgender individuals.

Under U.S. law, an officer can only perform a pat search on the street if the officer has a reasonable, articulable suspicion, based on his or her observation of the individual's behavior, that the individual is armed and could be dangerous to the officer and/or the public.[350] In the United States, courts have taken different views about the legitimacy of cross-gender "pat" searches, as thorough pat searches require some contact with the genital area, even though the individual is still clothed.[351]

In AI's survey, police departments were asked whether they had any policies regarding strip searches of transgender persons. Out of the 29 police departments responding to AI's survey only seven (24 percent) reported having a policy.[352] Four police departments reported that they do not perform strip searches and the following departments reported that they do not have a policy or a practice governing strip searches of transgender persons: Bridgeport, Connecticut; Wilmington, Delaware; Atlanta, Georgia; Honolulu, Hawaii; Baltimore, Maryland; Boston, Massachusetts; Jackson, Mississippi; Omaha, Nebraska; Manchester, New Hampshire; Albuquerque, New Mexico; Memphis, Tennessee; San Antonio, Texas; Virginia Beach, Virginia; Seattle, Washington; and Cheyenne, Wyoming.

In Los Angeles, Chicago, New York and San Antonio, AI found that generally speaking, the policy of law enforcement agencies is to have officers with the same genitally determined sex conduct searches of transgender persons. In other words, a transgender woman who has not undergone sex reassignment surgery will be searched by a male officer, and a transgender man who has not undergone sex reassignment surgery will be searched by a female officer.

- **Chicago:** Chicago Police Department told AI that they have the "same policy to perform a strip-search on any other arrestee." Reportedly searches are conducted by officers of the same sex, and it appears that unless a transgender woman has undergone sex reassignment surgery she will be searched by a male officer and unless a transgender man has undergone sex reassignment surgery he will be searched by a female officer. Officials told AI, "Transgender is only clothing. You would have to ask them what sex they are, in private," and said that they inquire into whether an individual has undergone surgery.[353] This was confirmed by reports from

---

[348] AI interview with San Antonio Police Department, 4 December 2003.

[349] General Comment 16 to Article 17 of the ICCPR, "Compilation of General Comment and General Recommendations Adopted by Human Rights Treaty Bodies," UN Document HRI/GEN/Rev.3, 15 August 1997.

[350] Terry v Ohio, 392 U.S. 1 (1968).

[351] In the state of Washington, a court decided that such searches of women by men amounted to cruel and unusual punishment, in violation of the U.S. Constitution [Jordan v Gardner, 986 F.2d (9th Cir., 19930]. In a later case, male and female correctional officers successfully sued the director of the Nevada Department of Prisons to prevent him transferring male officers out of a female facility and transferring female officers into the facility. The court decided that it was not against the law for male correctional officers to conduct clothed body searches of female inmates which include touching their breast and genital areas, unless there was evidence (as had been presented in Washington) that the women would suffer severe distress. Even if there was such evidence, the court held, cross-gender searching would be legal if it could be shown to be necessary for security reasons because there were not enough female correctional officers to conduct all searches [Carl v Angelone, 883 F.Supp.1433 (D.Nev., 1995)]. Principle 5(2), Body of Principles for the Protection of All Persons Under Any Form of Detention, G.A. res. 43/173, annex, 43 U.N. GAOR Supp. (No. 49) at 298, U.N. Doc. A/43/49 (1988), provides that measures which are designed solely to protect the rights and special status of women are not considered discriminatory.

[352] Birmingham, Alabama; Los Angeles, California; Jacksonville, Florida; Chicago, Illinois; Lexington, Kentucky; Kansas City, Missouri; Las Vegas, Nevada. It should be noted that not all of these departments appear to have a specific policy relating to transgender detainees; for example, Birmingham, Alabama reported that its policy was "Same as any person—person of same [biological] gender must conduct search."

[353] AI interview with Chicago Police Department, 19th District, 25 February 2004.

Chicago-area advocates.[354]

- **Los Angeles:** Los Angeles Police Department responded to AI's survey and stated that they do have a policy on the searching of transgender persons: "Officers search same-sex detainees."

- **New York:** Although the NYPD did not respond to AI's survey, it did allow AI representatives to interview officials at the police headquarters and also at four precincts. NYPD officials told AI that they do not have a specific policy regarding searches of transgender individuals.[355] However, officials at one precinct told AI that existing procedures do allow for frisk searches to determine genitally determined sex.[356] One NYPD official told AI, "Searches are based on biology regardless of what they think they are,"[357] and officials also told AI that if a person has had sex reassignment surgery, officers of the same sex would search them.[358] In another meeting with NYPD officials, however, AI was told, "If you tell the officer you want a woman to search the top and male to search the bottom, we'll accommodate you as best possible."[359]

- **San Antonio:** In response to AI's survey, SAPD indicated that they do not have any policies or procedures regarding strip-searching transgender people. Chief Ortiz also told AI that the department had no specific policy on searching transgender individuals but "if they are dressed as a female we are calling a female officer." However, as noted above, Deputy Chief Jeffrey Page indicated that "it would depend on what the officer believed at the time" and an individual "may be dressing like a female, but if I know you're male I'm going to search you."[360] It's clear that there is no firm policy, and comments made by Page appear to suggest that a male officer would search a transgender woman. San Antonio's Sheriff's Department told AI that a transgender woman is searched as a man during the intake procedure.

6.1.2
INAPPROPRIATE SEARCHES OF TRANSGENDER INDIVIDUALS

AMNESTY INTERNATIONAL received several reports that officers use pat searches or strip searches to determine an individual's sex. Transgender individuals and advocates report that, during street encounters and traffic stops, police officers regularly demand that persons they perceive to be transgender reveal their "real" gender, at times asking inappropriate and abusive questions such as "Do you have a dick?" In several cases, AI has heard of police officers performing full or partial searches of transgender or gender variant individuals in public, either on the street or in police facilities in full view of other detainees and law enforcement officers. Searches of transgender women are reportedly frequently marked by the officer's insistence that transgender women are men. Repeated and unnecessary searches of transgender individuals in police custody, by both police officers and medical professionals, have also been reported.

- **Chicago:** An African American transgender woman reports that after being arrested in December 2004, she was repeatedly subjected to police officers gathering and staring at her, making comments such as "Do you know what that is?" She reported being searched three times, including at the processing center, where one of the arresting officers searched her vaginally, but not anally. She told AI that she suspected that the search was to find out about her sex and for the benefit of curious officers, rather than for a legitimate purpose.[361]

---

[354] AI interview with Anonymous, Chicago, 25 February 2004.

[355] AI interview with Dep. Inspector Douglas Rolston, Dep. Inspector Monahan, Office of Management Analysis and Planning, NYPD 115th Precinct, New York City, 22 March 2004.

[356] AI interview with Dep. Inspector Monahan, Office of Management Analysis and Planning, NYPD 77th Precinct, New York City, 22 March 2004.

[357] AI interview with Deputy Inspector Douglas Rolston, 115th Precinct, Jackson Heights, New York, 22 March 2004.

[358] AI interviews with Deputy Chief John Gerrish, Office of Management, NYPD, Administration Meeting, New York City, 24 March 2004; Detective Adam Damico, Community Relations, and Lt. Sam Ortiz, NYPD Midtown South Precinct, New York City, 22 March 2004.

[359] AI interview with Dep. Ins. June Roberts, Internal Affairs, NYPD, New York City, 24 March 2004.

[360] AI interview with Dep. Chief Jeffrey Page, San Antonio Police Department, San Antonio, 4 December 2003.

[361] AI telephone interview with Anonymous (Name on File with AIUSA), Chicago, 7 March 2005.

- **Los Angeles:** A Native American transgender woman reports that she was standing near a tree at 2:30 a.m., smoking a cigarette, when an officer pulled up, got out of the patrol car, hit her and shoved her up against a tree, pulling her hair back roughly. He reportedly told her, "I'm going to have to ask you to remove your underwear," claiming that she had concealed something on her person, and pulled down her miniskirt and underwear, spreading her legs. The officer demanded to know "where the drugs were," and when she responded that she didn't have any, took off her shirt and made her take off her bra, leaving her standing naked in the middle of the street. She told AI, "People were driving by. I was so embarrassed."[362]

- **New York:** A Latina transgender woman was approached by two white police officers in a car on her way home from a nightclub in 2000. One officer leaned out the window and began to ask her personal questions about her anatomy: "Are your breasts implants or hormones?" and "What's up with your genitalia?" The officer then asked her to show him her breasts. Michelle told AI, "I didn't know what to do, I couldn't think and was worried that if I didn't do what he said I'd provoke him and he'd maybe get out of the car, maybe arrest me for something I didn't do." She complied with his request and the officer then let her go.[363]

- **San Antonio:** An African American transgender woman told AI that while on her way to work as a dancer in October 2001, she was reportedly stopped by a police officer while crossing the street. When the officer went to search her she reportedly told him, "I'm a transsexual" and "My breasts are real." She asked him to call a female officer to search her. The officer reportedly became offended and said, "Let me see if you are" and then grabbed her right breast. The officer said, "I'm not going to call anybody." She was then arrested for jaywalking and soliciting. During her time in detention she was searched twice: once at the processing center and once at the Bexar County Jail. Both of the times she was searched in full view of male detainees and was searched by male officers, even though she reportedly objected both times.[364]

- **Germantown, Pennsylvania:** After police had been called to a domestic incident in 2002, it was reported to AI that, "the cops had to frisk "EF" [a transgender woman]. I witnessed the cop cupping both of her breasts as he searched her person for weapons. While the other cop looked on, the one doing the search looked at him and made a mocking face …. They did not try very hard to hide their disrespect or disdain in front of "EF", but after she had gone they literally laughed out loud in front of Lisa and I, making many derogatory remarks such as 'Did you see the size of the tits on that freak?' until we informed them that we too were transsexuals. At that they held their tongues."[365]

- **San Francisco:** A transgender woman was arrested by the San Francisco Police Department on a misdemeanor charge. After reportedly being told she was "under arrest for bad fashion," she was strip-searched. One officer commented that she had "a pretty big dick for a woman."[366]

AI is concerned by reports that transgender people are victims of sexual abuse during searches. Such abuse includes the use of sexually offensive language; male staff touching transgender women's breasts and genitals when conducting searches; female staff touching transgender men's genitalia; and male or female staff and other detainees watching transgender detainees while they are naked. In San Antonio, Sheriff Lopez told AI that following a complaint by an inmate, three officers had recently been suspended for fondling a transgender woman's breasts.[367]

---

362 AI interview with Client of GLASS Mobile Unit, Los Angeles, 29 October 2003.

363 AI interview with Michelle Sosa, Positive Health Project, New York City, 24 February 2004.

364 AI interview with Anonymous, San Antonio AIDS Foundation, 5 December 2003.

365 As reported by Rachel Thompson. Emails from Rachel Thompson to Amnesty International USA, 19 March 2004 and 7 April 2005. "EF" is an acronym given by AI to protect the identity of the individual concerned – name on file with AIUSA.

366 Chris Daley, Elly Kugler and Jo Hirschmann, "Walking While Transgender," The Ella Baker Center for Human Rights and TransAction, San Francisco, April 2000, v, quoting an incident reported to Community United Against Violence.

367 AI interview with Sheriff Ralph Lopez, Bexar County Sheriff's Department, San Antonio, 5 December 2003.

AI recommends that if a frisk or search is necessary under governing legal standards, transgender persons should be searched by two officers of the gender(s) requested by the transgender individual, consistent with maintenance of physical integrity and human dignity of the person. If a transgender individual does not specify a preference, then the search should be conducted by officers of the same gender presentation (e.g. a transgender female expressing no preference should be searched by a female officer). Advocates also argue that thorough training is critical, as practices used to alter body shape to conform with gender identity, such as "binding" of breasts or wearing a prosthetic penis, may, during a pat-down by an untrained officer, be perceived as concealed weapons or means of concealing them.[368]

AI believes that searches and frisks to determine an individual's genitally determined sex are never justified and constitute cruel, inhuman and degrading treatment, in contravention of international law.[369] It is essential that all police departments develop policies and conduct training on issues relating to searches of transgender individuals, and searches should not be conducted for the purpose of determining gender. The implementation of such policies should be carefully monitored and officers should be held accountable for failing to adhere to the requirements.

---

[368] AI interviews with Shirley Bushnell, Van Ness Recovery House Prevention Division, Los Angeles, 2 October 2003; Staff Member of an FtM Transgender Support Organization, and Simmi Ghandi, Los Angeles Chapter, Incite! Women of Color Against Violence, Los Angeles, 28 October 2003. See also: Murray D. Scheel and Claire Eustace, *Model Protocols on the Treatment of Transgender Persons by San Francisco County Jail*, National lawyers Guild and City and County of San Francisco Human Rights Commission, 7 August 2002.

[369] Article 7, ICCPR, G.A. res. 2200A (XXI), 21 U.N. GAOR Supp. (No. 16) at 52, U.N. Doc. A/6316 (1966), 999 U.N.T.S. 171, *entered into force* 23 March 1976.

6.2
TREATMENT IN DETENTION/HOLDING CELLS

6.2.1
FAILURE TO PROTECT LGBT INDIVIDUALS FROM OTHER DETAINEES
HOUSING OF LGBT DETAINEES: DETENTION POLICIES AND PROCEDURES

THE PLACEMENT OF LGBT INDIVIDUALS in relation to other detainees has an important impact on their dignity and safety, in particular for transgender individuals. While the primary focus of this section is the treatment of transgender individuals in detention, it is important to note that gay, lesbian and bisexual individuals may also be targeted for abuse while in detention. Further research needs to be done to address this issue in greater depth.

Out of the 29 police departments responding to AI's survey, 17 (59 percent) report having no policy on detention of transgender people,[370] only nine (31 percent) reported having any policy, two (seven percent) failed to provide a response and one department indicated that it does not, itself, detain individuals.[371] Police authorities in the U.S. generally place transgender individuals into male or female holding cells based on their genitalia and in some cases transgender individuals may be held in separate holding cells.[372]

- **Chicago:** Reportedly the Chicago Police Department and Cook County detention facility do not have an official detention policy regarding the housing of transgender individuals.[373] Chicago Police Department officials told AI that placement determination is made based on whether a transgender individual is pre- or post-surgery, but that "it is common sense" to hold him or her in a separate cell, which they do "as much as possible."[374] In response to AI's survey, CPD reported that they have a "practice" whereby the watch commander can make a determination to house an arrestee separately, if necessary.

- **Los Angeles:** In response to AI's survey, the LAPD indicated that detention of transgender individuals is "based on their genitalia." According to the ACLU of Southern California there is a significant LGBT population detained in the Los Angeles County jail at any given time.[375] Following a lawsuit initiated by the ACLU in the early 1980s, a special unit, known as K-11, was created for LGBT and HIV-positive individuals at the jail.[376] It appears, based on the LAPD's response to AI's survey, that as a matter of policy, however, transgender individuals are not placed in K-11, but rather in the men's or women's section of the detention facility, depending on their "genitalia."

- **New York:** While the NYPD's stated policy is that they will detain transgender individuals in gender-segregated facilities based on their genitally determined sex, NYPD officials told AI that they try to isolate transgender individuals where possible for protection, and noted that there is rarely more than one person in a cell at any

---

[370] These departments are: Birmingham, Alabama; Anchorage, Alaska; Bridgeport, Connecticut; Wilmington, Delaware; Atlanta, Georgia; Lexington, Kentucky; Baltimore, Maryland; Boston, Massachusetts; Jackson, Mississippi; Manchester, New Hampshire; Albuquerque, New Mexico; Portland, Oregon; Memphis, Tennessee; San Antonio, Texas; Salt Lake City, Utah; Virginia Beach, Virginia; and Cheyenne, Wyoming.

[371] AI notes that this is a problem not only in the U.S. but, according to one study, also in Europe and Australia. See Petersen, M., Stephens, J., Dickey, R. & Lewis, W, "Transsexuals within the Prison System: An International Survey of Correctional Services Policies," *Behavioural Sciences and the Law*, 1996, Vol. 14, pp. 219-229.

[372] For post-operative transgender individuals who have had their genitalia surgically modified to resemble those of their desired gender this practice may not pose a problem; however, pre- and non-operative transgender individuals face serious problems. See, Darren Rosenblum, "'Trapped' in Sing Sing: Transgendered Prisoners Caught in the Gender Binarism," *GIC TIP Journal, Transgendered in Prisons*, University of Michigan Law School, Winter 2002.

[373] Following an incident where police detained a young transgender woman and refused to segregate her from other detainees, Kate Walz from First Defense Legal Aid contacted the Equal Employment Opportunity Commission (EEOC) to enquire about transgender detention standards. She was reportedly informed that there were no such standards: AI interview with Kate Walz, Formerly of First Defense Legal Aid, Chicago, 24 February 2004. Also reported by participants at a TYRA drop-in evening meeting, Chicago, 25 February 2004.

[374] AI interview with Chicago Police Department, 19th District, 25 February 2004.

[375] AI interview with Martha Matthews, former staff attorney, ACLU Foundation of Southern California, 3 October 2003.

[376] AI interview with Martha Matthews, former staff attorney, ACLU Foundation of Southern California, 3 October 2003; see *Block v. Rutherford*, 468 U.S. 576 (1984).

given time, since precincts usually have between 10 and 12 holding cells.[377]

- **San Antonio:** SAPD indicated in response to AI's survey that they do not have any policies or procedures regarding the detention of transgender people. San Antonio's Bexar County Sheriff's Department, which runs the county jail system, told AI that a "female impersonator" who had not had surgery must be classified as male. Accordingly, a pre-operative transgender woman will be housed with men.[378]

PLACEMENT OF LGBT INDIVIDUALS: PLACING INDIVIDUALS AT RISK

An African American transgender woman told AI she was dressed in "drag" when they detained her in "the tank"[379] with males at the Bexar County Jail, San Antonio. When she asked why they were putting her in with the men, an officer told her, "Oh, bitch, you're going to like it," she reported. While in the tank she said that she started screaming, "They're going to attack me." Finally, a female officer came and the transgender woman reports saying to her, "Miss, I'm a transsexual"—the officer told her to "get the fuck out." After nearly eight hours in the tank, without food, she was taken to her own cell. She also reports that officers refused her access to the medicine she takes for HIV.[380]

AI HAS PREVIOUSLY FOUND that certain groups of detainees, including LGBT people, may be especially at risk of violence from other detainees. AI heard several reports of LGBT individuals being placed in cells with other detainees and, based on their sexual orientation or gender identity, being subjected to verbal, physical or sexual abuse by other detainees. In some cases of abuse against LGBT detainees by other inmates, it appears that officers have not taken appropriate measures to ensure their safety, or have failed to intervene in dangerous situations. In some instances reported to AI, officers have contributed to an atmosphere conducive to attacks against LGBT individuals by "outing" LGBT people to other detainees,[381] conducting degrading searches in plain view of others, or by engaging in homophobic or transphobic verbal abuse. AI is concerned that "outing" of LGBT individuals could lead to abuse and misconduct by other detainees. When police and prison authorities, as agents of the state, fail to protect inmates from violence at the hands of other detainees and prisoners, they can be held accountable for torture or ill-treatment. Institutional and societal homophobia and transphobia means that police and prison officials are often able to act, secure in the knowledge that their behavior will not be investigated thoroughly, or indeed at all. One of the consequences of this climate of impunity is that people whose rights have been violated are silenced.

As described above, AI has found that the majority of police departments surveyed do not have any policy on the housing of transgender detainees. According to an advocate in Chicago, "what often happens is that they don't know what to do with them."[382]

- **New York:** In November 2003, a transgender man was reportedly handcuffed to a pole because police officers did not know where to house him.[383]

Policies where a transgender person's genitally determined sex determines the location in which they will be detained in gender-segregated facilities, regardless of their gender identity or expression or their legal gender, have serious implications and increase the risk of transgender individuals being subjected to serious human rights abuses, including cruel, inhuman and degrading treatment and torture. AI's findings indicate that transgender detainees are at high risk of violence from other prisoners; transgender women in particular may be at heightened risk of torture or ill-treatment if they are placed in male jails or holding cells, as such placement may put an individual at risk of physical or sexual assault.

---

[377] AI interview with Kevin Zatariski, LGBT Liaison to the Commissioner, and Commissioner John Fyfe, Training, NYPD, Administration Meeting, New York City, 24 March 2004.

[378] AI interview with Sheriff Ralph Lopez, Bexar County Sheriff's Department, San Antonio, 5 December 2003.

[379] "Tank" is American slang for a room where a prisoner is kept; jail or jail cell.

[380] AI interview with Anonymous, San Antonio AIDS Foundation, San Antonio, 5 December 2003.

[381] Anonymous Client of Gay Men's Health Crisis, New York, 19 March 2004.

[382] AI interview with Anonymous, Chicago, 25 February 2004.

[383] AI interview with Anonymous, 23 March 2004.

- **Washington, D.C.:** Patti Shaw, a transgender woman arrested in a domestic dispute, was placed in a male cell-block at the D.C. Superior Court after authorities determined they had no procedure for changing her gender from male to female in the court's criminal record system (even though she had identification that had been legally corrected to reflect her gender; this identification had been issued after she had undergone sex-reassignment surgery). In the courthouse cellblock, male prisoners called her names, were lifting up her skirt, exposing their penises and masturbating in front of her, and reportedly sexually assaulted her.[384] The guards allegedly did nothing to intervene and protect her.[385]

- **New York:** A white transgender woman called the police for assistance following a dispute with a neighbor in New York who made transphobic remarks, including "fucking freak," and threatened her with a knife in June 2001. On arrival the police arrested the transgender woman as well as the neighbor. The police officer reportedly said to his partner, "Put the freak in the car too; they are all prostitutes and crackheads anyway." When the woman told the officer that she was self-employed he reportedly responded, "Oh, really? What corner of 9th Avenue is yours?"[386] Even though she requested to be segregated and her identification said she was female, she was put into the male cell. She reports being strip-searched in front of 20 to 30 people. During the search, officers allegedly remarked, "Hey, if you get cold maybe the faggot will take it up the ass and keep you warm." They kept bringing other officers past the cell and saying, "This is the new exhibit from the Bronx Zoo: faggot or freak in a cage." One of her cellmates exposed himself and reportedly urinated on her. She said that she started to have an asthma attack and alleged that officers told her that if she went to the hospital she would have to go to Rikers (jail), where she would be lost in the system for seven days for making them fill out six pages of paperwork. They reportedly made her sign a form waiving medical care.[387]

In New York, advocates reported to AI that detention and holding cell conditions, and the associated risks, are significant contributing factors to transgender individuals pleading guilty, sometimes to false charges. They charge that conditions are often so dangerous, and NYPD officers' failure to act to prevent abuse so pervasive—the officers often partake in the abuse or instigate it themselves—that transgender individuals may be willing to have a criminal record rather than run the risk of being detained in these facilities.[388]

Advocates stress the need for housing decisions to be made on a "case-by-case basis" and urge against creating "blanket housing policies for this vulnerable population."[389] Bearing in mind the need for personal safety, some advocates recommend that transgender individuals be permitted to make a determination, based on their own assessment and experience, as to where it would be safest for them to be detained in gender-segregated facilities and that, should conditions lead an individual to change their assessment in this regard, requests for relocation should be immediately accommodated.[390] AI notes that the National Lawyers Guild and the San Francisco Human Rights Commission has developed a "model protocol" on the treatment of transgender persons.[391]

---

[384] Lou Chibbaro Jr., "Trans woman reports sexual assault in D.C. male cellblock: Incident prompts police to consider changing record system," *Washington Blade*, 28 November 2003.

[385] AI interview with Gigi Thomas and Cyndee Clay, HIPS, Washington, D.C., 20 November 2003; telephone interview with Jessica Xavier, Transgender Activist, 24 March 2004.

[386] Insinuating that she was a sex worker.

[387] New York City Police Watch Incident Report Form, 28 June 2001.

[388] AI interviews with Dean Spade, Sylvia Rivera Law Project, New York City,19 February 2004; Anonymous, New York City, 26 February 2004; Stephen Edwards, Attorney, New York City, 18 February 2004.

[389] Alexander L. Lee, *Nowhere to Go But Out: The Collision Between Transgender and Gender-Variant Prisoners and the Gender Binary in America's Prisons*, Boalt Hall School of Law, Spring 2003.

[390] For example, San Francisco County Jail currently has a policy that requires that "all transgender inmates … will be assigned housing based on their gender identity, not their genitalia" and that "an individualized assessment for appropriate housing will be made for each inmate, and reviewed periodically thereafter …. As part of the housing assessment for vulnerability, jail staff will ask the inmate his or her own opinion of his or her vulnerability." Murray D. Scheel and Claire Eustance, *Model Protocols on the Treatment of Transgender Persons by San Francisco County Jail*, National Lawyers Guild and City and County of San Francisco Human Rights Commission, 7 August 2002.

[391] Murray D. Scheel and Claire Eustance. *Model Protocols on the Treatment of Transgender Persons by San Francisco County Jail*, National Lawyers Guild and City and County of San Francisco Human Rights Commission, 7 August 2002. See also Alexander L. Lee, *Nowhere to Go But Out: The Collision Between Transgender and Gender-Variant Prisoners and the Gender Binary in America's Prisons*, Boalt Hall School of Law, Spring 2003.

U.S. authorities must ensure that safe housing appropriate to a transgender individual's gender is provided for while in detention. AI recommends that authorities should immediately begin consultations with transgender organizations to identify best practices in making housing decisions in a detention facility. AI recommends that when deciding where to house a transgender detainee, authorities should take into consideration the transgender individual's opinion as to where it would be safest for them to be detained in gender-segregated facilities. The individual's assessment should be central, if not necessarily determinative, as to where he or she should be housed.

As noted above, LGB individuals are also at risk of physical and sexual abuse at the hands of other detainees in holding cells, jails and prisons.[392] For example, in Los Angeles, it was reported that a 40-year-old white gay male was detained in Men's Central Jail in Los Angeles in March 2003, where he was subjected to homophobic slurs. Inmates reportedly hit him with broomsticks and officers reportedly "allowed it to happen." He also reports being denied the medical attention he needed.[393]

AI has not been able to find national documentation on how widespread is the concept of segregated cells for LGBT individuals in the U.S., nor the extent of policies regarding placement in protective detention. As noted above, however, in Los Angeles a special unit, known as K-11, was created for LGBT and HIV-positive individuals. While the conflation of LGBT people and HIV is problematic,[394] the K-11 unit represents an improvement over previous conditions for LGBT detainees in Los Angeles. AI is concerned, however, at reports which indicate that problems remain related to the housing of LGBT individuals. Officers charged with screening detainees for placement in K-11 are alleged to rely on stereotypical notions of who is LGBT.[395] Authorities in Los Angeles told AI that individuals who are not gay or transgender attempt to gain placement in the K-11 cell because it is perceived to be safer, and that they therefore carefully screen applicants. The vigorous screening process has reportedly resulted in humiliating, degrading and potentially dangerous situations. For example, an advocate reported an incident in late 2003 in which officers denied a request by an African American gay man to be placed in the K11 cell because he did not conform to the stereotype of a gay man.[396] Such stereotypical assumptions of sexual orientation and gender identity or expression as well as race negatively affect the treatment of those who do not neatly fit into categories.

SEGREGATION

THE SOLUTION THAT MANY AUTHORITIES REPORTEDLY USE to prevent abuse by other detainees is to separate detainees who may be at risk of abuse from the rest of the detainee population. AI recognizes that this may be done for an individual's safety; however, it has resulted in abuses in some instances. Any such segregation, regardless of its rationale, must avoid further marginalization or stigmatization of lesbian, gay, bisexual and transgender people or rendering them at further risk of torture, ill-treatment or discriminatory treatment. The line between prisoner protection and transphobic or homophobic discrimination is easily blurred by authorities, and prison officials can sometimes conceal discriminatory behavior and remain unaccountable for their actions by claiming they are acting to protect LGBT prisoners. AI is concerned that housing LGBT individuals in administrative segregation may mean

---

[392] According to Human Rights Watch, "Many gay inmates, even those who are openly gay outside of prison, carefully hide their sexual identities while incarcerated … because inmates who are perceived as gay by other inmates face a very high risk of sexual abuse." *"No escape: male rape in U.S. prisons,"* Human Rights Watch, April 2001. See also: *Faulty Investigation by Texas Corrections Department Led to Grand Jury's Failure to Indict Rape Suspects*, American Civil Liberties Union, 26 February 2004, www.aclu.org/Prisons/Prisons.cfm?ID=15098&c=26. AI interview with Martha Matthews, former staff attorney, and Sharon Murphy, chapter coordinator, ACLU, Los Angeles, 3 October 2003.

[393] LAGLC Anti-Violence Project incident report form, Los Angeles, March 2003.

[394] The segregation of HIV-positive prisoners has led to a deprivation of access to programs and facilities. See: *Amnesty International Concerned About Treatment of Prisoners Infected with HIV/AIDS* (AI Index: AMR 51/22/00), 1 February 2000; *HIV-Infected Prisoners Threatened with Retaliation While Conditions of Confinement Deteriorate* (AI Index: AMR 51/108/2000), 1 July 2000.

[395] AI interview with Martha Matthews, former Staff Attorney, ACLU of Southern California, Los Angeles, 3 October 2003.

[396] AI interview with Anonymous Advocate, Los Angeles, 29 January 2004.

that they are housed in punitive conditions purely on the basis of their sexual orientation, gender identity or gender expression. AI believes that placement in solitary confinement is not a satisfactory placement option, since isolation poses significant risks to an individual's well-being.

- **San Antonio:** A 17-year-old gay white boy was arrested and taken to the county jail. In a public area, officers asked, "Is anyone homosexual?" The boy told AI, "I didn't want to say it in front of everybody." He later pulled an officer to one side and told him, but told AI that he wished he had not done so. "They were 'mean' and called me 'princess.'" They placed him in a cell at the back of the station. He was worried that they had forgotten about him, until the next day when someone came by and asked, "Who is this boy? Why is he in here?" He was released and charges were later dropped.[397]

The Convention on the Rights of the Child provides that a child should be detained only ''in conformity with the law [...] as a measure of last resort and for the shortest appropriate period of time."[398]

6.2.2
VERBAL, PHYSICAL AND SEXUAL ABUSE BY GUARDS

Terry Phalen, a 41-year-old gay man, was awaiting a bond hearing on auto theft charges in the Cook County Criminal Courts Building, Chicago, in October 1999 when, he alleged, deputies used homophobic epithets and punched him, threw him to the floor and stomped on him while he was in custody of the Cook County Sheriff. In 2002 it was reported that Phalen was to receive $65,000 from the county under a proposed settlement.[400]

As noted in the verbal, physical and sexual abuse section, AI has heard several accounts of officers engaging in verbal, physical and sexual abuse against LGBT detainees in police stations or jails following arrest. For example, in Los Angeles, AI heard of verbal abuse during booking after arrest, including "Oh look, I've got another faggot here" or "Come look at this," or "These are the people who get AIDS."[401] AI also heard reports of verbal abuse of gay men in detention, including one officer who reportedly said, "I'll take the fag up to housing."[402] Reports to AI further indicate that verbal abuse of LGBT individuals in detention may be common, in particular against transgender detainees, and frequently target their gender identity or expression.

- **Los Angeles:** A 38-year-old African American transgender woman arrested for petty theft in March 2000 was reportedly taken to the county facility, where one officer said, "you're no female" and laughed. He allegedly later called her "he/she."[403] Some transgender women have reported that when officers move them through this facility, they yell, "Man coming through."[404] According to one African American transgender woman, when she was brought in to the county jail, the two arresting officers asked, "Where do we put this one?" to which a deputy responded, "It has tits and ass, so let's put it in the queer tank."[405]

Reports of physical abuse of LGBT individuals in detention include the following:

---

[397] AI interview with Anonymous, Esperanza Center Community Meeting, San Antonio, 4 December 2003.

[398] See further: UN Convention on the Rights of the Child (CRC), G.A. res. 44/25, annex, 44 U.N. GAOR Supp. (No. 49) at 167, U.N. Doc. A/44/49 (1989). The CRC has been ratified by every country in the world except Somalia and the U.S., both of which have signed it. The U.S. signed the CRC in February 1995. As a signatory, the U.S. is obliged under international law to refrain from acts that would defeat the object and purpose of the treaty.

[399] Mickey Ciokajlo, "Deputies' Beating Case to be Settled for $65,000," *Chicago Tribune*, 4 June 2002, pg. N2.

[400] Frank Main, Carlos Sadovi, "Sheriff's Officers in Chase Off the Force," *Chicago Sun-Times*, 5 June 2002, pg. 1.

[401] AI interviews with Anonymous Clients of GLASS Mobile Unit, Los Angeles, 29 October 2003; Shirley Bushnell, Van Ness Recovery House Prevention Division, Los Angeles, 1 October 2003; Anonymous Transgender Service Provider, Los Angeles, 2 October 2003.

[402] Anti-Violence Project Incident Report, 4 January 2001.

[403] Anti-Violence Project Incident Report, 5 July 2000.

[404] AI interview with Shirley Bushnell, Van Ness Recovery House Prevention Division, Los Angeles, 1 October 2003.

[405] AI Interview with Members of GLASS focus groups I and II, Los Angeles, 29 January 2004.

- **Boston:** A lesbian of color was arrested and detained in a police holding cell. When she asked one of the police officers to loosen her handcuffs, she was told to "shut up, bitch." The woman objected to the officer's remark and the officer responded "You want to act like a man, I'll treat you like a man!" Reportedly, the woman began yelling, and the officer entered her cell and began to physically assault her. She bent down and reportedly bit the officer, whereupon three other officers then entered the cell and allegedly beat her. She was subsequently shackled and charged with assault on a police officer.[406]

In some instances reported to AI, the abuse of LGBT detainees in police holding cells and jails in the U.S. has taken a sexual form. For example, in Chicago, a transgender woman told AI that until around 2000, sexual misconduct was common in holding cells and she was frequently pressured into performing sexual favors in exchange for letting her go, or for food.[407]

- **Chicago:** An African American transgender woman told AI that while at a processing center in December 2004, one officer approached her in the waiting room and asked, "What kind of sex do you like to have?" He indicated his interest in having sex with her once she was released and detailed the specific sexual activities he wanted to engage in with her.[408]

- **San Francisco:** In 2002, a transgender woman filed a suit against the City of San Francisco for repeated sexual assaults by a male Sheriff's Deputy while she was held in San Francisco County Jail. According to her attorneys, the deputy isolated her and ordered her to "strip naked, masturbate and show him her body, and dance for his arousal."[409]

OTHER CONCERNS ABOUT CONDITIONS IN DETENTION

Holding cells often have fewer amenities and services than long-term detention centers due to their transitory nature.[410] While AI is not aware of any national study on holding cells, local investigations have revealed serious lapses in ensuring the rights of detainees, for instance by failing to provide hygienic and safe conditions, access to bathrooms, running water and medical attention.[411] This would violate international standards under the UN Standard Minimum Rules for the Treatment of Prisoners. AI has also heard allegations that LGBT individuals have been denied access to restrooms, telephones, medication, food and water while in NYPD custody.[412]

- **New York:** A transgender man, detained subsequent to a raid on a fundraising event in November 2003, reported that during the approximately 12 hours he and others were detained at the 77th precinct, they were given neither food nor water, despite repeated requests.[413]

[406] AI interview with Rebecca Young, National Drug Research Institute, New York City, 10 March 2004.

[407] AI interview with Anonymous Client, Rafael Center, Chicago, 26 February 2004.

[408] AI interview with Anonymous (name on file with AIUSA), Chicago, 7 March 2005.

[409] Shortly after the lawsuit was filed, the Sheriff's Department fired the officer. See: Rachel Gordon, "SF Jailer Allegedly Fired in Sex Case—Transgender Person Suing for Assault," *S.F. Chronicle*, 12 November 2002.

[410] One international study found that "The police holding cell is seen as a temporary facility and is thus not generally given the attention it deserves as an important part of the custodial chain. As a result, it has become a weak link in the criminal justice process…" Dissel, Amanda and Kindiza, Ngubeni, "The Conditions of Custody: Police Holding Cells," *Crime and Conflict*, No. 10, pp. 32-36, Autumn 2000.

[411] For example, David Shepardson, "Detroit Holding Cell Ripped," The Detroit News, 20 November 2002. Statistics used were from *Investigative Findings Letter from the Special Litigation Section of the Civil Rights Division of the Department of Justice to the Corporation Counsel for the City of Detroit*, 4 April 2002, available at: http://www.usdoj.gov/crt/split/documents/dpd/detroit_4_4.htm. See also: *2002-2003 Grand Jury Report, Detention/ Holding Facilities*, http://www.solanocourts.com/grandjury/REP-RES/10Holding.pdf

[412] AI interview with Kate Barnhart, Neutral Zone, New York City, 11 February 2004; "Police Overreact as Thousands of NY Queers Protest Shepard's Death," AnythingThatMoves.com, 27 March 1999.

[413] AI interview with Anonymous, New York City, 23 March 2004.

AI heard accounts from LGBT detainees and other detainees who had experienced problems in accessing medication while in police holding cells in Chicago,[414] Los Angeles,[415] New York[416] and San Antonio.[417] Such issues are of particular importance for detainees suffering from illnesses that require a regimented intake of medication in order to be managed, such as diabetes or HIV. Access to hormones is only available if a physician will confirm they have been prescribed in a particular case. As a result, low-income transgender individuals who are unable to afford medical care and secure hormones through formal markets are unable to receive them while in detention.

AI is concerned by reports that transgender individuals may be denied access to personal items related to an individual's gender identity or expression, i.e., personal items appropriate to gender presentation such as wigs and bras. A recent pilot study of the provisions for transsexual and transgender people in the criminal justice system in the United Kingdom recommended as a best practice that authorities should ensure the right to continue reasonable expression of the personal sense of gendered self and appropriate related appearance while in detention.[418] AI has also received reports from transgender women that they have been laughed at by officers while in detention; had their wigs, bras, make-up, purses and prosthetic devices snatched, stomped on and confiscated; are forced to wear clothing inconsistent with their gender identity; are denied the opportunity to wear a bra even when medically indicated; and are detained with males.[419]

Such treatment is in contravention of the ICCPR, which mandates that "[a]ll persons deprived of their liberty shall be treated with humanity and with respect for the inherent dignity of the human person."[420]

AI urges authorities to review their detention policies and practices for LGBT individuals and bring them in line with obligations required by international standards, including the requirement to ensure the safety and dignity of individuals in detention. AI believes that all those in the custody of authorities must be protected from gender-based violence and other forms of torture or ill-treatment, whether at the hands of staff or other detainees.

---

[414] AI interview with Lisa Tonna, Director of Advocacy and Legislative Affairs, Chicago AVP/Horizons, Chicago, 28 October 2003.

[415] AI interviews with Martha Matthews, former staff attorney, and Sharon Murphy, chapter coordinator, ACLU of Southern California, 3 October 2003; Anonymous Gay and Bisexual Men's Service Provider, Los Angeles, 28 October 2003; Anonymous Tramnsgender Service Provider, 2 October 2003.

[416] AI interview with 10 members of ACT UP, Monthly Meeting, New York City, 3 March 2004; Dean Spade, Sylvia Rivera Law Project, New York City, 19 February 2004; Kate Barnhart, Neutral Zone, New York City, 11 February 2004. See, Emily Gest, "NYPD Agrees to Let Suspects Take Meds," New York Daily News, 4 March 2002.

[417] AI interview with two anonymous transgender women, San Antonio AIDS Foundation, San Antonio, 5 December 2003.

[418] Dr. Stephen Whittle, Paula Stephens, A Pilot Study of Provisions for Transsexual and Transgender People in the Criminal Justice System, and the Information Needs of their Probation Officers, The Manchester Metropolitan University, 14 May 2001. The ICTLEP has likewise framed standards for the protection of transsexuals in prisons, which urge that transgender persons be ensured access to medications as well as to personal items appropriate to their gender presentation and human dignity: Proceedings from the International Conference on Transgender Law and Employment Policy, pages 3, 134-141 (1993) and pages 83-86 (1994).

[419] AI interview with RL, Client, Rafael Center, Chicago, 26 February 2004; Anonymous Client of GLASS Mobile Unit, Los Angeles, 29 October 2003; Members of GLASS focus group, Los Angeles, 28 January 2004; AI meeting with community activists, Los Angeles, 26 January 2004; Shirley Bushnell, Van Ness Recovery House Prevention Division, Los Angeles, 1 October 2003.

[420] Article 10.1 ICCPR, G.A. res. 2200A (XXI), 21 U.N. GAOR Supp. (No. 16) at 52, U.N. Doc. A/6316 (1966), 999 U.N.T.S. 171, entered into force 23 March 1976.

7

POLICE RESPONSE TO CRIMES AGAINST LGBT INDIVIDUALS
FEAR OF REPORTING; POLICE FAILURE TO RESPOND AND INAPPROPRIATE POLICE RESPONSE

SYSTEMIC DISCRIMINATION FOSTERS VIOLENCE against LGBT people around the world, including in the United States. What all forms of homophobic and transphobic violence have in common is ignorance and prejudice within society that gives rise to such violence, official discrimination that allows it and the impunity that sustains it. States have an obligation not only to address the violence itself but also the discrimination that gives rise to the violence.[421]

The fact that such acts are perpetrated by private individuals rather than agents of the state does not absolve the authorities of their responsibility: the state may be held accountable under international human rights standards when these abuses persist owing to the complicity, acquiescence or lack of due diligence of the authorities. The concept of due diligence describes the threshold of effort which a state must undertake to fulfill its responsibility to protect individuals from abuses of their rights. The Special Rapporteur on violence against women has held that "... a State can be held complicit where it fails systematically to provide protection from private actors who deprive any person of his/her human rights."[422] Due diligence includes taking effective steps to prevent abuses, to investigate them when they occur, to prosecute the alleged perpetrator and bring them to justice in fair proceedings, and to ensure adequate reparation, including compensation and redress. It also means ensuring that justice is dispensed without discrimination of any kind. State inaction can be seen in a range of different areas. These include inadequate preventive measures; police indifference to abuses; homophobia in the court system; and failure to define abuses as criminal offences. Most LGBT victims of violence find access to legal redress and reparations difficult, if not impossible. Impunity and indifference habitually surround many acts of violence against LGBT people.

AI considers that acts of violence against lesbians, gay men, and bisexual and transgender people in the home or community constitute torture and ill-treatment for which the state is accountable when they are of the nature and severity envisaged by the concept of torture and ill-treatment in international standards, and the state has failed to fulfill its obligation to act with due diligence.

AI is concerned that U.S. authorities are failing to act with due diligence to prevent and investigate crimes against LGBT people. AI's findings indicate that many police departments do not have well-developed policies and do not train their officers adequately on how to respond appropriately to crimes committed against LGBT individuals. Reports to AI indicate a pattern of police failing to respond or responding inappropriately to "hate crimes,"[423] domestic violence and other crimes against LGBT individuals, particularly crimes against LGBT individuals of color,

---

[421] A/56/156, para. 21 (Special Rapporteur on torture); E/CN.4/1997/47, para. 8 (Special Rapporteur on violence against women); Report of the Special Rapporteur on extrajudicial, summary or arbitrary executions to the 57th session of the Commission on Human Rights, E/CN.4/2001/9, paras. 48-50; Report of the Special Representative of the Secretary-General on human rights defenders to the 57th session of the Commission on Human Rights, E/CN.4/2001/94, para. 89(g).

[422] Report of the Special Rapporteur on violence against women, its causes and consequences, 04/01/1996, UN Doc E/CN.4/1996/53 para 32.

[423] "Hate Crime" – Used in this report to describe crimes that are motivated by discrimination on grounds such as race, sexual orientation, or gender identity or expression. Over past decades, the problem of violence motivated by discrimination in the U.S. has resulted in the introduction of the "hate crimes" legislation. This legislation may make a criminal act motivated by discrimination a distinct crime in the criminal code, or it enhances penalties for a crime when it is motivated by discrimination. While international law calls for violence motivated by discrimination to be punished, a question remains under international law of whether such violence must be penalized by special legislation, or whether it can simply be punished through existing criminal laws.

immigrants and other marginalized individuals.[424] Reportedly, "masculine appearing" women and gay men may be perceived by some law enforcement officers to not require or deserve protection from violence.[425] LGBT victims of crimes told AI that police officers seem uncomfortable interacting with them, and perform only a cursory investigation in order to exit as quickly as possible.[426] AI also received a number of reports suggesting that officers responding to a crime against LGBT individuals often focus their attention on the victim's sexual orientation, gender identity or expression, at times explicitly or implicitly blaming the victim for what happened to him or her.[427]

According to reports to AI, police frequently respond according to transphobic, homophobic, racist or class-based stereotypes and assumptions rather than performing a proper assessment of the situation. This may mean, for example, that when officers respond to a call for assistance in an LGBT domestic violence incident, transgender and gender variant survivors, immigrant survivors and survivors of color may be arbitrarily arrested.[428]

As many LGBT individuals and advocates expressed a fear of reporting crimes against them, this section will initially examine these concerns. The section will then outline patterns in police response to crimes against LGBT individuals, with a particular focus on how police respond to hate crimes and domestic violence. When LGBT individuals report these crimes they have to reveal their sexual orientation or gender identity and as such the likelihood of misconduct and discriminatory treatment is heightened.

7.1

FEAR OF REPORTING CRIMES

REPORTS TO AI INDICATE that LGBT people often do not report crimes against them, in particular hate crimes and domestic violence, because they are reluctant to reveal their sexual orientation or gender identity to responding officers, and because they fear homophobic or transphobic treatment at the hands of police officers.[429] Reportedly, reluctance to contact the police is particularly pronounced among transgender women.[430] Deterrents to reporting include

---

[424] AI interviews with Patti Buffington, Executive Director, Genesis House, Chicago, 26 February 2004; Julia Garcia, La Opportunidad, Los Angeles, 30 October 2003; Representatives of New Immigrant Community Empowerment (NICE) and Council of Pakistan Organization (COPO), New York City, 9 March 2004.

[425] AI interview with C. Nicole Mason, Executive Director, National Women's Alliance, Washington, D.C., 10 October 2003.

[426] AI interviews with Andy Thayer, CABN, Chicago, 15 September 2003; RL, Client, Rafael Center, Chicago, 18 February 2004; Julia Garcia, La Opportunidad, Los Angeles, 30 October 2003; Anonymous Gay and Bisexual Men's Service Provider, Los Angeles, 27 October 2003; Marshall Wong, HR Commission Hate Crime Reporting Unit, Los Angeles, 27 January 2004; Anonymous, APICHA Outreach Workers, New York City, 30 March 2004; Mark Reyes, Bronx Lesbian and Gay Health Consortium, New York City, 11 March 2004; New York Gay and Lesbian Center Anti-Violence Project Administration, New York City, 23 February 2004; Al Thurk, San Antonio, 2 March 2004; Annette Lamoreaux, ACLU Texas, Houston, 1 December 2003; M'Bwende Anderson, NYAC, Washington, D.C., 16 March 2004; telephone interview with Robbyn Stewart, New York City, 21 January 2004.

[427] AI interviews with Rick Garcia, Executive Director, Equality Illinois, Chicago, 14 November 2003; Dan Biggs and Karen S., Chicago Recovery Alliance, Chicago, 2 February 2004; Miranda Stevens, TYRA, Chicago, 25 February 2004; Matt Pulling and Susan Holt, STOP Domestic Violence Program, Los Angeles, 30 September 2003; George Unger, Los Angeles chapter, PFLAG, 3 October 2003; Jih-Fei Cheng, APICHA, New York City, 8 March 2004; Basil Lucas, Hate Crimes Coordinator and Director of Police Relations, NYG&LC AVP, New York City, 23 February 2004; Hank, Esperanza Center, Community Meeting, San Antonio, 4 December 2003; Rick Gipprich, San Antonio Rape Crisis Center, San Antonio, 2 December 2003; GiGi Thomas and Cyndee Clay, HIPS, Washington, D.C., 20 November 2003; Jessica Xavier, Transgender Activist, Washington, D.C., 24 March 2004.

[428] AI interviews with Gelsys Rubio, Director, Latino Counseling Services, Chicago, 25 February 2004; LGBT Rights Advocate, Chicago, 12 November 2003; Lora Branch, Director, City of Chicago Department of Public Health, Chicago, 26 February 2004; Ujima Moore, Amassi, 29 January 2004; Matthew Pulling and Susan Holt, STOP Partner Abuse/Domestic Violence Program of the Los Angeles Gay and Lesbian Center, 30 September 2003; Staff of Jeff Griffith Center, Los Angeles Gay and Lesbian Center, 29 January 2004; New York Gay and Lesbian Center Anti-Violence Program Administration, New York City, 23 February 2004; Sean Kosofsky and Crystal Witt, The Triangle Foundation, Detroit, 19 March 2004; C. Nicole Mason, Executive Director, National Women's Alliance, Washington, D.C., 10 October 2003.

[429] A study of gay men and lesbians found that approximately one third of hate crime victims reported the incident to law enforcement. Herek, GM, Cogan J, and Gillis, RJ, *The Impact of Hate Crime Victimization in Hate Crimes Today: An Age-Old Foe in Modern Dress*, American Psychological Association, 1998. NCAVP's 2003 report found that only 39 percent of victims report incidents to the police: *Anti-Lesbian, Gay, Bisexual, and Transgender Violence in 2003*, National Coalition of Anti-Violence Programs, 2004 Preview Edition.

[430] AI interviews with Susan Holt and Matthew Pulling, STOP Domestic Violence Program, Los Angeles Gay and Lesbian Center, 1 October 2003; David Bonfanti, Gay and Lesbian Adolescent Social Services, Los Angeles, 28 January 2004; Michelle Sosa, Gender Identity Project, New York City, 3 February 2004.

that in contacting the police a person's sexual orientation or gender identity may be revealed to family members, friends, landlord or employers.[431] LGBT individuals who are survivors of domestic violence reportedly hesitate to contact law enforcement for fear of being arrested, or because they worry about how their partner would be treated in police custody because of his or her LGBT identity.[432]

A number of other factors further contribute to underreporting, including fear of treatment based on race or ethnicity, age, immigration status,[433] socioeconomic status, language and cultural barriers, and fear of being arrested for participation in criminalized activity, including sex work.[434]

- **New York:** An undocumented lesbian from Trinidad, who was living in secret with her U.S. citizen partner, was reportedly dragged out of the apartment where she was living and locked in the basement of the family home by her brother after he discovered she was a lesbian, in 2001. She was reportedly too afraid to contact the police because she had no immigration documents. AI is concerned that she may have been returned to Trinidad where her parents were reportedly arranging for her to be placed in a psychiatric hospital.[435]

AI is concerned that these factors compound and foster a climate of impunity for perpetrators of hate crimes, as well as other crimes. AI believes that police departments need to conduct effective outreach to members of LGBT communities to develop strategies to deal with crimes against LGBT individuals, and to encourage individuals to come forward to report crimes against them. Such outreach must extend to marginalized LGBT communities such as homeless LGBT youth and sex workers.[436] **(See further discussion in Accountability section.)** Furthermore, it is crucial that police officers are trained adequately on how to respond appropriately to crimes against LGBT people.

---

[431] Prior to the 2003 decision in *Lawrence*, criminal sodomy laws further deterred reporting, since survivors faced potential criminal prosecution when reporting crimes to the police.

[432] AI interviews with Joanne Archibald and Gail Smith, CLAIM, Chicago, 14 November 2003; Susan Holt and Matthew Pulling, STOP DV Program, Los Angeles Gay and Lesbian Center, Los Angeles, 1 October 2003; Nohelia Canales and Roger Coggan, Los Angeles AVP, 28 January 2004; Margaux Delotte-Bennett, Sexual Minority Assistance League, Washington, D.C., 20 November 2003.

[433] Undocumented immigrants may fear deportation or other reprisals if they contact law enforcement, and furthermore, language barriers and lack of appropriate victim services also act as deterrents. AI notes that LGBT individuals could potentially be deported to a country where their life may be endangered on the basis of their sexual orientation, gender identity or expression. Advocates also noted that the post-911 scrutiny of immigrants has further affected their ability and willingness to come forward with reports. AI interviews with Gelsys Rubio, Director, Latino Counseling Services, Chicago, 25 February 2004; Roger Coggan and Nohelia Canales, Anti-Violence Project, Los Angeles Gay and Lesbian Center, 28 January 2004; Anonymous Gay and Bisexual Men's Service Provider, Los Angeles, 28 October 2003.

[434] AI interviews with Lora Branch, Director, City of Chicago Department of Public Health, Chicago, 26 February 2004; Anonymous Transgender Service Provider, Los Angeles, 2 October 2003; Ujima Moore, Amassi, 29 January 2004; Marshall Wong, Hate Crimes Reporting Unit, Los Angeles Human Relations Commission, 27 January 2004; Members of FIERCE!, New York City, 22 January 2004; Jih-Fei Cheng, APICHA, New York City, 8 March 2004.

[435] AI was unable to establish whether or not she has been returned to Trinidad. AI interview with Pradeep Singla, Attorney, New York, 19 February 2004. AI telephone interview with Pradeep Singla, Attorney, New York, 13 July 2005.

[436] Eleven out of 29 police departments (38 percent) responding to AI's survey have a liaison officer.

7.2

HATE CRIMES

Several youth drove by a Latina transgender woman in their car, stopped, and attacked her, stabbing her and beating her with a baseball bat. When LAPD officers responded, they reportedly focused on determining the woman's "real" gender, demanding her driver's license, which identified her as female, and refusing to accept this documentation. Officers allegedly demanded that responding paramedics verify the woman's genitally determined sex to confirm that she was male. The paramedics refused to do so. Police also reportedly harassed witnesses to the crime, many of whom were also transgender women, inquiring about their immigration status.[437]

In 2002, a 21-year-old white transgender individual[438] was reportedly subjected to transphobic verbal and physical harassment by a group of young girls. When he attempted to report the incidents to the police, he alleges they told him they could not intervene, since the conduct was not criminal. After several weeks of ongoing attacks, he told the girls that he'd hurt them if they did not stop. Reportedly, the girls' parents complained to the police, who arrested him for "assault." Advocates told AI they attempted to explain the context of the situation to the police, but were advised by an officer that the situation was a result of the young person's "chosen lifestyle." Reportedly, he was placed in an interrogation room and questioned about his transgender identity, and he was kept in custody overnight, where officers refused advocates' requests to segregate him from other detainees. He was released the following day and charges against him were dropped.[439]

CRIMES COMMITTED AGAINST INDIVIDUALS based on prejudice against or hatred of their identity—be it race, nationality, gender, sexual orientation or gender identity or expression—take place worldwide, including in the U.S. What distinguishes a hate crime from other crimes is not the act itself—for example, assault—but the gender, sexual orientation, gender identity, racial, religious or ethnic bias that motivates the commission of the crime.

Over past decades, the problem of violence motivated by prejudice in the U.S. has resulted in the introduction of hate crimes legislation. This legislation may make a criminal act motivated by discrimination a distinct crime in the criminal code, or it enhances penalties for a crime when it is motivated by discrimination. While international law calls for violence motivated by discrimination to be punished, a question remains under international law of whether such violence must be penalized by special legislation, or whether it can simply be punished through existing criminal laws.[440]

Before looking closer at police responses to hate crimes, the following section will look at general issues pertaining to hate crimes involving LGBT individuals in the US.

---

[437] AI interviews with Emily Frydrych and Ricardo Hernandez, Anti-Violence Project, Los Angeles Gay and Lesbian Center, 30 September 2003; Domestic Violence Advocate (name on file with AIUSA), 29 September 2003.

[438] The transgender individual was biologically male and identified himself as a "he" though he dressed like a woman.

[439] AI interview with Kate Walz, Attorney, Formerly of First Defense Legal Aid, Chicago, 24 February 2004.

[440] See for example Article 4 (a), ICERD, 660 U.N.T.S. 195, *entered into force* Jan. 4, 1969.

7.2.1

HATE CRIMES: BACKGROUND
DOCUMENTATION AND STATISTICS

California: Gwen Araujo, a young transgender Latina woman, was murdered on 3 October 2002 after acquaintances at a party learned that she was transgender. She was kicked and beaten with a soup can and iron skillet, smashed with a shovel and strangled with a rope. According to court testimony, at one point, Gwen was punched so hard in the face that a wall behind her head "indented and cracked." Her body was then driven into the Sierra Nevada Mountains and buried in a shallow grave. Three men who reportedly said she had deceived them into believing she was biologically female are facing murder and hate-crime charges.[441]

THE FEDERAL GOVERNMENT has collected data on the number and type of hate crimes occurring in the U.S. since 1990 and the FBI collects information on crimes motivated by homophobia. In 2003, the FBI reported that hate crimes committed on the basis of sexual orientation accounted for 1,430 (19 percent) out of the 7,489 reported incidents.[442] These statistics depend on reports from local law enforcement agencies and do not reflect the extent of all hate crimes in the U.S.[443] In 2003, NCAVP received 2,051 reports of anti-LGBT incidents from just 28 locations.[444] Out of the 29 police departments responding to AI's survey, 21 (72 percent) report that they do track statistics of hate crimes based on an individual's sexual orientation.[445] However, police departments in Atlanta, Georgia; Honolulu, Hawaii; Jackson, Mississippi; Kansas City, Missouri; Manchester, New Hampshire; and San Antonio, Texas reported that they do not track statistics of hate crimes based on sexual orientation.[446]

While documentation of hate crimes based on gender identity or expression is inadequate, and therefore the scale of the problem is grossly underestimated, indications from non-governmental organizations suggest that crimes based on gender identity or expression against transgender individuals are committed at an alarming rate.[447] The advocacy organization Remembering our Dead has documented 92 bias-motivated murders of transgender people in the U.S. since 1998, notwithstanding the lack of any formal documentation of hate crimes based on gender identity.[448] A survey by the advocacy and lobbying group Gender Public Advocacy Coalition (GenderPAC) found that almost 60 percent of transgender-identified people surveyed had experienced some form of harassment or abuse,

---

[441] John M. Glionna, "Keeping Focus on Victim in Retrial; Transgender advocates publicize the details of the latest proceeding against three men accused in the slaying of teenager Gwen Araujo." *Los Angeles Times*, 5 July 2005; *Anti-Lesbian, Gay, Bisexual and Transgender Violence in 2002*, 2003 Preliminary Edition, National Coalition of Anti-Violence Programs.

[442] *Hate Crime Statistics 2003*, Federal Bureau of Investigation, U.S. Department of Justice, November 2004.

[443] Local law enforcement agencies are not legally required to report hate crimes. Only 11,909 law enforcement agencies (67 percent) reported to the FBI in 2003. Furthermore, agencies in states that have laws obliging them to report data frequently do not comply. *Hate Crime Statistics 2003*, Federal Bureau of Investigation, U.S. Department of Justice, November 2004. Reportedly, only 63 agencies in New York State (12 percent) submitted data to the FBI in 2002. *FBI Releases Annual Statistics on Hate Crime*, National Coalition of Anti-Violence Programs, 28 October 2003.

[444] Clarence Patton, *Anti-Lesbian, Gay, Bisexual, and Transgender Violence in 2003*, National Coalition of Anti-Violence Programs, 2004 Preview Edition.

[445] Birmingham, Alabama; Anchorage, Alaska; Los Angeles, California; Bridgeport, Connecticut; Wilmington, Delaware; Jacksonville, Florida; Chicago, Illinois; Lexington, Kentucky; Baltimore, Maryland; Boston, Massachusetts; Omaha, Nebraska; Las Vegas, Nevada; Albuquerque, New Mexico; Fargo, North Dakota; Portland, Oregon; Philadelphia, Pennsylvania; Memphis, Tennessee; Salt Lake City, Utah; Virginia Beach, Virginia; Seattle, Washington; and Cheyenne, Wyoming.

[446] The remaining two police departments responding to AI's survey failed to provide a response to this question.

[447] In a study of violence and discrimination against transgender people in Ohio, 28 percent of the 94 people surveyed reported experiencing verbal abuse in the last 30 days, 45 percent in the last 12 months, and 67 percent at some point in their lives. *GenderPAC (Gender Public Advocacy Coalition) Transgender Violence Survey*, conducted by Emilia Lombardi, Research Coordinator, 1997. See also: Minter, Shannon and Christopher Daley, *Trans Realities: A Legal Needs Assessment of San Francisco's Transgender Communities*, National Center for Lesbian Rights and Transgender Law Center, 2003; Xavier, J., *Final Report of the Washington Transgender Needs Assessment Survey*, Washington, D.C., Administration for HIV and AIDS, Government of the District of Columbia, 2000, http://www.gender.org/resources/dge/gea01011.pdf; and NCAVP, *FBI Releases Annual Statistics on Hate Crimes, Reports Deficiencies Underscore Continuing Need for Improved Federal Hate Crime Tracking*, 28 October 2003.

[448] Gwendolyn Ann Smith, *Remembering Our Dead* http://www.gender.org/remember/. See also: http://groups.msn.com/PeopleofGender/dayofremembrance.msnw.

directed at them because of their non-normative expression of gender.[449] Out of the 29 police departments responding to AI's survey, 17 (59 percent) report that they do track statistics of hate crimes based on an individual's gender identity. Police departments in Atlanta, Georgia; Honolulu, Hawaii; Boston, Massachusetts; Jackson, Mississippi; Kansas City, Missouri; Las Vegas, Nevada; Manchester, New Hampshire; San Antonio, Texas; Salt Lake City, Utah; and Virginia Beach, Virginia, i.e., 10 out of 29 (34 percent), reported that they do not track statistics of hate crimes based on an individual's gender identity.[450] AI is further concerned to note that the FBI does not monitor hate crimes on the basis of gender identity and expression.

Advocates point out that a lack of documentation and coordination between federal, state and local agencies and community groups impedes efforts to examine, respond to and prevent violence.[451] For the four cities studied, AI found disparities between the hate crimes reported by authorities and hate crimes documented by advocacy organizations:

- **Chicago:** In 2003 the Chicago Police Department documented 31 reports (24 percent) of hate crimes based on sexual orientation, making this the second largest group of hate crimes (following racially motivated hate crime, numbering 56 reports).[452] 28 of these crimes were against gay men. In 2003, AVP Chicago received reports of 56 LGBT hate crimes.

- **Los Angeles:** According to the Los Angeles County Commission on Human Relations, 192 hate crimes based on sexual orientation were documented in 2002 by law enforcement agencies within the county. Hate crimes based on sexual orientation were the second most prevalent (after crimes based on race). Eight hate crimes based on gender identity were reported.[453] In 2003, the Anti-Violence Project of the Los Angeles Gay and Lesbian Center received 433 reports of hate crimes based on sexual orientation or gender identity.

- **New York:** An NYPD spokesman reported a significant increase in the number of anti-LGBT hate crimes.[454] The Gay and Lesbian Anti-Violence Project report said homophobic incidents throughout the city increased 43 percent and the number of victims went up 53 percent during the second half of 2003 over the same period in 2002. Overall, the NYG&LAVP ended the year with an almost unprecedented 26 percent increase in reports of anti-LGBT violence, from 513 in 2002 to 648 in 2003.[455] According to the NYG&LAVP, insufficient funds are available to ensure that every jurisdiction within New York State tracks hate crimes according to their mandate, and such efforts are not consistent.[456]

- **San Antonio:** In response to Amnesty International's survey, the San Antonio Police Department indicated they do not keep any data on the victims of hate crimes based on sexual orientation or gender identity. According to the Texas Department of Public Safety, the number of hate crimes reported based on sexual orientation in 2003 was 57, making up 18.4 percent of the total of hate crimes for all categories in 2003.[457]

The likelihood of LGBT individuals being targeted for violence also depends on such factors as gender, race, age, ethnicity, and immigrant and economic status. LGBT people of color may be at a higher risk of experiencing hate

---

[449] The sample size of the survey was 402. *GenderPAC (Gender Public Advocacy Coalition) First National Survey of Transgender Violence.* 13 April 1997.

[450] The remaining two police departments responding to AI's survey failed to provide a response to this question.

[451] NCAVP, *Anti-Lesbian, Gay, Bisexual, and Transgender Violence in 2003*, Clarence Patton, 2004 Preview Edition; CRD, *ICERD Shadow Report, RACIAL AND ETHNIC DISCRIMINATION IN THE UNITED STATES, The Status of Compliance by the United States Government with the International Convention on the Elimination of All Forms of Racial Discrimination*, 21 September 2000.

[452] *Hate Crimes in Chicago, Annual Report – 2003*, Chicago Police Department, available at: http://egov.cityofchicago.org/webportal/COCWebPortal/COC_EDITORIAL/HC03.pdf.

[453] *2003 Hate Crimes Report*, L.A. County Commission on Human Relations, p. 31.

[454] "Anti-gay Hate Crimes on Rise in NYC," The Associated Press, 12 March 2003.

[455] Clarence Patton, *Anti-Lesbian, Gay, Bisexual and Transgender Violence in 2003*, NCAVP, 2004 Print edition, available at: http://www.avp.org/.

[456] Only 63 agencies in New York State (12 percent) submitted data to the FBI in 2002. *FBI Releases Annual Statistics on Hate Crime*, NCAVP, 28 October 2003.

[457] Hate crimes based on sexual orientation were third highest to hate crimes committed on the basis of race (52.6 percent) and ethnicity/national origin (19 percent). See: *2003 Crime in Texas, The Texas Crime Report*, Texas Department of Public Safety, 2004.

crimes, as statistics show most hate crimes are motivated by race.[458] 51 percent of LGBT individuals reporting hate crimes to the NCAVP in 2003 were people of color.[459] LGBT immigrants may also be targeted because of xenophobia, particularly in the aftermath of 11 September 2001.[460] In Los Angeles in 2002, the majority of hate crimes reported against transgender individuals was committed against low-income transgender women of color in areas known to be frequented by street-based sex workers.[461] Nevertheless, AI has found that hate crimes motivated by more than one prejudice mostly go unrecorded or are incompletely recorded. In fact, the FBI only recorded three multiple bias crimes in 2002.[462]

Some civil rights organizations have noted that hate crime statistics and prosecutions rarely, if ever, include crimes perpetrated by law enforcement or other government agents.[463] As described in this report, AI has heard a number of reports of officers engaging in verbal, physical and sexual abuse against LGBT people, motivated by homophobia and transphobia. AI believes that statistical data on hate crimes committed by officials should be recorded.

- **Houston, Texas:** A "cross-dresser,"[464] was stopped for a traffic violation in Houston in November 2003. The policeman yelled and verbally abused her, saying, "What do you think you are anyway? ... Are you supposed to be a man or a woman?" The officers reportedly poked her and shoved her face on the trunk of the car before taking her to the station, claiming that they needed to "check out her story." They were reportedly demeaning regarding her appearance and repeatedly insisted that she was a man. She was searched by a male officer. They also made comments about her wife, threatening to tell her.[465]

HATE CRIME LAWS

The main federal hate crime statute, 18 U.S.C. §245 (1994), was enacted as part of the Civil Rights Act of 1968. It prohibits the use of force, or threat of force, to injure, intimidate or interfere with a person based on race, color, religion or national origin only and does not include hate crimes committed based on sexual orientation or gender identity.[466] The statute is also confined to several enumerated circumstances where federal authority would be triggered, for instance, participating in voting and polling, participating in court proceedings or enrolling in or participating in public school or college. Individual states and cities are left to enact their own hate crime legislation and as a result, there is substantial variation from state to state and city to city in terms of the degree and nature of protection from hate crimes available. Many jurisdictions have enacted sentence enhancement statutes increasing penalties for crime motivated by a statutorily impermissible discrimination. State statutes may include a range of provisions requiring the collection of statistics on hate crimes, creating civil causes of action for hate crime victims, or requir-

---

[458] Incidents motivated by race make up 48.8 percent of all hate crimes. *Crime in the United States 2002*, Federal Bureau of Investigation, Department of Justice, October 2003.

[459] *Anti-Lesbian, Gay, Bisexual, and Transgender Violence in 2003*, NCAVP, 2004 Preview Edition, p. 36. A Missouri study found that African American gays and lesbians (16 percent and 12 percent) reported higher rates of hate crimes than white (11 percent and nine percent) or Hispanic (six percent and seven percent) gays and lesbians. *The Pulse, A Health Assessment of the Lesbian, Gay, Bisexual, And Transgender (LGBT) Community in the Kansas City, Missouri, Bi-State Metropolitan Area*, The Lesbian and Gay Community Center of Kansas City and the Kansas City, Missouri Health Department, 3 April 2004, p. 73.

[460] See: *Anti-Lesbian, Gay, Bisexual and Transgender Violence in 2002*, NCAVP, 2003. See also: *Is War an LGBT Issue?*, American Friends Service Committee and National Youth Advocacy Coalition, 6 March 2003, available at http://www.zmag.org/content/showarticle.cfm?SectionID=51&ItemID=3188.

[461] AI interview with Marshall Wong, Los Angeles County Commission on Human Relations, Los Angeles, 27 January 2004. See also: *Anti-Lesbian, Gay, Bisexual and Transgender Violence in 1999*, NCAVP, April 2000, which found that one in six of all incidents of anti-LGBT violence and harassment in San Francisco were perpetrated against low-income, transgender women of color, making them proportionately the most likely members of the LGBT community to be targeted for violence.

[462] *Crime in the United States 2002*, Federal Bureau of Investigation, Department of Justice, October 2003.

[463] Katherine Whitlock, *In a Time of Broken Bones, a Call to Dialogue on Hate Violence and the Limitations of Hate Crimes Legislation*, *Justice Visions Working Paper*, American Friends Service Committee, 2001.

[464] Cross-dresser: A person who chooses sometimes to wear clothing conventionally associated with another gender. They may or may not adopt a different gender identity when cross-dressing.

[465] As reported in an AI interview with Vanessa Edwards Foster, Activist, Co-founder and Chair of National Transgender Advocacy Coalition (NTAC) and Executive Director of Texas Gender Advocacy (TGAIN), Houston, 30 November 2003.

[466] 18 U.S.C. §245 (1994) The statute only protects a victim if they are partaking in six enumerated federally protected activities at the time a hate crime is committed. (1. enrolling or attending public school; 2. participating in a service or facility provided by a state; 3. employment by any private or state employer; 4. service as a juror; 5. traveling in or using a facility of interstate commerce; and 6. enjoying the services of certain public establishments).

ing training for law enforcement personnel to properly identify and investigate hate crimes.[467]

Although some states and local authorities in the U.S. have taken legislative steps to address crimes motivated by discrimination, many state hate crime laws do not cover gender identity or sexual orientation. 33 states including the District of Columbia have enacted state hate crime statutes that include sexual orientation,[468] while only 10 states include gender identity/expression.[469]

For the four cities studied in more detail, AI found the following:

CHICAGO	State of Illinois	City of Chicago
Hate crime law includes sexual orientation	YES[470]	YES[471]
Hate crime law includes gender identity	NO	NO
Is training statutorily required for law enforcement on hate crimes?	YES[472]	YES[473]
Is documentation of hate crimes required by statute?	YES[474]	YES[475]

LOS ANGELES	State of California	City of Los Angeles
Hate crime law includes sexual orientation	YES[476]	No Hate Crime Law[477]
Hate crime law includes gender identity	YES[478]	N/A
Is training statutorily required for law enforcement on hate crimes?	YES[479]	N/A
Is documentation of hate crimes required by statute?	YES[480]	N/A

---

467 Troy Scotting, "Hate Crimes and the Need for Stronger Federal Legislation," *34 Akron Law Review* 853, 867-869 (2001).

468 Arizona, California, Colorado, Connecticut, Delaware, District of Columbia, Florida, Hawaii, Illinois, Iowa, Kansas, Kentucky, Louisiana, Maine, Maryland, Massachusetts, Michigan, Minnesota, Missouri, Nebraska, Nevada, New Hampshire, New Jersey, New Mexico, New York, Oregon, Pennsylvania, Rhode Island, Tennessee, Texas, Vermont, Washington, Wisconsin. See further: National Gay and Lesbian Task Force, http://www.thetaskforce.org/downloads/hatecrimesmap.pdf.

469 California, Connecticut, District of Columbia, Hawaii, Maryland, Minnesota, Missouri, New Mexico, Pennsylvania, Vermont See further: http://www.nctequality.org/resources.asp.

470 § 720 I.L.C.S. 5/12-7.1(a) Hate Crime.

471 The City of Chicago has also enacted a hate crime ordinance that includes sexual orientation but not gender identity. Chicago Code of Ordinances § 8-4-085 Hate Crimes.

472 The State requires the Department of State Police to provide training to State Police officers in identifying, responding to, and reporting all hate crimes. § 20 I.L.C.S. 2605/55a (31) Powers and Duties.

473 The ordinance provides for the training of law enforcement personnel in identifying and reporting a hate crime. Chicago Code of Ordinances § 2-120-518 (b) and (d) Hate Crimes.

474 The State requires the Department of State Police to collect and disseminate information relating to hate crimes on a monthly basis. § 20 I.L.C.S. 2605/55a (31) Powers and Duties.

475 The ordinance provides for the collecting and disseminating of statistics of hate crimes on a monthly basis. Chicago Code of Ordinances § 2-120-518 (b) and (d) Hate Crimes.

476 California's hate crime statute provides for penalty enhancements where a felony or attempted felony committed against a person or their property is primarily motivated by actual or perceived "race, color, religion, nationality, country of origin, ancestry, disability, gender or sexual orientation." Cal. Pen. Code § 422.75 (2004).

477 The City of Los Angeles has not enacted a Hate Crime Ordinance, see: http://lacodes.lacity.org/NXT/gateway.dll?f=templates&fn=default.htm.

478 "Gender" is defined in the statute as "the victim's actual sex or the defendant's perception of the victim's sex, and includes the defendant's perception of the victim's identity, appearance, or behavior, whether or not that identity, appearance, or behavior is different from that traditionally associated with the victim's sex at birth." Cal. Pen. Code § 422.76 (2004).

479 The statute mandates hate crime law training for all law enforcement officers, including training on the impacts of hate crimes on survivors, indicators of and procedures for reporting and documenting hate crimes, as well as techniques and methods for handling reports in an appropriate manner. Cal. Pen. Code § 13519.6 (2004).

480 Cal. Pen. Code § 13519.6 (2004).

NEW YORK	State of New York	New York City
Hate crime law includes sexual orientation	YES[481]	YES[482]
Hate crime law includes gender identity	NO	YES[483]
Is training statutorily required for law enforcement on hate crimes?	NO	NO
Is documentation of hate crimes required by statute?	NO	NO

New York City has enacted its own hate crime ordinance prohibiting "discriminatory harassment" on the basis of a person's actual or perceived race, creed, color, national origin, gender, sexual orientation, age, marital status, disability, alienage or citizenship status.[484]

SAN ANTONIO	State of Texas	City of San Antonio
Hate crime law includes sexual orientation	NO[485]	No Hate Crime Law
Hate crime law includes gender identity	NO	N/A
Is training statutorily required for law enforcement on hate crimes?	NO	N/A
Is documentation of hate crimes required by statute?	NO[486]	N/A

AI received reports that police officers may profile people of color as perpetrators of LGBT hate crimes.[487] AI is concerned by statements to AI by officials in Los Angeles suggesting that people of color may be profiled as perpetrators of hate crimes committed against the LGBT community. Although officials in West Hollywood maintained that they do not engage in racial profiling, they claimed that "90 percent of hate incidents come in the summertime from young Latino and black males that are coming from other parts of L.A. and then just cruising around."[488]

While AI believes authorities must act to protect, investigate and bring to justice the perpetrators of crimes against LGBT individuals, hate crimes statutes frequently call for enhanced penalties and it should be noted that AI strongly opposes any penalty that results in the application of the death penalty. Authorities should also ensure that hate crime penalty enhancements are not applied in a discriminatory manner. The International Convention on the Elimination of All Forms of Racial Discrimination obliges states to eradicate racial discrimination.[489]

[481] The New York State Legislature enacted the Hate Crimes Act of 2000, which went into effect 8 October 2000. The legislation requires that an offense be recorded as a "hate crime" if a person commits a specified offense because of a belief or perception regarding the race, color, national origin, ancestry, gender, religion, religious practice, age, disability or sexual orientation of a person. N.Y. C.L.S. Penal § 485.05 (1)(a) and (b) (2004).

[482] The New York City Council enacted a "Discriminatory Harassment" ordinance on 22 January 1993. New York City Municipal Code §8-603. Available at: http://www.nyc.gov/html/cchr/html/ch6.html#3.

[483] The definition for "Gender" for Discriminatory Harassment includes "Gender Identity" in its definition. New York City Municipal Code §8-102(23).

[484] New York City Administrative Code, Title VIII, Ch. 6, Sec. 3.

[485] The State of Texas currently has a statute that enhances the penalty for a crime committed because of the defendant's bias or prejudice against a group identified by race, color, disability, religion, national origin or ancestry." Tex. Code. Crim. Proc. Art. 42.014 (2004).

[486] The State requires that local law enforcement agencies report offenses based on bias to the Department of Public Safety of the State of Texas. The Department of Public Safety must then summarize and analyze the information received and submit an annual report with the governor and the legislature containing the summary and analysis. However, it follows that as sexual orientation and gender identity/expression are not included in the hate crime statute, such documentation and analysis does not take place for hate crimes against LGBT individuals. Tex. Gov't Code § 411.046 (a) and (b)(2004).

[487] AI interviews with Joey Mogul, Attorney, Queer to the Left and People's Law Center, Chicago, 12 November 2003; Glenn Magpantay, Sin Yen Ling and Khin Mai Aung, Asian American Legal Defense and Education Fund, New York City, 4 February 2004.

[488] AI interview with Anonymous, Los Angeles, 29 September 2003.

[489] Art. 2, ICERD, 660 U.N.T.S. 195, *entered into force* Jan. 4, 1969.

TRAINING

Out of the 29 police departments responding to AI's survey, eight (28 percent) report that they do not train officers on issues relating to hate crimes against LGBT individuals. The eight police departments that do not offer training on LGBT hate crimes are: Birmingham, Alabama; Wilmington, Delaware; Baltimore, Maryland; Boston, Massachusetts; Jackson, Mississippi; Omaha, Nebraska; Philadelphia, Pennsylvania; and Memphis, Tennessee.

7.2.2
POLICE RESPONSE TO HATE CRIMES

In 2003, an immigrant transgender woman working as a street vendor was attacked by three women who did not want her in the neighborhood. The women allegedly surrounded her and began verbally abusing and threatening her, using strong and derogatory language regarding transgender women. When the police were called by bystanders, officers reportedly responded, "If they kill her, call us."[490]

FAILURE TO RESPOND

In some cases, police officers reportedly refuse to take a complaint of a potential hate crime. Officers reportedly have trivialized incidents or stonewalled attempts to file complaints.[491] According to the NCAVP, police refused complaints by victims in 14 percent of all cases reported to law enforcement in the cities covered by NCAVP's study.[492]

- **New York:** On 28 September 2001, two lesbians of color report that they were followed by two men in a car in Brooklyn who persisted in harassing them, making intimidating comments. The women report that when the men in the car pulled in and cut them off, they ran into a nearby fast food restaurant, followed by the men. The men proceeded to verbally and physically assault them in front of the restaurant staff; one reportedly yelled at one of the women: "I'm going to kill you, bitch. You're not a man, shorty, you need to know that. I'm gonna put you in your place. Get the fuck out of the neighborhood. Get the fuck out of Brooklyn." The two women later called 911, and police officers arrived at their location. However, as soon as one of the women said that the crime was based on homophobia, the officers reportedly left without further investigating the incident or taking a complaint. The officers reportedly also told the ambulance attendants responding to the women's call that they were not needed, although one of the women was reportedly bleeding from the head due to a blow struck by one of the men. The woman's companion stated, "It was ridiculous. There she was running down the street bleeding and chasing after the ambulance."[493]

Reports to AI indicate a difference in experience for larger LGBT organizations or institutions, in comparison to the experiences of individuals, particularly transgender individuals, LGBT people of color, youth, immigrants and homeless individuals.[494] Police response reportedly varies by neighborhood with institutional racism playing a role in poorer policing in certain areas. Incidents in more affluent communities or neighborhoods with a higher concentration of LGBT individuals reportedly receive better responses, while response to incidents in Black and Latino/a communities is not as good.[495]

---

[490] AI interview with Julia Garcia, La Opportunidad, Los Angeles, 30 October 2003.

[491] AI interviews with Andy Thayer, CABN, Chicago, 15 September 2003; Staff Member, Equality Illinois, Chicago, 14 November 2003; Anonymous, Los Angeles, 29 September 2003; Simmi Ghandi, INCITE! LA, Los Angeles, 28 October 2003; Two Anonymous Members, FIERCE! Member Meeting, New York City, 2 March 2004; Mark Reyes, Bronx Lesbian and Gay Health Resource Consortium, New York City, 11 March 2004; Basil Lucas, Hate Crimes Coordinator and Director of Police Relations, NYG&L AVP, New York City, 23 February 2004; Hank, Community Member, Esperanza Center, Community Meeting, San Antonio, 4 December 2003; Al Thurk, San Antonio, 2 March 2004; Staff of a National Latino LGBT Organization, Washington, D.C., 19 November 2003; M'Bwende Anderson, NYAC, Washington, D.C., 16 March 2004.

[492] *Anti-Lesbian, Gay, Bisexual, and Transgender Violence in 2003*, NCAVP, 2004 Preview Edition.

[493] Copwatch Intake Form, 2001, on file with AIUSA.

[494] AI interview with Robert Woodworth, LGBT Center, New York City, 11 February 2004.

[495] AI interviews with Wendell Glenn, GLASS, 31 October 2003; Marshall Wong, Hate Crimes Reporting Unit, Los Angeles Human Relations Commission, 27 January 2004; Mark Reyes, Bronx Lesbian and Gay Health Consortium, 11 March 2004.

- **Denver, Colorado:** April Mora, a 17-year-old lesbian of African American and Native American heritage, was reportedly attacked because of her gender expression and perceived sexual orientation in March 2002. Four men allegedly jumped out of a car and slashed her with razor blades, carving "dyke" into her forearm and "R.I.P." onto her stomach.[496] Reportedly the police did not respond appropriately: "They just think that I did it to myself. ... I think they're saying that because I choose to look like this, I deserve it or something. It's as if—if I want to look like a guy, I should get beat up like a guy." Mora's girlfriend's mother reported, "One police officer was so rude ... when they first pulled up, they were asking my daughter if [she and Mora] had been fighting ... They asked April how many drugs they were on. They tore my room up searching for the blade and a bloody shirt. They said they were looking for a razor blade and that the wounds looked self- inflicted."[497] Mora stated, "I'm black and Indian, but I look Chicano. I think if we were white, the cops and people would treat us differently."[498]

FAILURE TO IDENTIFY HATE CRIMES

AI has heard several reports indicating that law enforcement officers frequently fail to properly identify hate crimes.[499] In 2003, NCAVP reported 80 cases in which bias classification was refused. Failure to identify crimes motivated by discrimination may be due to lack of proper training and expertise. AI has heard that police often do not know what questions to ask, even if there are signs that the crime is a hate crime. Interviews with advocates and officials indicate that there is an over-reliance by officers on survivors to articulate discrimination as a motive, or officers focus exclusively on whether a slur was used by an attacker, in order for a hate crime investigation and prosecution to be considered.[500] Officers should be trained to exercise appropriate sensitivity, as LGBT individuals may not feel safe to bring their sexual orientation or gender identity to their attention and as such may be reluctant to report a homophobic slur or comment.

- **Los Angeles:** A Latino gay man reported that he returned home late one night from a volleyball game to find "faggot," followed by his name, and "vamos ensenar a ser hombre" (we'll teach you to be a man) scrawled across his door. The message was reportedly signed by his upstairs neighbors. He called the police, who did not respond until approximately five hours later. When they arrived, they reportedly had to locate the appropriate code for a hate crime in their manual, noting that they don't often use it, and frequently list hate crimes as "something else." The officers then asked him if there had been any other incidents of verbal or physical abuse. When he told him there had not, but that he was fearful that there would be following this incident, the officers told him that there was nothing they could do because the threat was not a physical one, and merely promised to patrol the area more frequently at night.[501]

- **New York:** A gay Latino man was murdered in the Bronx in August 2002. Reports indicate that he had been stabbed 46 times and asphyxiated. There was reported to be writing on the walls in his apartment, where he was found: "Crips hate fags." Advocates report several concerns in connection with the investigation of the case, including that police failed to post an "information wanted" notice until January 2003 – five months after the murder. An advocate told AI that they met with the community affairs officers at NYPD to obtain updates on the case but it did not appear that any real work was being done in terms of investigating the case. The advocate expressed to AI that in his view, "If the victim was not Latino and gay, more would have been done."[502]

---

[496] "An Interview with April Mora, GPAC Talks with Teen Attacked in CO," *GenderPAC National News*, 3 April 2002, available at: http://www.tgcrossroads.org/news/archive.asp?aid=169.

[497] Rhonda Smith, "Police Question Anti-Gay Attack on Colo. Lesbian Teen," *New York Blade News*, 5 April 2002, at: http://www.tampabaycoalition.com/files/405PoliceQuestionAttackLesbianHappened.htm.

[498] "Denver Teen Attacked for Her Gender Expression, 'I don't look like a girl,'" *TG Crossroads*, 29 March 2002, available at: http://www.tgcrossroads.org/news/archive.asp?aid=167.

[499] AI interviews with Cara Thaxton, Victim Advocacy Coordinator, and Lisa Tonna, Director of Advocacy and Legislative Affairs, Center on Halsted / Horizons Community Services, Chicago, 23 February 2004; Andy Thayer, CABN, Chicago, 15 September 2003.

[500] AI interview with Inspector Monahan, Office of Management Analysis and Planning, NYPD, 77th Precinct Meeting, New York City, 22 March 2004; Chief Dennis Blackmon, Hate Crimes Task Force, NYPD Administration Meeting, New York City, 24 March 2004; Scott Millington, Los Angeles County District Attorney – Hate Crime Suppression Unit, Los Angeles, 29 January 2004; Capt. Michael Downing, LAPD – Hollywood/Wilcox Station, Los Angeles, 26 January 2004; Chief Albert Ortiz, SAPD, San Antonio, 4 December 2003; Sheriff Ralph Lopez, Bexar County Sheriff's Department, San Antonio, 5 December 2003.

[501] AI interview with Outreach staff of Anonymous Gay and Bisexual Men's Service Provider, Los Angeles, 28 October 2003.

[502] AI interview with Mark Reyes, Bronx Lesbian and Gay Health Resource Consortium, New York City, 11 March 2004.

- **San Antonio:** Al Everton, a white gay man aged 74, died on 8 October 2003, reportedly after being struck in the left temple by a baseball bat. Before he died, Everton told family, friends and authorities that his attacker, who he identified as a neighbor, called him a "fucking faggot" as he hit him with the bat. The neighbor had allegedly had previous scuffles with Everton and his partner and made homophobic remarks.[503] Everton had originally refused to go to the authorities because he did not want the police to know that he was gay.[504] Amnesty International was told by Everton's partner that one of the detectives called to the scene had made homophobic remarks, saying, "You're one of those goddamn fucking queers." The crime was never investigated as a hate crime or as a homicide and no charges have been filed. Authorities claim that altercation was the motive, whether or not the attacker used homophobic slurs while striking Everton with the bat.[505] Everton's partner tried to contact the local FBI field office and was reportedly told, "If he's not a woman we cannot do anything about it." The case has reportedly now been labeled "cold"/"closed."[506]

In some instances, it appears that any indication of "mixed motives" for a crime, (e.g., although homophobic slurs were used, the victim was also robbed) means that a case is discounted as a hate crime. Following intense debate on whether "mixed motive" considerations had led to a low prosecution rate of hate crimes, an amendment to the Illinois Hate Crime Statute providing that the existence of other motives is immaterial came into effect in 2003.[507] However, in other jurisdictions, "mixed motive" issues are still of concern:

- **San Antonio:** Chief Ortiz of San Antonio Police Department told AI that if homophobic slurs are used during a robbery then it would not be a hate crime, it would be a robbery. The Chief further indicated that if homophobic slurs were used, i.e., where "the alleged perpetrator called the victim 'queer and all that good stuff,' then it's not a hate crime, but if they say the perpetrator was lying in wait and then beat me when I came out of a gay bar, then we would investigate it as a hate crime." Advocates claim that since July 2002, three murders were reportedly committed within a one-mile radius of the area's gay club scene.[508] The SAPD says the crimes were motivated by robbery and not linked to each other.[509]

Hate crimes may take the form of sexual violence against LGBT individuals and AI is concerned that officers do not investigate whether an individual's sexual orientation or gender identity or expression may have contributed to the motivation for a rape or sexual assault. Only 24 percent (seven) of police departments responding to AI's survey reported they have a policy or practice governing investigation of sexual assault of LGBT individuals. AI heard reports of several lesbian women who were targeted and raped by men in San Antonio, and that law enforcement failed to investigate these crimes as possible hate crimes.[510] When asked about these allegations, SAPD Chief Ortiz indicated that a victim's sexual preference would not be part of the police report unless the victim raises it.[511] Chief Ortiz indicated that he did not recall "there being a major problem" with the rape of lesbians and suggested that if advocates are aware of any specific cases that he would be willing to follow up. Advocates have expressed concern

---

[503] AI interview with Al Thurk, San Antonio, 2 March 2004.

[504] Matt Lum, "Alamo City to Dialogue Hate, Remember Victim," TXTriangle.com, Vol. XII, Issue 8, 26 November-4 December 2003.

[505] According to SAPD, the officer involved in the case stated that the case "may have been carried as a hate crime because of the statement," but that the "assault was not motivated by the complainant's sexual orientation … [but] may have been motivated by the suspect's belief that the complainant may have been the person who reported that the suspect had a dog in the apartment, causing the suspect to have to get rid of the animal." According to SAPD, this case was not handled as a murder due to the attending physician documenting that the cause of death was not a result of his injuries sustained in the attack. Email from Michael Schwab, San Antonio Police Department, to AI, 5 December 2003.

[506] Interview with an anonymous reporter, San Antonio Current, San Antonio, 3 December 2003.

[507] *Chicago Police Department: Hate Crimes Report 2002*, available at:
http://egov.cityofchicago.org/webportal/COCWebPortal/COC_EDITORIAL/HateCrimes02_1.pdf.

[508] Two victims were reported to have been gay or bisexual, but one was believed to be unrelated even thought it was in the same area.

[509] Martin Herrera, "Murders Near Gay Neighborhood Prompt Community Vigilance," 28 September 2002,
http://www.texastriangle.com/archive/1051/news4.htm; telephone interview with Martin Herrera, GLCCSA, San Antonio, 15 January 2003.

[510] AI interviews with Members of Esperanza, San Antonio, 16 October 2003; Christie Lee Litleton, Gay and Lesbian Community Center of San Antonio, San Antonio, 16 October 2003.

[511] AI interview with Chief Albert Ortiz, San Antonio Police Department, San Antonio, 4 December 2003.

that failure to consider how the identity of rape survivors may have impacted such crimes may have hindered the investigation.

- **Chicago:** A white bisexual woman reports that she was sexually assaulted by a co-worker at the restaurant where she works. When she reported it to the police, they interrogated her for an hour and a half and said, "We know from the people you work with that you identify as lesbian/ bisexual." They threatened to call her girlfriend and tell her she was "cheating on her." Police allegedly convinced her to sign a statement that the man who assaulted her was not responsible.[512]

BLAMING THE VICTIM OF A HATE CRIME

AI also heard reports of officers directly or indirectly suggesting that survivors are in some way responsible for crimes committed against them; for example, indicating that the person "asked for it" or "provoked" an attack.[513] The NCAVP call the perception among law enforcement officers, prosecutors and judges that victims somehow "deserve" what happened to them "one of the most formidable barriers to bringing hate crimes offenders to trial."[514]

- **Detroit, Michigan:** In 2003, two men physically attacked a lesbian couple at a party in Detroit. The first officers responding to the incident allegedly left when they discovered the women were lesbians. As the party was on the border of two police departments, officers from another police department subsequently arrived. The women pointed out their attackers, who fled. The officers focused their questioning on the women, suggesting that they had been to blame for the incident and asking, "Were you in there making out in front of people?" and ignoring the women's requests for medical attention as result of their injuries.[515]

- **Los Angeles:** An Asian Pacific Islander transgender woman reportedly complained to the Internal Affairs Bureau (IAB) that officers responding to a hate crime committed against her refused to take pictures of her injuries. The IAB officer allegedly told her, "There's nothing to report, the officers didn't do anything wrong. You're not a victim of violence. If you didn't tell people you're a transsexual, people would leave you alone."[516]

VERBAL AND PHYSICAL ABUSE BY POLICE TOWARDS VICTIMS OF HATE CRIMES

AI has received reports of police being verbally or physically abusive when individuals have come forward to report a hate crime, inappropriately focusing on a survivor's sexual orientation or gender identity. Police responses to hate crimes are reportedly frequently abusive in cases involving transgender individuals.[517] Reports include the following:

- **Cincinnati, Ohio:** Spears, a 26-year-old gay man, was allegedly arrested after he was the victim of a homophobic crime. Spears alleges that while handcuffed and placed in the police car, he asked why he was being arrested. The officers stopped the car and reportedly maced him in the face and poked him with a nightstick when he squirmed to get away from the mace.[518]

---

[512] LAGLC AVP intake form, April 2003.

[513] AI interviews with: Miranda Stevens, TYRA, Chicago, 25 February 2004; Julio Rodriguez, President, ALMA, Chicago, 16 September 2003; Julia Garcia and Antonio, La Opportunidad, and Ralph Shower, Jovenes, Inc., 30 October 2003; George Unger, Los Angeles chapter, PFLAG, Los Angeles, 3 October 2003.

[514] *Anti-Lesbian, Gay, Bisexual, and Transgender Violence in 2003*, NCAVP, 2004 Preview Edition.

[515] AI interview with Crystal Witt , Triangle Foundation, Detroit, 19 March 2004.

[516] LAGLC Anti-Violence Project incident report, 22 October 1999.

[517] AI interviews with staff of the Jeff Griffith Center and Youth Program, Los Angeles Gay and Lesbian Center, 29 January 2004; Administration of NYG&L Anti-Violence Program, New York City, 23 February 2004. See also cases reported to Illinois Gender Advocates (formerly It's Time Illinois): *Discrimination 2002, 6th Report on Discrimination and Hate Crimes Against Gender Variant People*, Spring 2002.

[518] Eric Resnik, "Victim Sues Police Who Arrested Him with Basher," gaypeopleschronicle.com, 1 February 2002.

ADDITIONAL MEASURES BY POLICE DEPARTMENTS

In some cities, centralized units have been set up in order to develop expertise in how to handle hate crimes against LGBT individuals as well as others. Marshall Wong of the Hate Crimes Reporting Unit of the LAHRC told AI that centralized units are "the best way to have accountability for investigations and training issues."[519] However, reports indicate that despite the existence of such units, they do not always respond to LGBT hate crimes, and often depend on the ability of responding officers to identify the crime as a hate crime and to notify them of it.

AI welcomes the attempts by some police departments or precincts within larger police departments to improve police response to hate crimes. Reported initiatives include:

- **Chicago:** AI commends an initiative introducing bike patrols in the Lakeview area since 2002.[520] While advocates note it is difficult to measure the exact impact of the bike patrols, reported hate crimes fell by 50 percent in their first year.[521] The bike patrols reportedly have also had a positive impact in terms of outreach: one advocate told AI that some LGBT homeless youth call one of the bike patrol officers "Officer Smiley" because he is "nice and fair."[522] Individuals who have engaged in sex work reported that the bike patrols put in place because of gay hate crimes make them feel safer.[523] AI believes that the individuals selected for such duties should be provided with appropriate training, and similar initiatives should be encouraged.

- **Los Angeles:** In West Hollywood, police track "hate incidents," i.e., they monitor patterns in complaints which are homophobic or racist in nature, but do not amount to the level of a hate crime. Authorities maintain this approach has had some success in intervening against potential hate crimes.[524] AI supports this concept being explored in other police departments where there is a concentration of hate crimes based on sexual orientation or gender identity. Such initiatives could be an important step towards meeting obligations to prevent crimes against LGBT people.

- **Los Angeles:** Authorities in West Hollywood have attempted to conduct outreach and establish contacts with advocates in the transgender community. It is reportedly now an institutionalized practice to contact transgender advocates whenever a hate crime against a transgender individual is reported.[525] This has reportedly meant that transgender survivors and witnesses of hate crimes are far more likely to trust and work with police officers. A transgender woman was assaulted on Santa Monica Boulevard by three men who beat her with baseball bats, almost killing her. Los Angeles Sheriff's Department deputies arrived at the scene and immediately transported her to the hospital. Representatives of the transgender community were contacted, and acted as liaisons between the victim, the witnesses, who were also transgender women, and investigating deputies. Those responsible were apprehended and convicted.[526]

---

[519] AI interview with Marshall Wong, Hate Crimes Reporting Unit, Los Angeles Human Relations Commission, 27 January 2004.

[520] Local activists, advocates, churches and businesses working together as the Lakeview Coalition were able to convince police officials to attempt this initiative. AI interview with Matt Gross, Director, Lakeview Coalition, Chicago, 18 September 2004.

[521] AI interview with Matt Gross, Director, Lakeview Coalition, Chicago, 18 September 2004.

[522] AI interview with Karen Stanczykiewicz, Chicago Recovery Alliance, Chicago, 27 February 2004.

[523] AI interview with Patti Buffington, Executive Director, Genesis House, Chicago, 26 February 2004.

[524] AI interviews with Captain Long, Los Angeles County Sheriff's Department, West Hollywood Station, 29 January 2004; Richard Odenthal, West Hollywood Public Safety Manager, January 2004; Anonymous, 29 September 2003.

[525] AI interview with Shirley Bushnell, Van Ness Recovery House Prevention Division, Los Angeles, 1 October 2003.

[526] AI interviews with Richard Odenthal, West Hollywood Public Safety Manager, January 2004; Anonymous DV Advocate, (name on file with AIUSA), Los Angeles, 29 September 2003.

7.3

DOMESTIC VIOLENCE

DOMESTIC VIOLENCE IS A SERIOUS PROBLEM in the United States for both heterosexual and same-sex couples. Nevertheless, some advocates suggest that there may be a reluctance to acknowledge the issue of LGBT domestic violence and a fear that bringing attention to the problems will detract from progress toward equality.[527] Visibility and knowledge about LGBT domestic violence is minimal and survivors experience extreme isolation, a problem which is exacerbated by the scarcity of programs and resources that exist for LGBT domestic violence survivors.[528] Some advocates pointed to the absence of community-based and controlled alternatives in many jurisdictions, which exacerbates the vulnerability of LGBT survivors and means they have nowhere to go for protection from domestic violence.[529]

Individuals who come out to their families as lesbian, gay, bisexual and transgender, particularly young LGBT people, are often rejected and in some cases subjected to violence at the hands of their families.[530] NCAVP report that older LGBT individuals are also vulnerable to violence at the hands of family or caregivers.[531] AI was not able to obtain a significant amount of data regarding police response to family violence against LGBT individuals, due in part, according to some advocates, to reluctance on the part of LGBT individuals to share such difficult experiences.[532]

AI's research revealed that law enforcement responses to domestic and interpersonal violence involving LGBT individuals is inadequate and that police authorities are failing to act with due diligence to prevent and protect LGBT individuals from domestic violence, in contravention of international standards.

7.3.1

BACKGROUND
POLICE TRAINING AND POLICIES ON RESPONSE TO LGBT DOMESTIC VIOLENCE

POLICE DEPARTMENTS should have policies on how to respond to LGBT domestic violence and officers must receive effective training on the issues. Only five out of 29 (17 percent) of police departments responding to AI's survey reported having specific policies on same-sex domestic violence.[533] 83 percent (24 out of 29) of responding departments reported that they provide some training to officers on same-sex domestic violence.[534] AI notes with concern that police departments in Wilmington, Delaware; Atlanta, Georgia; Baltimore, Maryland; and Omaha, Nebraska do not provide any training on same-sex domestic violence, but with the exception of Baltimore, Maryland, they do provide training on heterosexual domestic violence.[535]

---

527 AI interviews with Gelsys Rubio, Director, Latino Counseling Services, and Heather Bradley, Night Ministry, Chicago, 12 November 2003; Matt Pulling and Susan Holt, STOP Domestic Violence Program, Los Angeles, 30 September 2003.

528 Many support services for survivors of domestic violence including emergency shelters, transitional housing and counseling support groups are not available to LGBT individuals or do not offer LGBT-specific services. Pamela M. Jablow, "Victims of Abuse and Discrimination; Protecting Battered Homosexuals under Domestic Violence Legislation," 28 *Hofstra Law Review*, 1095, 2000.

529 AI interviews with Members of FIERCE!, New York City, 22 January 2004; Shante Smalls, 2 April 2004.

530 AI interviews with Shirley Bushnell, Van Ness Recovery House Prevention Division, Los Angeles, 1 October 2003; Asian Pacific AIDS Intervention Team Community Forum Meeting, Los Angeles, 29 January 2004; Carl Siciliano, Executive Director, Ali Forney Center, New York City, 13 February 2004.

531 Rachel Baum, *Lesbian, Gay, Bisexual and Transgender Domestic Violence in 2002*, NCAVP, Preliminary Edition 2003.

532 AI interview with Carl Siciliano, Executive Director, Ali Forney Center, New York City, 13 February 2004.

533 Los Angeles, California; Honolulu, Hawaii; Lexington, Kentucky; Kansas City, Missouri; and Portland, Oregon.

534 Birmingham, Alabama; Anchorage, Alaska; Los Angeles, California; Bridgeport, Connecticut; Jacksonville, Florida; Honolulu, Hawaii; Chicago, Illinois; Lexington, Kentucky; Boston, Massachusetts; Jackson, Mississippi; Kansas City, Missouri; Las Vegas, Nevada; Manchester, New Hampshire; Albuquerque, New Mexico; New York, New York; Fargo, North Dakota; Portland, Oregon; Philadelphia, Pennsylvania; Memphis, Tennessee; San Antonio, Texas; Salt Lake City, Utah; Virginia Beach, Virginia; Seattle, Washington; and Cheyenne, Wyoming.

535 Phoenix, Arizona failed to respond as to whether they do any kind of training on domestic violence.

For the cities studied, AI received the following information on how police departments train and respond to LGBT domestic violence:

- **Chicago:** The Chicago Police Department indicated in its survey response that it provides training on same-sex domestic violence "as needed" but that it does not have a specific policy or practice governing response to same-sex domestic violence. It went on to note that its existing domestic violence policy is not specific to same-sex couples, but that it covers all persons living in a household. In interviews with CPD officials, AI was told that all domestic violence is treated equally.[536]

- **New York:** NYPD did not respond to AI's survey but officials told AI that they do provide training on same-sex domestic violence and that NYPD has adopted a more inclusive definition of "family" in its Training Protocol.[537] Officials told AI that officers use the same procedures in cases of LGBT domestic violence as in cases of heterosexual domestic violence to determine who is the aggressor.[538]

- **Los Angeles:** LAPD responded to AI's survey, indicating that it does provide training on same-sex domestic violence and that it has a specific policy or practice governing responses to same-sex domestic violence pursuant to the California Penal Code and departmental policy. No further details were provided in the survey. LAPD officers are issued a small card ("palm card") summarizing procedures to be followed when responding to domestic violence calls.[539] Captain Garner of the 77th Division of the LAPD told AI that he was unaware of whether officers assigned to domestic violence in his division had received LGBT-specific training, but that no such training was provided at the division level.[540] LASD officials conceded that response "may depend on where you are in the county," describing the West Hollywood station as having the best training and response.[541]

- **San Antonio:** The SAPD responded to AI's survey indicating that they do not have any policies or procedures for responding to same-sex domestic violence.[542] However, they maintained that officers do receive training on the issue. Nevertheless, AI received reports from an official within SAPD that such training does not take place. It was reported that such training was withdrawn following an attempt to introduce it, when the trainer was subjected to harassment. The SAPD has a Critical Response Team which deals with emergency domestic violence situations, and while it reportedly receives additional training, the team does not receive training on LGBT domestic violence. Sheriff Lopez of the San Antonio Sheriff's Department told AI that the Sheriff's Department does not have any specific training on how to handle same-sex domestic violence situations: "It's handled exactly the same way as any other domestic violence [incident], no different."[543]

---

536 AI interview with Chicago Police Department, 19th District, 25 February 2004.

537 The NYPD's definition includes persons who: Are not legally married, but are currently living together in a family-type relationship; or Are not legally married, but formerly lived together in a family-type relationship, *Police Student's Guide: Domestic Violence*, 29 July 2003.

538 AI interviews with Inspector Monahan, Office of Management Analysis and Planning, NYPD – 77th Precinct, New York, 22 March 2004; Deputy Inspector Brian Conroy, NYPD – Midtown South Precinct, New York City, 22 March 2004; Deputy Chief John Gerrish, Office of Management Analysis and Planning, NYPD – Administration Meeting, New York City, 24 March 2004.

539 The card advises that the "officer shall make reasonable efforts to determine the dominant aggressor at any domestic violence incident, and directs officers to consider a number of factors, including history of domestic violence, credibility, existence of offensive and defensive injuries, the seriousness of injuries, the height and weight of the parties, use of drugs or alcohol, and criminal history of the parties. LAPD PC 13701.

540 AI interview with Captain Kenneth Garner, 77th District, LAPD, Los Angeles, 26 January 2004.

541 AI interview with Sheriff Baca, Captain Linda Castro and Jeff Prang, LASD, Los Angeles, 29 January 2004.

542 Sources indicate that SAPD does not have adequate procedures in place for dealing with domestic violence reports from LGBT individuals; for example, the forms SAPD use to record domestic violence incidents do not refer to same-sex domestic violence (just complainant and perpetrator, name, sex, DOB and ethnicity). Problems were also reported when LGBT partners wished to apply for a protection order. Forms are not designed for such situations, requiring survivors to put down "roommate" for relationship to the offender.

543 AI interview with Sheriff Ralph Lopez, Bexar County Sheriff's Department, San Antonio, 5 December 2003. While it appears that authorities in San Antonio are doing little to address LGBT domestic violence as a specific issue, AI notes the work undertaken by San Antonio Police Department's Victim Advocacy Section (a section of SAPD charged with the responsibility of providing integrated services to victims of violent crimes, with an emphasis on family violence) and observed that a representative attended a meeting at the Gay and Lesbian Center in San Antonio on domestic violence. The Victims Advocacy Service does offer services to same-sex domestic violence survivors. Lesbians may be able to access shelters. Men cannot, though VAS does offer survivors three nights in hotel accommodation if shelter accommodation is not a viable option.

A review of the content or effectiveness of policies and training curricula was outside the scope of this report. AI recommends that such reviews be undertaken as our findings suggest problems that belie the relatively high rate of reported training on domestic violence. Advocates in Chicago told AI that "police often do not know what to do," and that officers are often insensitive and exhibit a lack of understanding of power relationships inherent in domestic violence.[544] AI is concerned that few officers may actually receive specific training about how to respond to a situation of LGBT domestic violence; for example, in how to identify a situation as a LGBT relationship and how to distinguish the abuser. For instance, in addition to what AI heard from officials in Chicago and New York, the police department in Anchorage, Alaska responded to AI's survey that they provide training on same-sex domestic violence, but noted that "All domestic violence without respect to sexual orientation are handled the same." This suggests that the training may not provide officers with adequate tools and techniques to respond appropriately to LGBT domestic violence, including, for example, how to recognize that an incident has occurred in the context of an intimate relationship **(see below)**.

Furthermore, AI's survey only covered the largest city in each state and has no information on whether officers in smaller cities or rural areas are provided with training on how to respond to LGBT domestic violence situations.

7.3.2

POLICE RESPONSE TO LGBT DOMESTIC VIOLENCE

Marc Kajs, a 28-year-old gay man in Houston, Texas, was shot to death by his former lover after a history of threats and domestic violence. In a lawsuit filed against the City of Houston in 2000, Kajs' mother asserted that Kajs had "sought protection from the police several times before the shooting but was turned away by officers." Kajs had "complained to the police five times but nothing was ever done," the family's attorney stated. In one instance Kajs fled to a police station at 2:30 a.m., followed by his ex-lover. Though his ex-lover threatened him in front of a police officer, Kajs received no protection and "was sent out onto the street with the person stalking him and threatening him." Several days later, Kajs filed a report at Houston's Montrose storefront police station after receiving further threats against his life. He was turned away "because the domestic violence unit was closed on weekends." Hours later, Kajs was dead.[545]

AI HEARD A NUMBER OF REPORTS from national organizations and from advocates in all of the cities studied of inadequate police responses to LGBT domestic violence incidents, including allegations that officers frequently fail to respond, or respond in an inappropriate, racist, homophobic or transphobic manner. As a result, many members of LGBT communities, particularly people of color and immigrants, advocates claim, mistrust police and would not contact them in domestic violence situations. Reportedly, race, ethnicity and the social status of an individual may influence police response to domestic violence situations, including LGBT domestic violence.[546]

---

[544] AI interviews with Lora Branch, Director, City of Chicago Department of Public Health, Chicago, 26 February 2004; Cara Thaxton, Victim Advocacy Coordinator, and Lisa Tonna, Director of Advocacy and Legislative Affairs, Center on Halsted / Horizons Community Services, Chicago, 23 February 2004.

[545] Harvey Rice, "Judge again dismisses lawsuit over gay domestic violence case," *Houston Chronicle*, 4 February 2004. In response to pressure around this case and others, the police department created a different structure of the Family Unit: there are now local offices that are able to respond to domestic violence cases. AI interview with Annette Lamoreaux, ACLU, Houston, 1 December 2003.

[546] AI interviews with Gelsys Rubio, Director, Latino Counseling Services, Chicago, 25 February 2004; Kate Walz, Formerly of First Defense Legal Aid, Chicago, 24 February 2004.

POLICE FAILURE TO RESPOND TO LGBT DOMESTIC VIOLENCE

AI's findings suggest that police often fail to respond to domestic violence, including within the LGBT community. In some cases officers may fail to recognize that the incident has occurred in the context of an intimate relationship. Advocates in Chicago, New York, Los Angeles and San Antonio as well as in D.C. and San Francisco told AI that police often do not take LGBT domestic violence seriously.[547] AI heard reports of police failing to respond to domestic violence involving transgender individuals:

- **Los Angeles:** In September 2003, a homeless Mexican transgender woman was being abused by her boyfriend when police drove by but did not intervene, despite her pleas for help. She was severely beaten, requiring medical treatment. When officers eventually responded, after being called by a member of the public, they reportedly arrested her boyfriend for drug possession, but did not charge him with assaulting her.[548]

- **Los Angeles:** A young African American transgender woman reported that in 2001, she was living with her boyfriend, who became abusive. On several occasions when she called the police for assistance, they were initially very attentive, but once they discovered that she was transgender, they told her they could take him away for an hour, but there was nothing else they could do. On one occasion, she noticed them pointing and whispering. The fourth time she called the police, her boyfriend had "destroyed" her house and she had bruises all over her body, but the officers refused to take any action and simply left.[549]

Some advocates report that where police respond to domestic violence involving lesbian couples, officers will simply "try to get the girls to calm down and get along," or see it as a "fair fight," failing to take such incidents as "real" domestic violence.[550] In San Antonio, AI heard from a Latina lesbian woman who told AI that when police responded to a domestic violence situation in her home, the police just "didn't know what to do with two women." Reportedly, her house was a mess and her partner had a gun, but while the police took the gun they did not remove her partner. She was forced to leave her home to escape the potentially dangerous situation.[551]

- **San Antonio:** A 17-year-old lesbian was killed by her 21-year-old partner in October 2003. Allegedly, the police report notes that one of the responding police officers indicated that he had been called to the home "a lot."[552]

Police reportedly also do not take domestic violence involving two men seriously.[553] In some cases, officers have reportedly told men that both will have to be arrested, and suggest that instead one of them should just leave.[554] Advocates report that officers reportedly respond in such a way that would suggest that "men can fight their own battles."[555] AI also spoke with a white gay man in Chicago who reported that police were reluctant to take action when he called for help in a domestic violence situation, and suggested that he had somehow provoked his partner through infidelity.[556]

---

547 AI interviews with Deborah Benford, Affinity, Chicago, 17 September 2003; Linda, Member of GLASS Focus Group I & II, Los Angeles, 28 January 2004; Ben Shepherd, Activist, New York City, 6 May 2004; Anonymous, Gay Officer's Action League, New York City, 14 April 2004; Jane Shaefer, Victim Advocate Services, San Antonio Police Department, San Antonio, 3 December 2003; Shawna Virago, Director, Domestic Violence Project, Communities United Against Violence, San Francisco, 31 July 2002; Nicole Mason, Executive Director, National Women's Alliance, Washington, D.C., 10 October 2003.

548 AI interview with Anonymous, Gay and Lesbian Adolescent Social Services, Los Angeles, 28 January 2004.

549 AI interview with Members of GLASS focus group, Los Angeles, 28 January 2004.

550 AI interview with Matthew Pulling and Susan Holt, 30 September 2003; Staff from an HIV/AIDS Service Provider for African American Gay and Bisexual Men, Washington, D.C., 19 November 2003.

551 Domestic violence meeting, Gay and Lesbian Community Center of San Antonio, 15 October 2003.

552 AI interview with Anonymous (name on file with AIUSA), 3 December 2003.

553 AI interviews with LGBT Rights Advocate, Chicago, 12 November 2004; Aonoymous Gay and Bisexual Men's Service Provider, 27 October 2003; Jeffrey King, In the Meantime Men, 2 October 2003; Staff from an HIV/AIDS Service Provider for African American Gay and Bisexual Men, Washington, D.C., 19 November 2003.

554 AI interview with an anonymous domestic violence advocate in Los Angeles, 29 September 2003.

555 New York Anti-Violence Project, New York City, 23 February 2004.

556 Telephone interview with Anonymous, Chicago, 21 January 2004.

- **New York:** In 2003, a gay Brazilian man called police for help in a domestic violence situation, expressing fear for his life. When police responded, they reportedly took the apartment keys away from alleged perpetrator but took no further action. Two hours later, the man who called the police was found dead. The AVP told AI that normally in such situations, the Domestic Violence unit is mandated to respond, which did not happen in this case.[557]

- **Anonymous Location:** An officer responding to a domestic violence incident involving two gay men reportedly told one of them, "You're not hurt that bad, quit crying, don't be a sissy." When the victim expressed fear of his abuser and refused to press charges against him, he reports being taunted by the officers. The officers refused to take the man to a hospital to receive treatment for his two black eyes and a compound fracture of the arm. Ultimately, he had to walk to the emergency room. Reportedly, his partner is a police officer, and he suspected that that had a hand in the poor treatment that he suffered.[558]

ARREST AND THREATS TO ARREST BOTH PARTIES OR THE VICTIM OF DOMESTIC VIOLENCE

> "It's really, really common for the victim to be arrested as the batterer."
> Matthew Pulling, Staff Counselor, Stop Partner Abuse/Domestic Violence Program of the Los Angeles Gay and Lesbian Center[559]
>
> A transgender woman was reportedly choked by her male partner and chased through their apartment as she tried to defend herself, in 2002, in Washington, D.C. She managed to get him out of the apartment and called the police, who responded by arresting her, handcuffing her and forcing her down the stairs. Her alleged abuser was not arrested. She reports that as soon as officers saw her identification, they began referring to her by male pronouns, calling her "mister." She was detained for over seven hours at the police station, and was charged with civil assault against her alleged abuser. The charges against her were subsequently dismissed.[560]

According to advocates in Chicago, New York, Los Angeles, San Antonio, San Francisco and Washington, D.C., the police have greater difficulty in identifying the abuser when responding to LGBT domestic violence calls.[561] Because of a misconception among law enforcement that a determination of domestic violence is based primarily on the sex of the people in the couple, many simply assign the label of mutual abuse and arrest both parties in a situation involving violence in an LGBT relationship. AI heard a number of reports of police officers arresting or threatening to arrest both parties when responding to LGBT domestic violence in Chicago, New York, Los Angeles, San Antonio and Washington, D.C.[562] Gay men and "masculine appearing" lesbian couples are reportedly particularly at risk of being arrested under an assumption that the situation involves "mutual combat."[563]

- **New York:** Two gay Latino men were involved in a domestic dispute in New York. The police officers reportedly told them that if the police were called again, they would both be arrested. The officers left without taking any action.[564]

---

[557] AI Interview with Administration of NYG&L Anti-Violence Program, New York City, 28 January 2004.

[558] AI interview with Attorney (name of attorney, organization and location on file with AIUSA), 15 March 2004.

[559] AI interview with Matthew Pulling, Staff Counselor, Stop Partner Abuse/Domestic Violence Program of the Los Angeles Gay and Lesbian Center, Los Angeles, 30 September 2003.

[560] AI interview with Cyndee Clay and GiGi Thomas, HIPS, Washington, D.C., 20 November 2003.

[561] AI interviews with Staff, Rafael Center, Chicago, 14 November 2003; Anonymous, Los Angeles, 29 September 2003; Chuck Stewart, Ph.D., Los Angeles, 29 January 2004; Administration of NYG&L Anti-Violence Program, New York City, 23 February 2004; Andrew Thomas, Attorney, San Antonio, 4 December 2003; Shawna Virago, Director, Domestic Violence Project, Communities United Against Violence, San Francisco, 31 July 2002; Staff from an HIV/AIDS Service Provider for African American Gay and Bisexual Men, Washington, D.C., 19 November 2003; HIPS, 20 November 2003.

[562] AI interviews with Anonymous Transgender Service Provider, Los Angeles, 2 October 2003; Jane Shaefer, Victim Advocate Services, San Antonio Police Department, 3 December 2003; Staff from an HIV/AIDS Service Provider for African American Gay and Bisexual Men, Washington, D.C., 19 November 2003; Cyndee Clay and GiGi Thomas, HIPS, Washington, D.C., 20 November 2003; AVP Horizons intake form, Chicago, July 2002.

[563] AI interviews with Ujima Moore, Amassi, 29 January 2004; Matthew Pulling and Susan Holt, Stop DV Program, LAGLC, Los Angeles, 30 September 2003; Staff of Jeff Griffith Center, Los Angeles Gay and Lesbian Center, Los Angeles, 29 January 2004.

[564] AI interview with Members of SOMOS, New York, 23 February 2004.

STONEWALLED

- **New York:** A black transgender woman told AI, "Me and my roommate (she's also a black MTF) [transgender woman] got into an argument and we called the police. One of the cops that came treated us like 'dogs.' He was saying things like, 'Next time I come down here I'm going to arrest both of you.' My roommate and I refer to each other by our female names. The officer said, 'First, let's stop this.' His attitude was, 'this is absurd.' They didn't help us in any way."[565]

AI is concerned by comments made by law enforcement officials in San Antonio suggesting that police may arrest both parties. Serious concerns were raised about San Antonio Police Department's response to domestic violence, including that SAPD appears to have an unwritten policy to threaten survivors of domestic violence with arrest if they repeatedly call for assistance.[566] This was confirmed by Chief Ortiz, who told AI that officers use threat of arrest as a "tactic in combative relationships" and say, "'if you call again one of you is going to be arrested'... We use it all the time—that's just a bluff. If they are not the problem, then it doesn't deter them from reporting." [567] AI is extremely concerned by such a practice and calls upon SAPD to desist from using such tactics and communicate this change in policy immediately to all officers.

When police do attempt to identify the abuser in an LGBT domestic violence situation, reports to AI suggest that transgender and gender variant survivors, immigrant survivors, survivors of color, the person perceived to be of lower socioeconomic status or the biggest and youngest person are reportedly often assumed to be the abusers and arrested.[568] The Los Angeles Gay and Lesbian Center's STOP Partner Abuse/Domestic Violence Program has found the erroneous arrest of survivors of LGBT domestic violence to be so prevalent that it maintains a group for LGBT survivors referred by courts for mandatory batterer's intervention.[569]

- **Los Angeles:** A gay Filipino man was reportedly beaten on several occasions by his partner, a white U.S. citizen, who was reportedly addicted to drugs and alcohol. When police responded to one altercation, they reportedly arrested the Filipino man and threatened to report him to immigration authorities, saying: "You're not a citizen. We should deport you, you shouldn't be hitting Americans; you're not an American." The Filipino man was sentenced to 52 weeks of batterer's intervention in court.[570]

AI heard reports of arrests of transgender domestic violence survivors in Los Angeles, Chicago, New York, San Antonio, San Francisco and Washington, D.C.[571] An assumption that transgender people are "deviant" or "mentally ill" and more likely to commit heinous and violent crimes is a common element of transphobia and may play into decisions by officers to automatically arrest the transgender person when responding to a domestic violence situation.

- **San Antonio:** A transgender woman called the police because her boyfriend had broken some of her personal things and a window. On arrival, the boyfriend told police that she was bipolar. The police arrested and handcuffed the transgender woman while she was in tears, telling them that she had called the police for help. On

565 AI interview with transgender woman, New York, 26 February 2004.

566 AI interviews with Anonymous (name on file with AIUSA), 3 December 2003; Domestic Violence Advocate, 2 December 2003.

567 AI interview with Chief Albert Ortiz, San Antonio Police Department, San Antonio, 4 December 2003.

568 AI interviews with Gelsys Rubio, Director, Latino Women's Services - Latino Counseling Services, Chicago, 25 February 2004; LGBT Rights Advocate, Chicago, 12 November 2003; Lora Branch, Director, City of Chicago Department of Public Health, Chicago, 26 February 2004; Ujima Moore, Amassi, 29 January 2004; Matthew Pulling and Susan Holt, STOP Partner Abuse/Domestic Violence Program of the Los Angeles Gay and Lesbian Center, Los Angeles, 30 September 2003; Staff of Jeff Griffith Center, Los Angeles Gay and Lesbian Center, 29 January 2004; Administration of NYG&L AVP, New York City, 23 February 2004; Sean Kosofsky and Crystal Witt, The Triangle Foundation, Detroit,19 March 2004; C. Nicole Mason, Executive Director, National Women's Alliance, Washington, D.C., 10 October 2003.

569 AI interview with Matthew Pulling and Susan Holt, STOP Partner Abuse/Domestic Violence Program of the Los Angeles Gay and Lesbian Center, Los Angeles, 30 September 2003.

570 AI interview with Matthew Pulling, STOP, Domestic Violence Program, Los Angeles Gay and Lesbian Center, 30 September 2003.

571 AI interviews with members of San Antonio AIDS Foundation, San Antonio, 5 December 2003; Members of GLASS Focus Group Meeting, Los Angeles, 28 January 2004; Dean Spade, Attorney, Sylvia Rivera Law Project, New York, 19 February 2004; Jennifer Rakowski, Communities United Against Violence, San Francisco, 23 October 2004; Cyndee Clay and GiGi Thomas, HIPS, Washington, D.C., 20 November 2003.

arrival at the police station, the intake forms required her to use her male name and she was then held in a male holding cell, even though she told them that she was transgender and didn't want to be put in with the men. She was reportedly held for two hours before being released.[572]

21 out of 29 (72 percent) police departments responding to AI's survey reported have mandatory arrest policies, i.e., officers are required to make an arrest when responding to a domestic violence call.[573] In the absence of training that enables an officer to make an appropriate assessment as to who should be arrested, this requirement may lead to prejudiced police response.

Furthermore, AI heard reports in Chicago and San Antonio that language barriers present significant problems for the immigrant population. Reportedly, if the abuser speaks better English, appears more in control of the situation and/or is a citizen, police are more likely to believe his or her version of the situation, leading to an arrest of the victim.[574] AI heard reports that officers may use the abuser to translate for the survivor. While police officials in Chicago maintained that they call officers with appropriate language skills, or use translation services over the phone,[575] advocates reported that police are "often disrespectful" and make "no effort" to accommodate those who need translation services.[576]

- **Chicago:** A Latina woman had reportedly been beaten by her partner over a period of time, and neighbors had repeatedly called the police, who usually did not intervene. On one occasion, her abusive partner called the police, claiming she had been abused. Despite the long history of abuse, the victim was arrested and mandated to counseling. An LGBT domestic violence advocate told AI that the abusive partner was fluent in English and was for that reason taken more seriously by police. The victim was monolingual Spanish, unfamiliar with her rights in the United States and was "unable to defend herself verbally with police. As with most same-sex domestic violence cases, the police assume both parties liable, and the one that can speak up and makes the first accusations is considered the victim."[577]

VERBAL ABUSE BY POLICE RESPONDING TO LGBT DOMESTIC VIOLENCE

> In San Antonio, one officer responding to a same-sex domestic violence call reportedly said, "I know we are supposed to be tolerant but that's a bunch of bull, they should all be killed."[578]

AI heard reports in all four cities studied of officers making homophobic or transphobic comments when responding to LGBT domestic violence situations.[579]

---

[572] AI interview with Caseworker (anonymous), San Antonio AIDS Foundation, San Antonio, 5 December 2003.

[573] Birmingham, Alabama; Anchorage, Alaska; Los Angeles, California; Bridgeport, Connecticut; Wilmington, Delaware; Atlanta, Georgia; Honolulu, Hawaii; Lexington, Kentucky; Jackson, Mississippi; Kansas City, Missouri; Omaha, Nebraska; Las Vegas, Nevada; Manchester, New Hampshire; Albuquerque, New Mexico; Fargo, North Dakota; Portland, Oregon; Memphis, Tennessee; San Antonio, Texas; Salt Lake City, Utah; Virginia Beach, Virginia; and Seattle, Washington.

[574] AI interview with Gelsys Rubio, Director, Latino Counseling Services, Chicago, 25 February 2004.

[575] AI interview with Chicago Police Department, 19th District, 25 February 2004.

[576] AI interview with Gelsys Rubio, Latino Counseling Services, and Heather Bradley, Night Ministry, Lakeview Coalition, Chicago, 12 November 2004.

[577] AI interview with Gelsys Rubio, Director, Latino Counseling Services, Chicago, 25 February 2004.

[578] AI interview with Anonymous Advocate (name on file with AIUSA), 3 December 2003.

[579] AI interviews with Darron E. Bowden, Former Executive Director, First Defense Legal Aid, Chicago, 11 November 2004; Karen Stanczykiewicz, Chicago Recovery Alliance, Chicago, 27 February 2004. AI review of Horizons Anti-Violence Project, Case Intake/Incident Report Form, Chicago, 2000 to 2004. See also, Rachel Baum, *Lesbian, Gay, Bisexual and Transgender Domestic Violence in 2002*, National Coalition of Anti-Violence Programs, Preliminary Edition 2003.

AI heard that transgender individuals are targeted for verbal abuse by officers responding to domestic violence.[580] Officers have reportedly addressed survivors by the wrong pronoun, called transgender women "sir," and despite valid ID, have demanded, "What's your real name?"[581] AI also heard reports in San Antonio, including a report from a Latina transgender woman who was reportedly told by an officer "Shut up, faggot" when she reported that she had been assaulted by her boyfriend.[582]

Inappropriate comments made during police response to domestic violence involving lesbians and gays have also been reported, including "Which one of you is the wife?", "What is it that you don't see in women?" and comments suggesting that domestic violence involving two men was really the result of "kinky sex."[583]

Police need to be trained to undertake a more sophisticated and thorough assessment when responding to a LGBT domestic violence incident as the imbalance of power, which is at the center of domestic violence, is built and maintained on various issues of identity and social status including not just sexism but also issues of racism, classism, xenophobia, ageism, and community and occupational status.

Some police departments have responded to the call for improved service when responding to heterosexual domestic violence by creating specialized units or officers in domestic violence cases, and conduct outreach and work with survivors of domestic violence after the initial incident. Such units will only improve the treatment of LGBT survivors if the officers receive appropriate training.

Failure to protect, investigate and punish crimes against LGBT individuals amounts to a failure of the state's obligation to act with due diligence, in contravention of international legal standards.

---

[580] AI interviews with Anonymous Transgender Rights Advocate (name and organization on file with AIUSA), Chicago, 25 February 2004; Kate Walz, Formerly of First Defense Legal Aid, Chicago, 24 February 2004; Susan Holt and Matthew Pulling, STOP Partner Abuse/ Domestic Violence Program, Los Angeles Gay and Lesbian Center, Los Angeles, 1 October 2003; AI review of AVP Horizons intake forms, Chicago, 2000 to 2003.

[581] AI interview with Anonymous Transgender Rights Advocate (name and organization on file with AIUSA), Chicago, 25 February 2004; Karen Stanczykiewicz, Chicago Recovery Alliance, Chicago, 27 February 2004.

[582] AI interview with Anonymous, San Antonio AIDS Foundation, San Antonio, 5 December 2003.

[583] AI interview with South Asian Network, 29 January 2004; LAGLC Anti-Violence Project incident report, 30 May 2000.

8

TRAINING AND ACCOUNTABILITY

SUMMARY

TWENTY-EIGHT PERCENT OF RESPONDING POLICE DEPARTMENTS do not provide training on LGBT issues. When training on LGBT issues does take place it is frequently not provided in a systematic, ongoing manner, but is limited to a session provided for new recruits at the police academy. Amnesty International is concerned at reports that often the training which does exist reinforces stereotypes and fails to change perceptions of bias.

Anecdotal evidence suggests that there are few openly gay or lesbian officers in the U.S., and few higher ranking officers nationwide are women, people of color or openly LGBT.[584] Nevertheless, only four of the 29 responding departments reported any kind of affirmative action hiring practice for LGBT individuals (14 percent).

Community outreach efforts such as LGBT liaisons or community boards are in place in some jurisdictions, but are often underfunded, overstretched or have a very limited mandate. Marginalized and disenfranchised individuals are frequently not seen as part of the "community" by police and are often not included in outreach efforts or welcome at community board meetings. There is a widespread sentiment among people of color and immigrant LGBT communities that law enforcement authorities are not particularly accountable to their communities. Furthermore, advocates charge that "quality of life" policies and practices are discriminatory against the poor and the economically disenfranchised. Young LGBT people are increasingly being pushed out of gentrifying neighborhoods and targeted for abuse, both by police and some members of the community. As one NYC advocate put it, "Whose quality of life is the City concerned about?"—noting that police departments tend to cater to the needs of the more affluent members of the community and less to the marginalized and disenfranchised segments of the community.[585]

Reports to AI suggest that many individuals do not come forward with complaints about police officer conduct, including LGBT individuals. AI received a number of complaints of hostility or attempts to dissuade people from making complaints at police stations. AI also heard several accounts of retaliation against LGBT individuals who reported police misconduct. Moreover, many departments have inadequate procedures for officers to report misconduct. Public trust in police internal oversight is further undermined by the lack of transparency and delays in investigations.

Internal oversight bodies are frequently not trained in handling complaints pertaining to LGBT individuals. Only 45 percent (five of 11) of responding internal affairs departments told AI that they train their staff on LGBT issues, and of these, only two have mandatory training. In many cases, complaints are ruled "unfounded" since no corroborating evidence is found. This is particularly problematic for marginalized communities who are less likely to be believed by investigators, and who may not have witnesses to support their account. In the event that an officer is found to be culpable for misconduct, disciplinary decisions are often inadequate and there is little consistency from case to case. Reports indicate that a low number of officers are suspended or fired, even for serious abuses.

Internal oversight bodies often focus their energies on identifying individual perpetrators at the expense of examining systemic issues and policy review. While early intervention systems are increasingly being explored in order to identify problem officers, these systems frequently do not collect data regarding issues of discrimination, and

---

[584] Reportedly 91 percent of uniformed personnel at the rank of captain or above are white in the NYPD. See for example: "The State of Blacks in Law Enforcement 2004," at http://www.lopezclan.com/100blacks/kelly%20report%20card.pdf.

[585] AI interview with Joo-Hyun Kang, former Executive Director, Audre Lorde Project, New York City, March 16, 2004.

are rarely mined for systemic manifestations of such issues. AI is concerned that this results in the systems having limited utility in addressing police misconduct against marginalized groups.

Independent oversight and control has been instituted in many cities across the U.S.; however, seven out of 29 responding police departments (24 percent) indicated to AI that they do not have an external review process. Among existing review boards, AI's findings indicate a lack of training and expertise in LGBT issues, raising concerns about their ability to respond to and investigate complaints made by this population. External review boards are also frequently limited by inadequate funds, staff and access to information, and have been criticized for failing to perform sufficient outreach. Advocates also point out that often, external review bodies are not truly independent and lack any real power, such as subpoena power, to be truly effective. Independent monitors have been instituted in some cities to monitor the internal disciplinary process of police departments, reviewing systemic issues within the department. This type of monitoring could potentially assist in identifying systemic misconduct against marginalized communities.

Very few criminal cases involving excessive use of force or discriminatory practices are brought against individual police officers. Civil lawsuits may provide financial compensation to individual survivors, but are unlikely to be filed by marginalized and disenfranchised individuals and rarely serve to hold either police departments or individual officers accountable. Federal lawsuits have resulted in drawing up of "Consent Decrees"[586] in several cities, instituting reforms. However, insufficient resources are available to investigate such issues and as of 2004, to AI's knowledge, no such lawsuits have included discriminatory treatment on the basis of sexual orientation or gender identity.

8.1

BACKGROUND

ADVOCATES CHARGE THAT POLICE CULTURE has been—and in many cases still is—characterized by racism, sexism, homophobia and transphobia.[587] These biases result in misconduct and abuse by law enforcement, particularly against these groups, and the impunity of those who perpetrate such violations. Previous AI reports have highlighted problems in U.S. police departments with use of excessive force, in particular against communities of color, but also against homeless, mentally ill and LGBT individuals. Evidence of discriminatory treatment and bias in police contacts with members of the black, Latino and Asian communities is widely documented by NGOs, commissions of inquiry, in court cases and lawsuits, and by countless individual testimonies.[588]

Amnesty International and other organizations have pointed to the need for effective accountability measures in order to address many of these concerns. However, police departments have frequently resisted reforms of accountability and oversight measures, and officers reportedly often continue to block such measures, even if they are adopted.[589] Some advocates have pointed out that police unions have played a significant role in restricting disciplinary

---

[586] A "Consent Decree" is a court decree to which all parties agree.

[587] AI interview with Lisa Tonna, Director of Advocacy and Legislative Affairs, Horizons, Chicago, 23 February 2004; LGBT Rights Advocate, Chicago, 12 November 2003; Staff Member of an FtM Transgender Support Organization, Los Angeles, 28 October 2003; Kamau Franklin, People's Law Collective, New York City, 21 May 2004; Jesse Ehrensaft-Hawley, Director, FIERCE!, New York City, 12 February 2004; Anonymous, Gay Officers Action League, New York City, 14 April 2004.

[588] See: *Race, Rights and Police Brutality* (AI Index: AMR 51/147/1999), 1 September 1999.

[589] For example, the independent monitor of the Consent Decree between the Department of Justice and LAPD reported that LAPD officers were resistant to the decree. See: *Report of the Independent Monitor for the LAPD – Third Quarterly Report*, Office of the Independent Monitor of the Los Angeles Police Department, 15 May 2002, p.3, available at: http://www.lapdonline.org/pdf_files/boi/3rd_quarterly_report_02_05_15.pdf; see also: *Race, Rights and Police Brutality* (AI Index: AMR 51/147/1999),1 September 1999, available at: http://web.amnesty.org/library/Index/ENGAMR511471999?open&of=ENG-USA; *Shielded from Justice—Police Brutality and Accountability in the United States*, Human Rights Watch, June 1998, available at http://www.hrw.org/reports98/police/index.htm; Mark Worth, "When Cops Investigate Themselves," *The Washington Free Press*, June 1993, at http://www.washingtonfreepress.org/03/Cops1.html.

reviews and measures by adhering to limitations on investigation procedures and cumbersome appeals processes, and some external complaint systems have been set up in the face of strong opposition from police unions.[590] While unions try to serve the best interests of their members, AI is concerned about such barriers to effective investigations and disciplinary action to the extent that they contribute to the impunity of violators of human rights.

Effective reform requires commitment from the top ranks, and there must be a fundamental understanding of all individuals as deserving of equal rights. This must be instituted on every level of policing and management, including training, recruitment, supervision, outreach to communities and accountability measures.

8.2
TRAINING

69 PERCENT (20 out of 29) police departments responding to AI's survey reported that they provide training on issues relating to LGBT individuals or communities.[591] 28 percent (eight out of 29) of police departments responding to AI's survey reported that they do not have any training on LGBT issues. The eight police departments that do not provide training are: Bridgeport, Connecticut; Wilmington, Delaware; Atlanta, Georgia; Baltimore, Maryland; Omaha, Nebraska; Memphis, Tennessee; Virginia Beach, Virginia; and Cheyenne, Wyoming.[592]

International law and standards require states to provide law enforcement with training on human rights standards.[593] While international standards do not directly require law enforcement to receive training on LGBT issues, some standards do require training to sensitize officers to particular identities. For example, the need for gender-sensitive training of law enforcement personnel has frequently been stressed in the context of violence against women.[594]

In the United States, officers receive training, often at a police academy, before being able to serve on the police force. There are no federal guidelines as to the length or content of such trainings; these are set by each state. Furthermore, there is usually also a stipulation that officers must receive some in-service training after joining the force.

---

[590] Barriers to successful disciplinary or criminal action include special procedural protection afforded to police officers in some departments, often won through pressure by police unions. For example, a sophisticated monitoring system acquired by the Chicago Police Department in 1994 was reportedly shelved after opposition from the police union and was still not in use by late 1997. Amnesty International, *Rights for All*, 1 October 1998, (AI Index: AMR 51/035/1998). Advocates in Chicago told AI that the police union continues to be a major impediment to bringing perpetrators of misconduct to justice. AI interviews with Darron E. Bowden, Former Executive Director, First Defense Legal Aid, Chicago, 11 November 2004; Justice Coalition of Greater Chicago, Monthly Meeting, 17 September 2003; Anonymous Civil Rights Attorney (name and organization on file with AIUSA), Chicago, 17 September 2003.

[591] Birmingham, Alabama; Anchorage, Alaska; Los Angeles, California; Jacksonville, Florida; Honolulu, Hawaii; Chicago, Illinois; Lexington, Kentucky; Boston, Massachusetts; Jackson, Mississippi; Kansas City, Missouri; Las Vegas, Nevada; Manchester, New Hampshire; Albuquerque, New Mexico; New York, New York; Fargo, North Dakota; Portland, Oregon; Philadelphia, Pennsylvania; San Antonio, Texas; Salt Lake City, Utah; and Seattle, Washington.

[592] One police department responding to the survey did not provide a response to this question.

[593] Article 10 (1) Convention against Torture and Other Cruel, Inhuman or Degrading Treatment or Punishment, G.A. res. 39/46, [annex, 39 U.N. GAOR Supp. (No. 51) at 197, U.N. Doc. A/39/51 (1984)], *entered into force* 26 June 1987 (prescribes that education and information regarding the prohibition of torture be fully included in the training of law enforcement personnel); *Declaration of Basic Principles of Justice for Victims of Crime and Abuse of Power*, G.A. res. 40/34, annex, 40 U.N. GAOR Supp. (No. 53) at 214, U.N. Doc. A/40/53 (1985) (requires the police to receive training to sensitize them to the needs of victims); Principle 3, Body of Principles for the Protection of All Persons under Any Form of Detention or Imprisonment, G.A. res. 43/173, annex, 43 U.N. GAOR Supp. (No. 49) at 298, U.N. Doc. A/43/49 (1988); Rules 46 and 47, Standard Minimum Rules for the Treatment of Prisoners, adopted 30 August 1955, by the First United Nations Congress on the Prevention of Crime and the Treatment of Offenders, U.N. Doc. A/CONF/611, annex I, E.S.C. res. 663C, 24 U.N. ESCOR Supp. (No. 1) at 11, U.N. Doc. E/3048 (1957), amended E.S.C. res. 2076, 62 U.N. ESCOR Supp. (No. 1) at 35, U.N. Doc. E/5988 (1977); Article 6(3), Declaration on the Protection of All Persons from Enforced Disappearances, G.A. res. 47/133, 47 U.N. GAOR Supp. (No. 49) at 207, U.N. Doc. A/47/49 (1992); Principles 1, 11, and 19, Basic Principles on the Use of Force and Firearms by Law Enforcement Officials, Eighth United Nations Congress on the Prevention of Crime and the Treatment of Offenders, Havana, 27 August to 7 September 1990, U.N. Doc. A/CONF.144/28/Rev.1 at 112 (1990) (Training and clear guidelines shall be made available on all matters of police activities affecting human rights to all law enforcement officers).

[594] Paragraph 125 (f), The Beijing Declaration and Platform for Action, Fourth World Conference on Women, 15 September 1995, A/CONF.177/20 (1995) and A/CONF.177/20/Add.1 (1995); Committee on the Elimination of Discrimination against Women, General Recommendation 19, Violence against women, (Eleventh session, 1992), U.N. Doc. A/47/38 at 1 (1993), reprinted in Compilation of General Comments and General Recommendations Adopted by Human Rights Treaty Bodies, U.N. Doc. HRI/GEN/1/Rev.6 at 243 (2003), Sec. 24(b), Sec. 24(f).

AI believes that training on LGBT issues is essential; however, as noted above, 28 percent of police departments (eight out of 29) responding to AI's survey reported that they do not provide any training on LGBT issues. It is important to note that the police departments surveyed are in the largest city in every state and are more likely than smaller departments to develop training. Thus the problem may be wider than indicated by AI's survey.

Training on LGBT issues is often limited to a short session provided to new recruits at the police academy. While one police department reported that it provides 16 hours of training related to LGBT issues for new recruits, other police departments offer far less.[595]

In the cities that AI has both included in its survey and studied in more detail, we received the following information regarding LGBT training:

- **Chicago:** Chicago Police Department indicated that officers receive mandatory post-recruit training on LGBT-related issues "as needed."

- **Los Angeles:** Reportedly, formal cultural sensitivity training is provided at the training academy, which includes an LGBT component. According to LAPD, four hours of in-service mandatory training is also provided relating to LGBT issues.[596] It appears that the training referred to is "diversity" training, which not only covers LGBT issues, but also issues of race, national origin, ethnicity and gender, among others.[597]

- **New York:** The NYPD informed AI that their training curriculum was recently rewritten into a unified text that "teaches not to take action against people's differences."[598] The NYPD reported that the curriculum was sent for review and comment to community groups, including LGBT groups. The curriculum is taught over six months at the Academy by officers from the Gay Officers Action League (GOAL) and is developed with the input and guidance of the LGBT community. Trainings involve role-play, which are developed and conducted by GOAL, and include six hours of Cultural Awareness and Diversity Training and four and a half hours on LGBT issues.

- **San Antonio:** Chief Ortiz (SAPD) told AI that cadets go through six months of training at the academy and that during this training the cadets receive one full day dedicated to diversity training, which reportedly includes training on how to be sensitive to those with "alternative lifestyles."[599] In an interview with Bexar County Sheriff's Department, AI was told that there is no specific [LGBT] training: "it includes everyone."[600] Chief Ortiz told AI that there was nothing specific in either the academy or in-service training on transgender issues.[601] Amnesty International reviewed the Texas Commission on Law Enforcement Officer Standards and Education on Cultural Diversity and confirmed that there was no reference to transgender issues, and found only brief and cursory reference to lesbian, gay and bisexual issues, primarily in the section dealing with hate crimes.[602]

---

[595] For example, Birmingham, Alabama reported 16 hours of training. Police departments in Los Angeles, California; Atlanta, Georgia; Honolulu, Hawaii; and Manchester, New Hampshire reported four hours or less of LGBT-related training.

[596] LAPD response to Amnesty International survey, 11 December 2003.

[597] AI interview with Sgt. Don Mueller, West Hollywood Police Department, Los Angeles, 27 January 2004.

[598] AI interview with Commissioner James Fyfe, Training, NYPD, Administration Meeting, New York City, 24 March 2004.

[599] AI interview with Chief Albert Ortiz, San Antonio Police Department, San Antonio, 4 December 2003.

[600] AI interview with Sheriff Ralph Lopez, Bexar County Sheriff's Department, San Antonio, 5 December 2003.

[601] AI interview with Chief Albert Ortiz, San Antonio Police Department, San Antonio, 4 December 2003.

[602] Texas Commission on Law Enforcement Officer Standards and Education, Cultural Diversity.

Training experts as well as law enforcement officers speaking with AI on condition of anonymity noted that LGBT "sensitivity" or "diversity" training is often ineffective.[603] Officers AI met with in Los Angeles reported that training on LGB issues is generally "glossed over," and training with respect to transgender issues is extremely limited or non-existent. AI also heard reports from community organizations in Chicago, Los Angeles, New York and San Antonio, as well as from training experts,[604] that the limited training which does exist often reinforces stereotypes and fails to create learning experiences or to change perceptions of bias.

LGBT-SPECIFIC ISSUE TRAINING

San Antonio: AI received reports that during a training at the academy on same-sex domestic violence the trainer was subjected to harassment based on her perceived lesbian identity even though everyone knew that she was heterosexual and married. She reportedly said she would never do it again, and AI was told that there has been no training on same-sex domestic violence since then.[605]

TRAINING EXPERTS as well as police officers interviewed by AI stressed that practically oriented training is most effective, since this makes the issues concrete and provides useful tools that officers may use in situations involving LGBT individuals.[606] While AI was unable to undertake a thorough review of the content of police departments' trainings, our survey revealed that many police departments fail to provide officers with LGBT-specific training: for example, on enforcing public morals regulations; same-sex domestic violence; hate crime prevention, response and investigation; interaction with transgender individuals; and response to and investigation of crimes against LGBT individuals.

---

[603] AI interviews with anonymous official, Los Angeles, 27 October 2003; anonymous official, 1 November 2003; Shirley Bushnell, Peer Advocate/Outreach Worker, Van Ness Recovery House Prevention Division, Los Angeles, 1 October 2003; Chuck Stewart, Ph.D., Los Angeles, 29 January 2004; Sgt. Don Muller, West Hollywood Station, LASD, 27 January 2004; AnnJanette, Rosga, Ph.D., Assistant Professor, Sociology, University of Colorado, Boulder, 17 March 2004.

[604] AI interviews with Matt Gross, Director, Lakeview Coalition, Chicago, 18 September 2003; Heather Bradley, Outreach Worker, Night Ministry and Gelsys Rubio, Director, Latino Counseling Services, Lakeview Coalition, Chicago, 12 November 2003; Lisa Tonna, Director, Advocacy and Legislative Affairs, Horizons and Jacob Mueller, Administrative Assistant in the Office of Gay, Lesbian, Bisexual and Transgender Concern, University of Illinois at Chicago, 23 February 2004; Chuck Stewart, Ph.D., Los Angeles, 29 January 2004; Patricia Castillo, Executive Director, the Peace Initiative, San Antonio, 2 December 2003; telephone interview with AnnJanette Rosga, Ph.D., Assistant Professor, Sociology, University of Colorado, Boulder, 17 March 2004. See also: Samuel Walker, Geoffrey P. Alpert and Dennis J. Kenney, *Early Warning Systems: Responding to the Problem Police Officer*, National Institute of Justice, Research in Brief, July 2001, pp. 3, 4. Walker et al. note that while observing officers from the New Orleans Police Department participating in a Professional Performance Enhancement Program, they found that officers were actively engaged in components they perceived to be related to the practical problems of police work, but became disengaged in components they perceived to be "abstract, moralistic or otherwise unrelated to practical aspects of police work."

[605] AI interview with Captain Geraldine Garcia, Professional Standards Commander, Lt. Robert Hartle, Internal Affairs Director, Sgt. J.D. McKay, Internal Affairs Unit, San Antonio Police Department, 5 December 2003.

[606] AI interviews with Miranda Stevens, TYRA, Chicago, 25 February 2004; anonymous official, LASD, Los Angeles, 27 October 2003; Shirley Bushnell, Peer Advocate/Outreach Worker, Van Ness Recovery House Prevention Division, Los Angeles, 1 October 2003; Chuck Stewart, Ph.D., Los Angeles, 29 January 2004; Marcus De Maria Arana and Sergeant Stephen Thorne, San Francisco Human Rights Department and Police Department, San Francisco, 15 March 2004.

Strip Searches/Transgender	• 62 percent of all responding departments (18 out of 29) train their officers on how to do strip searches; only nine out of 29 (31 percent) report that they instruct their officers in how to strip search a transgender individual.
Same-Sex Domestic Violence	• 24 (83 percent) police departments reported providing training on issues around same-sex domestic violence. • 14 percent (four departments) reported that they do not train on issues around same-sex domestic violence.[607]
LGBT Hate Crimes	• 19 (66 percent) police departments reported providing training on hate crimes against LGBT individuals. • Eight (28 percent) police departments reported that they do not train officers on LGBT hate crimes.[608]
Sexual Assault of LGBT Individuals	• Most departments provide training regarding sexual assault (86 percent), but 52 percent (15 out of 29) of these do not touch on LGBT-specific issues in this regard.

In the four cities studied in greater detail, police departments reported providing the following LGBT-specific training:

	Searches of Transgender Individuals	LGBT Domestic Violence	LGBT Hate Crimes	Sexual Assault of LGBT	LGBT Sex Workers
CHICAGO	As Needed	As Needed	As Needed	As Needed	As Needed
LOS ANGELES	Yes	Yes[609]	Yes	No	No
NEW YORK[610]	Information not available	Yes	Information not available	Information not available	Information not available
SAN ANTONIO	No	Yes	Yes	No	No

Advocates noted that more sophisticated training regarding diversity in communities of color and LGBT communities is also required. For example, stereotypical assumptions that people of color are not LGBT may lead to inappropriate or insensitive reactions. Training on LGBT issues should not exist in a vacuum but needs to incorporate how issues such as race, age, gender, socioeconomics and immigration status impacts members of LGBT communities, and trainings on race and immigration should include LGBT issues and concerns.[611]

[607] AIUSA's survey did not ask whether training was provided on domestic violence incidents involving transgender individuals. One police department responding to AI's survey did not respond to this question.

[608] These departments are: Wilmington, Delaware (sexual orientation is included in the state's hate crime statute); Boston, Massachusetts (sexual orientation is included in the state's hate crime statute); Omaha, Nebraska (sexual orientation is included in the state's hate crime statute); Memphis, Tennessee (sexual orientation is included in the state's hate crime statute) Philadelphia, Pennsylvania (sexual orientation and gender identity are included in the state's hate crime statute; Birmingham, Alabama (sexual orientation and gender identity are not covered by a state hate crime statute); Baltimore, Maryland (sexual orientation and gender identity are not covered by a state hate crime statute); Jackson, Mississippi (sexual orientation and gender identity are not covered by a state hate crime statute). Two police departments responding to AI's survey did not provide a response to this question.

[609] While the LAPD reported in its response to AI's survey that training on domestic violence issues covers issues posed by domestic violence between same-sex couples, LAPD officials clarified that such training is limited to determining which party is the primary or dominant aggressor in any relationship, and does not focus on LGBT-specific scenarios, trends or factors. AI interview with Captain Downing, Hollywood-Wilcox Division, LAPD, 26 January 2003.

[610] NYPD failed to complete the survey sent to them by AI. Any answers that are entered were from official answers to questions in interviews with AI researchers.

[611] AI interviews with NEON, Chicago, 11 November 2003; Lisa Tonna, Director, Advocacy and Legislative Affairs at Horizons and Jacob Mueller, Administrative Assistant in the Office of Gay, Lesbian, Bisexual and Transgender Concern, University of Illinois at Chicago, 23 February 2004; Nohelia Canales and Roger Coggan, LAGLC AVP, Los Angeles, 28 January 2004; Francisco Lazala, Director of the SOMOS Project of the Latino AIDS Commission, New York City, 23 February 2004.

TRAINERS

IT IS ALSO IMPORTANT to recognize the role that a trainer plays in providing effective training. Reports to AI suggest that effective trainings have involved dedicated, well-respected officers with training expertise who collaborate closely with community members on the development and implementation of trainings.[612] Advocates have expressed concerns that trainings conducted without any input from community members do not properly convey the needs and rights of the groups in question.[613] Some police departments rely heavily or sometimes exclusively on unpaid LGBT organizations to provide training without any input or support from law enforcement trainers.[614] Other police departments ask officers who happen to be lesbian or gay to conduct trainings although they may not be professional trainers.[615] While AI recognizes the important role that LGBT organizations and LGBT officers have to offer in training police departments, AI's findings indicate that police departments themselves in many instances do not provide the support or commitment needed to ensure long-term institutionalized trainings on LGBT issues.

IN-SERVICE TRAINING

IT IS OF CONCERN that officers who have been on the force for longer periods may not have received any LGBT training, as few departments offer any systematized in-service LGBT training. This is particularly problematic in the event that such officers hold more senior positions and have supervisory responsibilities for less experienced officers. One of the New York organizations AI spoke with stated, "The trainings we did were doomed to failure—it was bottom-up training. You train the rookies but then you put them out there with the homophobic and transphobic officers. You've got to start from the top."[616]

- **New York:** NYPD told AI that trainings are held at the precinct and promotion levels, with each new recruit undergoing a special two-day orientation to a precinct upon reassignment, addressing issues of particular concern and relevance to that precinct, and conducted by the commanding officers.[617] LGBT community members, for example, participate in trainings conducted at the 6th precinct. However, one officer told AI that he and other LGBT officers had proposed putting together one-day training workshops on LGBT issues to be undertaken at the precinct level as well as during promotion. He reports that as yet, these trainings have not been realized.[618]

- **San Antonio:** Chief Ortiz (SAPD) told AI that all SAPD officers receive 40 hours of in-service training every year, which includes four to eight hours of cultural diversity training. AI was told that in the next cycle they will be covering ethnicity and that over time, the training covers age, gender and sexual orientation.

[612] AI interviews with Shirley Bushnell, Peer Advocate/Outreach Worker for the Van Ness Recovery House Prevention Division, Los Angeles, 1 October 2003; Sergeant Don Mueller, West Hollywood Police Department, Los Angeles, 27 January 2004; Margaux Delotte-Bennett, Sexual Minority Youth Assistance League, Washington, D.C., 20 November 2003; Cyndee Clay, Executive Director, HIPS, Washington, D.C., 20 November 2003. The use of ranking officers was also suggested by Roger Coggan and Nohelia Canales, AVP, Los Angeles Gay and Lesbian Center, 28 January 2004.

[613] AI interview with South Asian Network, 29 January 2003.

[614] AI interviews with law enforcement officer, 1 November 2003; Shirley Bushnell, Van Ness Recovery House Prevention Division, Los Angeles, 1 October 2003; Chuck Stewart, Ph.D., Los Angeles, 29 January 2004; Marshall Wong, Human Rights Commission – Hate Crimes Reporting Unit, Los Angeles, 27 January 2004; Lee Carpenter, Center for Gay and Lesbian Civil Rights, Philadelphia, 15 March 2004.

[615] AI interviews with anonymous official, LASD, Los Angeles, 27 October 2003; Anonymous, Gay Officers Action League, New York City, 14 April 2004; Patricia Castillo, Domestic Violence Advocate/Executive Director of the Peace Initiative, San Antonio, 2 December 2003; Marcus de Maria Arana and Sergeant Stephen Thorne, San Francisco Human Rights Commission and San Francisco Police Department, San Francisco, 15 March 2004.

[616] AI interview with Carrie Davis, Gender Identity Project, New York City, 3 February 2004.

[617] AI interview with Inspector Fitzgerald, Captain Hanley and Dep. Chief Gerrish, NYPD 6th Precinct, New York City, 15 March 2004.

[618] AI interview with Anonymous, Gay Officers Action League, New York City, 14 April 2004.

In some cities and counties, advocates have attempted to provide some form of in-service training and education to officers by conducting roll call trainings, where advocates have the opportunity to speak to officers for 10 to 20 minutes at staff meetings which take place before the beginning of a shift. Since there is no additional cost for administrators in terms of staff hours and advocates are usually willing to volunteer their services, police departments may be more receptive to requests from advocacy organizations to provide such trainings to their officers.[619]

AI is concerned that the limited time available during a roll call is not conducive to covering new or complex ground. Advocates told AI that with the proper support, roll call trainings may serve as useful reminders for officers, but that they cannot replace thorough training sessions.[620] Furthermore, AI has received reports of trainers who have endured transphobic and homophobic environments.[621]

- Washington, D.C.: In 2000, the organization Helping Individual Prostitutes Survive (HIPS) was invited to provide a sensitivity training at a roll call. HIPS told AI that it was a very negative experience—"one of the worst" experiences the organization has ever had. Reportedly, the presenters from HIPS were ridiculed by officers, who particularly targeted the transgender presenter who was belittled, ridiculed, laughed at and called "bad names." Reportedly, they "laughed her out of the room." According to HIPS, the officer who had invited them did nothing to halt the abuse. HIPS has not done roll call trainings since this incident.[622]

Condoning inappropriate treatment of trainers who act as representatives of LGBT communities reinforces the perception that members of LGBT communities are less deserving of rights than others. When supervisors stand by while their subordinates are openly hostile and homophobic or transphobic, they furthermore reinforce the belief among officers that human rights training is something they "have to" endure and that it bears little relation to policing in practice.

8.3

RECRUITMENT AND DIVERSITY ON THE FORCE

"… A police force representative of its community will enjoy improved relations with the community and will, consequently, function more effectively."[623]

U.S. Commission on Civil Rights

When it was discovered that a police officer was transgender in 2000, because of emails sent to other transgender women found on the officer's computer, the officer was pressured to leave the department. The officer told AI that after being called to the Police Chief's office, the Chief reportedly said, "I know about your other lifestyle… I can't have you working here. You've got a problem. There is something wrong with you. I've known you my whole life and this sickens and disgusts me… this is unacceptable." The Chief reportedly suggested that the officer get a doctor's note so that the officer could be off for six months and then leave the police department. The officer gave in to the pressure to leave. Since leaving the force, the officer told AI that former colleagues have made remarks such as "you disgust me" and "pervert."[624]

---

[619] AI interviews with Lisa Tonna, Director of Advocacy and Legislative Affairs, Horizons, Chicago, 23 February 2004; Patti Buffington, Executive Director of Genesis House, Chicago, 26 February 2004; NYPD 115th Precinct, New York City, 22 March 2004; Deputy Inspector Fitzgerald, Captain Hanley and Deputy Chief John Gerrish, NYPD 6th Precinct, New York City, 15 March 2004; Deputy Inspector Brian Conroy, Detective Adam Damico, Lieutenant Sam Ortiz, Inspector Monahan, NYPD Midtown South Precinct, New York City, 22 March 2004; Clarence Patton, Diane Dolon-Soto, Martine Barbier and Basil Lucas, NYG&L AVP, New York City, 23 February 2004.

[620] AI interviews with Lisa Tonna, Director of Advocacy and Legislative Affairs, Horizons, Chicago, 23 February 2004; Chuck Stewart, Ph.D., Los Angeles, 29 January 2004; Carmen Vazquez, Deputy Director, Empire State Pride Agenda, New York City, 8 April 2004; Marcus de Maria Arana, San Francisco Human Rights Commission, San Francisco, 15 March 2004.

[621] AI interviews with Lisa Tonna, Director of Advocacy and Legislative Affairs, Horizons, Chicago, 23 February 2004; Cyndee Clay, Executive Director, HIPS, Washington, D.C., 20 November 2003; official, San Antonio Police Department, Fall 2003.

[622] AI interview with Cyndee Clay, Executive Director, HIPS, Washington, D.C., 20 November 2003.

[623] See U.S. Commission on Civil Rights, Who Is Guarding the Guardians?, October 1981.

[624] AI telephone interview with Anonymous, 22 March 2004.

INTERNATIONAL STANDARDS AND GUIDELINES stress that law enforcement agencies should be representative of the community as a whole, noting that this is a prerequisite for the humane performance of law enforcement functions,[625] and stipulate, "The recruitment, hiring, assignment and promotions policies of police agencies shall be free from any form of unlawful discrimination."[626] While AI believes that demographics alone are unlikely to change the underlying culture, police forces should mirror the composition of the communities they police and include proper representation throughout the ranks of LGBT individuals, women and people of color.

Anecdotal evidence suggests there are relatively few LGBT officers who are in a position to be open about their sexual orientation or gender identity, although LGBT police officer associations exist in some larger cities; for example, GOAL in New York.[627] However, AI is only aware of a fairly small number of LGBT officers who serve on police forces in the U.S.[628]

Only four out of 29 responding police departments in Los Angeles, California; New York, New York; Fargo, North Dakota; and Salt Lake City, Utah reported any kind of affirmative action hiring practice for LGBT individuals. The Phoenix, Arizona police department did not make clear whether or not it maintained an affirmative action hiring practice for LGBT individuals, but indicated that it recruits at LGBT events.

Even in departments where relevant affirmative action policies exist, other factors impede appropriate diversity within the police force. The U.S. Commission on Civil Rights has noted that although police forces have tried to implement affirmative action policies for women and people of color, they have been unable to accomplish diversity, in part because claims of sexual and racial harassment and disparity in pay make police careers unattractive.[629] In light of pervasive homophobia and transphobia, it would follow that LGBT individuals face similar disincentives to seeking careers within police departments.

Some lesbian and gay officers (as well as one transgender officer) AI interviewed reported a predominantly positive experience when they came out. Others expressed frustration over transphobic or homophobic remarks from colleagues. Reports indicate that prejudice surfaces in everyday situations, including inappropriate comments in the locker room or via email and as screen savers.[630] Perceptions that such behavior and beliefs are somehow acceptable foster discrimination within the department, and moreover, it is unlikely that such attitudes would not impact treatment of members of the public on some level. Police officials told AI on several occasions that it is impossible to control what their officers think or believe, and that training on behavior is sufficient.[631] Nevertheless, this attitude allows such beliefs to go unchallenged. These discriminations intersect with other discriminations, including racism.

- **Los Angeles:** A gay law enforcement officer told AI, "If someone were to use words like 'nigger' or 'spic,' they would be immediately disciplined. However, if they use the word 'faggot,' generally nothing happens to them. Discipline only happens if someone steps forward, complains and says they are offended. Jokes and innuendoes in the locker room are still tolerated. This still happens rampantly across law enforcement. Racial jokes and slurs are immediately dealt with, regardless if there is a 'complaining party' or not, but with gay jokes, if no one complains, no one is disciplined. It needs to be seen as any other form of discrimination."[632]

[625] Preambular para. 8(a), UN Code of Conduct, G.A. res. 34/169, annex, 34 U.N. GAOR Supp. (No. 46) at 186, U.N. Doc. A/34/46 (1979).

[626] The United Nations High Commissioner for Human Rights, International Human Rights Standards for Law Enforcement, A pocket book, at http://www.ohchr.org/english/about/publications/docs/pocketbook.pdf.

[627] Gay Officers Action League, available at: http://www.goalny.org/.

[628] See further the organization Transgender Officers Protect and Serve (TOPS).

[629] The U.S. Commission on Civil Rights, *Revisiting Who Is Guarding the Guardians?*, November 2000, http://www.usccr.gov/pubs/guard/main.htm. (The United States Commission on Civil Rights is composed of eight Commissioners: four appointed by the President and four by Congress. The Commissioners serve six-year terms.)

[630] AI interviews with Lisa Tonna, Director of Advocacy and Legislative Affairs, Horizons, Chicago, 23 February 2004; Law Enforcement Officer, Los Angeles, 1 November 2003; Sgt. Don Mueller, West Hollywood Police Department, Los Angeles, 27 January 2004; Anthony Miranda, Latino Officers Association, New York City, 9 March 2004; Cyndee Clay, Executive Director, HIPS, Washington, D.C., 20 November 2003.

[631] AI interview with Commissioner James Fyfe, Training, NYPD Administration Meeting, New York City, 24 March 2004; Chief Steven Baum, San Antonio Parks Police, San Antonio, 4 December 2003.

[632] AI interview with Sgt. Donald M. Mueller, Los Angeles County Sheriff's Department, Los Angeles, 27 January 2004.

It must be made clear that any expressions of prejudice are unacceptable and will be disciplined appropriately. Discrimination within the police, including racism, sexism, homophobia and transphobia, must be rooted out and addressed in order for treatment of members of the public to change.

8.4

COMMUNITY ACCOUNTABILITY

> "In order for police to be effective, they need to understand that we're part of the community, not just policing the community."
> Richard Odenthal, former Captain of West Hollywood Division LASD, Public Safety Manager, City of West Hollywood[633]

DIVERSITY IN THE POLICE FORCE is only one potential marker of progress towards accountability and not an end goal in and of itself. Accountability to the communities they serve should be the guiding value of all law enforcement policies and practices. International guidelines suggest that involvement in and partnership with the communities is an important part of police work. The UN High Commissioner for Human Rights states that a prerequisite for the humane performance of law enforcement functions includes ensuring that "every law enforcement agency should be representative of and responsive and accountable to the community as a whole."[634] Principles for community policing include recommendations that police establish community outreach and public information programs; liaise regularly with all groups in the community; involve the community in identifying problems and concerns; and coordinate policies, strategies and activities with non-governmental organizations.[635]

AI's findings indicate the need for the police to work more proactively to build effective relationships with the communities they serve. Some community groups and activists have argued that one way to help this process and promote better accountability is for police departments to institute residency requirements for officers. AI's findings also demonstrate the need for local authorities to ensure that policing policies and practices serve the interests of all members of communities and do not result in systemic discrimination of targeted and marginalized groups.

Advocates in Chicago, Los Angeles, New York and San Francisco noted that police departments tend to focus their attention on older, wealthier members of the community, including business or property owners, to the exclusion of the needs and rights of the more marginalized and disenfranchised communities.[636] In some cities, "community boards" or beat meetings between police and local communities have been established, and these meetings provide an important channel of communication. However, they have been criticized for being dominated by police officials, and for only welcoming certain groups and individuals.[637] AI found a pattern of inadequate proactive outreach to LGBT communities, in particular to the more marginalized, including LGBT people of color and homeless youth. For example, in New York officials told AI, "Most of the young people who come to the Village don't live there; they don't have jobs there. It's too expensive for them anyway. They're not part of the community."[638]

Some police departments have instituted Advisory Boards and Task Forces which consist of community members who meet with officials on a regular basis to bring up issues of concern. AI is pleased to note that the West Hollywood

---

[633] AI interview with Richard Odenthal, former Captain of West Hollywood Division, LASD, Public Safety Manager, City of West Hollywood, January 2004.

[634] The United Nations High Commissioner for Human Rights, *International Human Rights Standards for Law Enforcement, A pocket book*, http://www.ohchr.org/english/about/publications/docs/pocketbook.pdf.

[635] Id.

[636] AI interviews with Andy Kim, Chicago Coalition for the Homeless, Chicago, 14 November 2003; Kate Walz, Formerly of First Defense Legal Aid, Chicago, 24 February 2004; Shirley Bushnell, speaking at an Asian Pacific AIDS Intervention Team Community Forum Meeting, Los Angeles, 29 January 2004; Sylvia Beltran and Alex Sanchez, Homies Unidos, Los Angeles, 27 January 2004; Q-Team, 1 November 2003; Sumiko Braun and Patrick Mangto, Ohana House, 28 January 2004; Carl Siciliano, Executive Director, Ali Forney Center, New York City, 13 February 2004; Yves Michel Fontaine, Clinical Coordinator of Gay Men's Health Crisis, New York City, 19 March 2004; Robert Woodworth, LGBT Center, New York City, 11 February 2004; Chris Daly, Transgender Law Center, San Francisco, 27 October 2003; Eric Schnabel, Queer Youth Training Collaborative Program Coordinator from LYRIC, San Francisco, 1 August 2002; Rachel Herzig, Field Organizer, Critical Resistance's national office, San Francisco, 23 October 2003.

[637] AI interview with Andy Kim, Chicago Coalition for the Homeless, Chicago, 14 November 2003.

[638] AI interview with NYPD 6th Precinct, New York, 15 March 2004.

Station of the LASD has a Gay and Lesbian Conference Committee, where, according to Sheriff Baca, anyone can walk in and participate. According to LASD officials, these are very effective, and allow them to stay in touch with community concerns.[639] The City of West Hollywood has established a Transgender Task Force which addresses policing issues, among others.[640] AI believes that such models may be a good idea provided that communities are effectively represented by those selected to be on the board.[641]

Some U.S. police departments have appointed officers to be LGBT liaisons, serving as a link between LGBT communities and the police. Only 11 of 29 responding police departments (38 percent) told AI they have an LGBT liaison officer.[642] Surveyed police departments without LGBT liaison officers are: Birmingham, Alabama; Anchorage, Alaska; Bridgeport, Connecticut; Wilmington, Delaware; Honolulu, Hawaii; Chicago, Illinois; Lexington, Kentucky; Jackson, Mississippi; Kansas City, Missouri; Omaha, Nebraska; Las Vegas, Nevada; Manchester, New Hampshire; Albuquerque, New Mexico; Memphis, Tennessee; San Antonio, Texas; Virginia Beach, Virginia; and Cheyenne, Wyoming.

AI found that while organizations and advocates generally expressed appreciation for LGBT liaisons, in many locations only one or two individuals cover a population of several million people, making it difficult to undertake substantive issues and to properly serve the entire LGBT community. In some cities, advocates charge that LGBT liaisons function merely as public relations managers, limiting their work to liaising with the larger mainstream organizations, with little or no input into police policy or training and lack of respect from the rest of the force. However, reports indicate that it can make a difference to have an advocate who understands police work as well as LGBT issues, depending on the mandate and personal impact of the liaison.[643]

- **Chicago:** Even though the Chicago Police Department indicated in its response to AI's survey that it does not have an LGBT liaison, AI learned that one precinct in the department has a LGBT liaison officer. This liaison has established an advisory group and invited representatives from various organizations to participate.[644] Furthermore, the Hate Crime Unit has a LGBT liaison to provide assistance or to report particularly sensitive cases.

- **Los Angeles:** LAPD has two officers assigned as LGBT liaisons who work under Chief Bratton. The LGBT Liaison for the West Hollywood Station of the LASD was described by several LGBT community members and activists as an effective advocate for LGBT concerns.[645]

- **New York:** The New York Police Department has one LGBT liaison. He explained to AI that he reports directly to the Commissioner on LGBT issues and that his role is to monitor LGBT protests and speak with council members, but that he doesn't conduct outreach to LGBT communities, although he remains in touch with some groups. While there are not LGBT liaisons at the precinct level, local outreach is the responsibility of Community Affairs officers at each precinct.[646]

---

[639] AI interview with Sheriff Lee Baca, Captain Linda Castro, LASD, and Mayor Jeffrey Prang, City of West Hollywood, Los Angeles, 29 January 2004.

[640] AI interviews with Sheriff Lee Baca, Captain Linda Castro, LASD, and Mayor Jeffrey Prang, City of West Hollywood, 29 January 2004; Richard Odenthal, former Captain of West Hollywood Division LASD, Public Safety Manager, City of West Hollywood, January 2004.

[641] While the U.S. Civil Rights Commission applauded the existence of the Boards as important in the context of implementation of a community policing model, it cautioned that station captains' use of their substantial discretion in selecting individuals from the community to serve on the Boards "is a source of concern." U.S. Civil Rights Commission, *Racial and Ethnic Tensions in American Communities: Poverty, Inequality, and Discrimination, Vol. V: The Los Angeles Report*, 1999.

[642] Surveyed police departments with LGBT liaison officers are: Phoenix, Arizona; Los Angeles, California; Jacksonville, Florida; Atlanta, Georgia; Boston, Massachusetts; New York, New York; Fargo, North Dakota; Portland, Oregon; Philadelphia, Pennsylvania; Salt Lake City, Utah; and Seattle, Washington.

[643] AI interview with Sgt. Don Muller, West Hollywood Station, LASD, 27 January 2004.

[644] The liaison is stationed at the 23rd Precinct.

[645] AI interviews with Susan Holt, STOP – Domestic Violence Program, Los Angeles, 30 September 2003; Shirley Bushnell, Van Ness Recovery House Prevention Division, Los Angeles, 1 October 2003.

[646] AI interview with Kevin Zatariski, LGBT Liaison to the Commissioner, and Deputy Chief John Gerrish, Office of Management Analysis and Planning, NYPD, administration meeting, New York City, 24 March 2004.

- **San Antonio:** Neither SAPD nor Bexar County Sheriff's Department has a member of staff designated to liaise with LGBT communities. Chief Ortiz (SAPD) told AI that he would be willing to meet on a regular basis with members of LGBT communities. AI urges SAPD to follow up on this commitment and also advises that outreach is undertaken to LGBT communities in San Antonio.

- **Washington, D.C.:** The Gay and Lesbian Liaison Unit (GLLU) in Washington, D.C. is staffed by four full-time officers and 10 volunteers and the head of the unit, Sgt. Brett Parson, reports directly to the Police Chief. The officers undertake police work as well as outreach, which was noted by the unit as an important factor in gaining respect and credibility within the police department. GLLU is also involved in training efforts within the police department.[647] LGBT organizations and advocates in D.C., including those representing marginalized populations such as sex workers and homeless youth of color, expressed great appreciation for the unit, praising individuals involved and the extensive outreach conducted. AI heard from one transgender woman of color who works as an advocate for sex workers that the unit "engages marginalized people and the LGBT community organizations in this city like no one ever has … I would call Brett before I called 911."[648]

Effective community outreach, whether in the form of LGBT liaisons or LGBT-specific task forces, must not be seen as isolated from the rest of the police department. Commitment to change must be a proactive effort department-wide, and reform must be supported and led by senior officials in order to truly impact the culture and actions of the police force as a whole.

8.5

LEADERSHIP AND SUPERVISION

> *As a leader in the Los Angeles County Sheriff's Department, I commit myself to honorably perform my duty with respect for the dignity of all people, integrity to do what is right and fight what is wrong, wisdom to use common sense and fairness in all that I do, and, finally, courage to stand against racism, sexism, anti-Semitism, homophobia and bigotry in all its forms.*
>
> Los Angeles Sheriff's Department Core Values

ACTIVISTS AND INDIVIDUAL POLICE OFFICERS also brought up the need for diligent supervision and commitment from leadership in order to achieve effective reform and any lasting change.[649] Moreover, to the extent that elected officials appoint police chiefs and influence the running of police departments, they must take responsibility for ensuring that police departments adhere to international human rights standards and operate in a transparent and inclusive manner.

Clear statements from senior police officials are an important step towards addressing institutional and cultural issues. AI is pleased to note, for example, that Sheriff Baca of the Los Angeles Sheriff's Department introduced an amendment to the department's core values, to include non-discrimination against sexual orientation.[650] Police departments are further encouraged to institute regular internal audits in order to identify institutional dynamics that may facilitate discrimination.

---

[647] The eight hours of sensitivity training provided to new recruits and personnel being promoted mentions GLLU as a resource. Furthermore, all officers are required to do 40 hours of training a year; of those, one hour is on sensitivity/awareness education, taught by Parson. AI interview with Sergeant Brett Parson, GLLU, 20 November 2003.

[648] AI interview with Gigi Thomas, Program Assistant, HIPS, Washington, D.C., 20 November 2003.

[649] AI interviews with Anonymous Civil Rights Attorney (name and organization on file with AIUSA), Chicago, 17 September 2003; Jeff Prang, Mayor of West Hollywood, in meeting with Los Angeles County Sheriff's Department Administration, Los Angeles, 29 January 2003; Richard Odenthal, West Hollywood Public Safety Manager, Los Angeles, January 2004; Sgt. Don Mueller, West Hollywood Police Department, Los Angeles, 27 January 2004.

[650] AI interview with Sgt. Don Mueller, West Hollywood Police Department, Los Angeles, 27 January 2004. See also: Sheriff Baca's speech, Inglewood Forum on Police Misconduct, 23 August 2002, available at: http://www.lacp.org/Page-1s/082302%20SheriffBaca.html.

Supervision and monitoring of operations in day-to-day police work is also important. Reports and lawsuits have documented the lack of diligent supervision as one of the root causes of police misconduct.[651] The findings of this report point to the need for particularly diligent supervision, monitoring and training in handling of the most marginalized communities—including LGBT people of color, youth, sex workers and homeless individuals.

Evaluations by supervisors of a police officer's performance are also a powerful way of sending a message about values and actions that the department believes are important. Some organizations believe police performance should be evaluated in a more holistic way than currently takes place, incorporating human rights aspects of policing. For example, issues of quality of service, perceptions of safety and confidence in policing can be measured by victim perception surveys.[652] The U.S. Commission on Civil Rights has suggested a system of rewards to incorporate and reinforce both the goal of crime prevention and protection of civil rights.[653]

---

[651] AI interview with Anonymous Civil Rights Attorney (name and organization on file with AIUSA), Chicago, 17 September 2003; Board of Inquiry into the Rampart Area Corruption Incident, Public Report, Los Angeles, 1 March 2000, at http://www.lapdonline.org/pdf_files/pc/boi_pub.pdf.

[652] The Department for International Development (UK), "Safety, Security and Accessible Justice: Putting Policy into Practice," July 2002, www.dfid.gov.uk.

[653] The U.S. Commission on Civil Rights, *Revisiting Who Is Guarding the Guardians?,* November 2000, http://www.usccr.gov/pubs/guard/main.htm.

8.6
ACCOUNTABILITY FOR POLICE MISCONDUCT AND ABUSE

8.6.1
COMPLAINT SYSTEMS

> "You want to root out any problems there may be. If you don't, they will come back and bite you."
>
> Captain Linda Castro, former Captain of West Hollywood Station of the LASD, explaining why she "went out of her way to actively encourage people to file complaints" of police misconduct.
>
> "Get complainants to tell the truth and then we wouldn't waste our time..."
>
> Comment made by a representative from San Antonio Police Department's Internal Affairs Unit when AI asked what would help make the processing of complaints easier.[654]
>
> A white lesbian wrote to AI describing an incident in July 2000, in St. Paul, Minnesota. She reports that while grocery shopping, a man repeatedly pushed his cart into her partner, eventually knocking her to the ground, and calling her a "dyke." As a result, she sustained a sprained wrist. The woman told AI that an officer stationed at the front of the store was called by a store employee, and "when we reported what had happened he informed us that he was off-duty (despite the fact that he was wearing his police uniform and badge and carrying his police-issue weapon). He said that if we wanted to press charges then he would have to arrest both my partner and the man since he did not know 'who started it.' When I informed him that the man had been following us for several minutes and had called my partner a 'dyke,' he told me that if we 'chose that lifestyle we had to expect some people to have a problem.' He refused to take a report and when we said we wanted his badge number he said that we could only get that if he arrested my partner." The woman took down his badge number and reported the incident to the police precinct, where she was informed that since the officer had not filed any incident report, she could not file a complaint against him. The woman contacted a LGBT newspaper about the incident. Shortly afterwards she was reportedly fired from her job working for the state of Minnesota. She told AI she was informed by her employers that her involvement in the incident was "conduct unbecoming a state employee."[655]

IN ORDER FOR POLICE DEPARTMENTS to be held accountable for misconduct and abuse, there must be an effective system in place for members of the public to make complaints.[656] Procedures for making complaints should be readily available, straightforward and be in all languages spoken in the community.

AI is concerned at reports in New York, San Antonio, Los Angeles, Chicago, Washington, D.C., Houston and San Francisco that suggest many people do not come forward with complaints about police officer abuse and misconduct, particularly LGBT people of color, LGBT homeless individuals, immigrants or youth.[657] Some individuals inter-

---

654 AI interview with Capt. Geraldine Garcia, Lt. Robert Hartle, and Sgt. J.D. McKay, Internal Affairs Bureau, SAPD, San Antonio, 5 December 2003.

655 Testimony submitted to AI by Anonymous (name on file with AIUSA), 25 March 2004; email from AI to Anonymous (name on file with AIUSA) 27 April 2005; email from Anonymous to AI, 27 May 2005.

656 Code of Conduct for Law Enforcement Officials, G.A. res. 34/169, annex, 34 U.N. GAOR Supp. (No. 46) at 186, U.N. Doc. A/34/46 (1979), preambular paragraph 8(a) (The Code of Conduct for Law Enforcement Officials prescribes that police agencies should be representative of and responsive and accountable to the community as a whole); Code of Conduct for Law Enforcement Officials, G.A. res. 34/169, annex, 34 U.N. GAOR Supp. (No. 46) at 186, U.N. Doc. A/34/46 (1979), preambular paragraph 8(d) and articles 7 and 8; Principles on Force & Firearms, principles 22-26 (The Guidelines for the Effective Implementation of the Code of Conduct for Law Enforcement Officials prescribe that effective mechanisms must be established to ensure the internal discipline and supervision of law enforcement officials); Code of Conduct for Law Enforcement Officials, G.A. res. 34/169, annex, 34 U.N. GAOR Supp. (No. 46) at 186, U.N. Doc. A/34/46 (1979), article 8. (Law enforcement officials who have reason to believe that a violation has occurred, or is about to occur, shall report the matter.)

657 AI interviews with Melinda Power, Westtown Community Law Office, Chicago, 24 February 2002; Members of Anonymous LGBT Youth Program, Los Angeles, 29 January 2004; Anonymous Gay and Bisexual Men's Service Provider, Los Angeles, 27 October 2003; Ujima Moore, Amassi, Los Angeles, 29 January 2004.

viewed expressed resignation or fear of coming forward due to an expectation of mistreatment by society in general and by police specifically.[658] A Chicago advocate explained the unlikelihood of transgender women coming forward to make a report, saying, "They expect to be demeaned and abused by the police, they tolerate that... [They do not report because] they feel nothing will be done."[659] Survivors of misconduct who were engaging in conduct that could result in criminal charges (such as sex work and lewd conduct) fear prosecution for the activity they were engaged in when the misconduct occurred.[660]

In contrast to these reports, police officials in Los Angeles, San Antonio, Chicago and New York expressed confidence in the complaint system to AI.[661] Seven out of 11 (64 percent) responding internal affairs departments told AI that they conduct outreach to specific communities to inform them of the availability of the complaint procedures. However, such outreach may involve simply providing written responses to requests for information on how to file a complaint.

AI found that complainants may face daunting and complex procedures when trying to make a complaint against a police officer. For example, the Internal Affairs Bureau in San Antonio requires a sworn and notarized statement from anyone making a formal complaint, and warns complainants of criminal liability for perjury for making a false complaint. While this may deter frivolous complaints, it could also have the effect of stifling complaints particularly from marginalized or indigent communities, who already fear that they will not be believed. Indeed, an official from the Internal Affairs Unit in San Antonio told AI that some people leave without making a complaint after being informed of the procedure.

Another obstacle individuals may face when to trying to make a complaint is the need to identify the individual officer. Advocates and members of the LGBT community in New York City indicated that one of the issues that prevent people from reporting misconduct is some officers' refusal to provide a badge number or name. One transgender attorney commented, "I've never had a negative interaction with the police when they don't cover their badges."[662]

AI heard that individuals sometimes feel more comfortable making a complaint if they can do so anonymously. In AI's survey, eight of 11 responding internal affairs bureaus (73 percent) accept anonymous complaints. Survey responses from Little Rock, Arkansas and Minneapolis, Minnesota indicate that these states do not accept anonymous complaints. A brochure regarding the San Antonio Internal Affairs Unit provided by San Antonio indicates that anonymous complaints will not proceed for serious or formal complaints. AI heard that in Chicago, according to a union contract, anonymous complaints are not allowed.[663] Some cities including New York[664] and Los Angeles also allow third parties to make complaints on behalf of the victim. However, AI heard from officials in San Antonio that such complaints cannot be made. AI heard in Los Angeles that anonymous and third party complaints have been successful in some instances where precinct commanders were willing to conduct extensive investigations within communities.[665] However, according to the Inspector General (who has the power to audit, investigate and oversee LAPD's handling of complaints of misconduct by police officers) there is a tendency to use the fact that an investigator was unable to speak with a complainant as an excuse not to investigate.[666] AI also heard from officials that anonymous and third party reporting poses a barrier to proper investigation. While AI appreciates that investigations may be difficult without detailed identifying information, the organization urges departments to seek other

---

[658] AI interview with Andy Kim, Chicago Coalition for the Homeless, Chicago, 14 November 2003.

[659] AI interview with Anonymous Transgender Rights Advocate (name and organization on file with AIUSA), Chicago, 25 February 2004.

[660] AI interview with Daniel, Client, Gay Men's Health Crisis, New York City, 19 March 2004; Jessica Xavier, Transgender Activist, Washington, D.C., 24 March 2004.

[661] AI interview with 115th Precinct Commander, New York, 22 March 2004.

[662] AI interview with Dean Spade, Sylvia Rivera Law Project, New York City. See also: *NYPD Adopts CCRB Policy Recommendation to Revise Patrol Guide Procedure Codifying an Officer's Obligation to Provide Identifying Information Upon Request*, New York City Civilian Complaint Review Board, Press Release, 27 June 2003.

[663] AI interview with Anonymous Civil Rights Attorney (name and organization on file with AIUSA), Chicago, 17 September 2003.

[664] Officials stated that third party complaints are accepted; however, they indicated that the name of the person subjected to police misconduct must be provided. AI interview with Lt. June Roberts, Internal Affairs, NYPD, Administration Meeting, New York City, 24 March 2004.

[665] AI interviews with Captain Downing, Hollywood-Wilcox Station, LAPD, 26 January 2004; Deputy Chief Michael Berkow, Internal Affairs Division, LAPD, 28 January 2004.

[666] AI interview with Andre Birotte and Nicole Bershon, Office of Inspector General, Los Angeles, 29 January 2004.

methods of pursuing such complaints, for example through tracking patterns, rather than focusing only on identifying individual officers who may have committed misconduct.

AI has received a number of reports from LGBT individuals who faced hostility, ridicule or attempts to dissuade them from making complaints at police stations.[667] Other organizations, investigative journalists and independent auditors, including some in Los Angeles and Chicago, have documented such issues, including intimidation of individuals wishing to make a complaint and failure to provide necessary information or forms.[668]

AI is particularly concerned about reports of retaliation against people who have come forward with complaints against police officers.[669] AI heard reports of officers charging the victim or potential witnesses with offenses such as resisting arrest, interfering with an arrest, or assault when they file or express an interest in filing a complaint.[670]

In addition to receiving reports of police abuse and misconduct from members of the public, international standards stipulate that police officers have an obligation to report violations of human rights to their superiors.[671] While nine of the 11 responding internal affairs departments indicated that they maintain procedures for officers to report misconduct, the remaining two departments[672] (18 percent) told AI they have no such procedures. Furthermore, the "code of silence" (an unwritten rule and custom that police will not testify against a fellow officer and that police are expected to help in any cover-up of illegal action)[673] has created a formidable barrier to reporting.[674] So-called "whistle-blowers" have allegedly faced ostracism and retaliation.[675] Nevertheless, while there are confidential re-

---

[667] AI interviews with Joey Mogul, People's Law Office, Chicago, 12 November 2003; Rashawn Lusk, Client, Rafael Center, Chicago, 18 February 2004; Anonymous, Los Angeles AVP Case Intake/Incident Report Forms; Basil Lucas, Hate Crimes Coordinator, Director of Police Relations, Administration of NYG&L AVP, New York City, 23 February 2004; Counselor, Streetworks Youth Drop-In, New York City, 5 March 2004; Erica Vargas, Positive Health Project – Transgender Tuesday Group, New York City, 24 February 2004.

[668] See: *Report of the Independent Commission on the Los Angeles Police Department*, Independent Commission on the Los Angeles Police Department, 1991; *Report of the Independent Monitor for the Los Angeles Police Department*, report for the quarter ending 30 June 2003, Office of the Independent Monitor of the Los Angeles Police Department, issued 15 August 2003; Jennifer E. Koepke, "The Failure to Breach the Blue Wall of Silence: The Circling of the Wagons to Protect Police Perjury," *Washburn Law Journal*, 39 Washburn L.J. 211, Winter 2000, p. 3.

[669] AI interviews with Kim Hawkins, Director, Peter Cicchino Youth Project of the Urban Justice Center, New York, 16 January 2004; Craig Futterman, University of Chicago, Legal Aid Clinic, 14 November 2003. See also: http://www.law.uchicago.edu/mandel/ of the Law Clinic at University of Chicago.

[670] AI interviews with Darron E. Bowden, Former Executive Director of First Defense Legal Aid, Chicago, 11 November 2003; Kate Walz, Formerly of First Defense Legal Aid, Chicago, 24 February 2004; Anonymous Transgender Service Provider, Los Angeles, 2 October 2003; Client, GLASS Mobile Unit, Los Angeles, 29 October 2003.

[671] Article 8, Code of Conduct for Law Enforcement Officials, G.A. res. 34/169, annex, 34 U.N. GAOR Supp. (No. 46) at 186, U.N. Doc. A/34/46 (1979).

[672] These were the Little Rock, Arkansas department and the Indianapolis, Indiana department.

[673] See e.g.: David Rudovsky, "Police Abuse: Can the Violence be Contained?", 27 Harv. C.R.- C.L. L. Rev. 465, 481 n. 60, 1992. Cited in Jennifer E. Koepke, "The Failure to Breach the Blue Wall of Silence: The Circling of the Wagons to Protect Police Perjury," *Washburn Law Journal*, 39 Washburn L.J. 211, Winter 2000, p. 11.

[674] For example, out of nearly 100 officers interviewed during a federal investigation into the torture of Abner Louima at the 70th Precinct in New York (most of whom had been granted immunity from prosecution in return for giving evidence), only two reportedly provided investigators with information. Louima was raped with a broomstick in the restroom of the precinct and suffered severe injuries. See: *Rights for All* (AI Index: AMR 51/035/1998), 1 October 1998. Failure by officers to report misconduct was highlighted by the Christopher Commission in L.A. in 1991; the Inspector General still cited four incidents where police officers failed to report misconduct in 2000 and three in 2001. *2001 Annual Report of the Office of Inspector General*, published April 2002, p. 70, at http://www.lacity.org/oig/documents/OIG2001annual.pdf).

[675] For example, more than 40 current and former Los Angeles police officers filed a class-action lawsuit in 2000 alleging that LAPD officials support the "code of silence" by retaliating against those who report misconduct. Many of the plaintiffs said they were forced out of the LAPD because they reported police abuses to their supervisors. Matt Lait and Scott Glover, "LAPD Sued by Whistle-Blowers," *The Los Angeles Times*, 25 August 2000, at http://www.truthinjustice.org/whistle.htm. See also: City of New York, Commission to Investigate Police Corruption and the Anti-Corruption Procedures of the Police Department – Commission Report (Mollen Commission), July 1994, pp. 54-56, available at http://www.parc.info/reports/pdf/mollenreport.pdf; Kimberly Edds, "Ex-Rampart Officers Testify They Signed False Reports to Cover Up Beating," *Metropolitan News-Enterprise*, 8 February 2002, at p. 3. Erwin Cherminsky, Law Professor at the University of Southern California, Maureen Murray, "Police Scandals Often More Than 'Bad Apples,' Tough to Clean Own House, Expert Says, Sweeping Reforms of 'Culture' Needed," *The Toronto Star*, 8 May 2004; *Domenech v. City of New York* (919 F. Supp. 702 (S.D.N.Y. 1996).

porting procedures for officers in some departments, officers reportedly still fear that their colleagues will retaliate against them.[676]

8.6.2
INTERNAL ACCOUNTABILITY MEASURES

ONCE A COMPLAINT HAS BEEN MADE it is usually investigated by a police department's internal affairs department. AI's survey results indicate that internal affairs departments do not train their staff specifically on LGBT issues: only 45 percent (five of 11)[677] of responding internal affairs departments told AI that they train their staff on LGBT issues, and of these only two have mandatory training.[678] This may impact their ability to identify and investigate sensitive issues impacting these groups.

Reportedly, only a relatively small number of complaints overall are sustained—some reports suggest that it may be as low as five percent.[679] One of the reasons behind this is a high number of cases where insufficient evidence is available to either confirm or deny the complaint—often in instances where the only evidence is the complainant's word against the officer's.[680] This is particularly concerning in light of the findings of this report, since the most marginalized individuals often may not be able to draw on witnesses, because the incident may have occurred in a desolate area, or because potential witnesses are transient, impossible to locate or afraid of coming forward.

In general, AI's findings suggest that when investigations of complaints against officers are undertaken internally by officers, complainants face substantial skepticism: Internal Affairs officials in San Antonio told AI that complainants often lie, and indicated that people who are being charged with a crime "automatically" file a complaint in order to deflect attention from their own actions.[681] Furthermore, reports indicate that Internal Affairs investigators are more likely to believe an officer's testimony when a complaint has been made by members of marginalized groups, such as sex workers or homeless individuals.[682] Independent inquiries into several large police departments have found that internal investigations of allegations of abuse lacked thoroughness and that officers were given the benefit of the doubt even if there was evidence of misconduct.[683]

AI is concerned by certain time limits that impact the ability to fully investigate and subsequently bring disciplinary action against an officer. Such restrictions have reportedly led to cases reaching the time limit before officers have been subject to disciplinary action, and the cases therefore have been dropped. Such problems have been reported in cities including New York, Los Angeles and San Francisco.[684] In 2002, San Francisco police officials re-

---

[676] AI interview with Chicago Advocate, Chicago, November 2003. See also: Erwin Cherminsky, Law Professor at the University of Southern California, Maureen Murray, "Police scandals often more than 'bad apples,'" 8 May 2004.

[677] The following Internal Affairs Departments train their staff members on LGBT issues: Minneapolis, Minnesota; Albuquerque, New Mexico; Fargo, North Dakota; Portland, Oregon; and San Antonio, Texas.

[678] Minneapolis, Minnesota and Albuquerque, New Mexico.

[679] For example, in 2004 the Office of Police Complaints of the District of Columbia sustained only five precent of cases. Annual Report, Government of the District of Columbia, Office of Police Complaints, January 2005. Between 1998 and 2002—the most recent year for which information is available—citizens made 13,703 charges against officers. OPS found evidence to support 847 of them (six percent). "Accounting for Police," *The Chicago Reporter*, November 2004, at http://chicagoreporter.com/2004/11-2004/police/police1.htm.

[680] AI interview with Melinda Power, Westtown Community Law Office, Chicago, 24 February 2002.

[681] AI interview with Capt. Geraldine Garcia, Professional Standards Commander, Lt. Robert Hartle, Internal Affairs Director, Sgt. J.D. McKay, Internal Affairs Unit, San Antonio Police Department Internal Affairs Bureau, San Antonio, 5 December 2003.

[682] AI interview with Anonymous, GLASS Mobile Unit, Los Angeles, 29 October 2003; Clarence Patton and Theresa Jefferson, NYG&L AVP, New York, 24 April 2002; Kamau Franklin, People's Law Collective, New York, 21 May 2004.

[683] See for example: Report of the Independent Commission on the Los Angeles Police Department ("The Christopher Commission"), published 9 July 1991, p. 160; The City of New York Commission to Investigate Allegations of Police Corruption and the Anti-Corruption Procedures of the Police Department ("The Mollen Commisssion"), published 7 July 1994, p.85 et seq.

[684] San Francisco and L.A. have a one-year and New York has an 18-month statute of limitation.

portedly planned to drop at least six disciplinary cases against officers because investigators had not completed the cases before the one-year statute of limitations expired, and therefore, no disciplinary action would be taken.[685] AI is particularly concerned that the Internal Affairs Unit in San Antonio only has 180 days to investigate from the date of the alleged misconduct, as stipulated by the police union contract.[686]

Public confidence in the complaints and disciplinary process is further undermined by the secrecy of police internal investigations. Some police departments have refused to provide information to victims, their families and their attorneys as well as to NGOs—in some instances on the grounds that "personnel matters" are not subject to disclosure under state confidentiality laws.[687] All 11 internal affairs departments responding to AI's survey reported that they provide information on the outcome of a complaint; however only three[688] provide the complainant with any justification for the decision.

AI notes the initiative by Internal Affairs in both Los Angeles and New York to utilize undercover surveillance operations of officers suspected of misconduct, after receiving complaints.[689] For example, in Los Angeles, officials told AI that when a sex worker alleged that an officer was sexually abusing women, an undercover operation was arranged to recreate the circumstances of the original complaint and the officer's conduct confirmed the allegations made by the complainant. However, such operations are very costly, and therefore only a limited number of such investigations can take place.[690]

DISCIPLINE

IN THE EVENT THAT A COMPLAINT IS SUSTAINED against an officer, disciplinary measures may often seem lenient compared to the alleged conduct. Even for serious abuses, reports indicate that a low number of officers are suspended or fired.[691] The lack of transparent and consistent guidelines for disciplinary measures has been cited by monitors and organizations as a factor contributing to a lack of consistency.[692]

---

[685] See Martin J. Mayer, Case Alert Memorandum to All Police Chiefs and Sheriffs, 24 November 2003, available at: http://www.jones-mayer.com/clientalerts/ca1819112403.asp; Amnesty International, Rights for All, 1 October 1998 (AI Index: AMR 51/035/1998).

[686] AI interview with Capt. Geraldine Garcia, Professional Standards Commander, Lt. Rob Hartle, Internal Affairs Director, and Sgt. J.D. McKay, Internal Affairs Unit, San Antonio Police Department, San Antonio, 5 December 2003.

[687] AI interview with Ruth Pena and Yvette Cruz, Comite Exigimos Justicia, Chicago, 13 November 2003; see: Rights for All (AI Index: AMR 51/035/1998), 1 October 1998; Response to the Board of Supervisors Regarding SFPD's Patterns of Withholding Information Requested for OCC investigations, The Office of Citizen Complaints, 23 April 2003, at p. 4.

[688] Bridgeport, Connecticut; Fargo, North Dakota; and Providence, Rhode Island.

[689] AI interview with Deputy Chief Michael Berkow, Internal Affairs Division, LAPD, Los Angeles, 28 January 2004.

[690] AI interview with Deputy Chief Michael Berkow, Internal Affairs Division, LAPD, Los Angeles, 28 January 2004.

[691] See: Amnesty International, Rights for All, 1 October 1998 (AI Index: AMR 51/035/1998); AI interview with Ruth Pena and Yvette Cruz, Comite Exigimos Justicia, Chicago, 13 November 2003.

[690] For example, The U.S. Commission on Civil Rights has noted that jurisdictions in the U.S. have varying interpretations of legal standards of reasonable behavior and the legitimate use of force. The U.S. Commission on Civil Rights, Revisiting Who Is Guarding the Guardians?, November 2000, http://www.usccr.gov/pubs/guard/main.htm.

PROACTIVE ACTIONS AND POLICY ISSUES

> "To change behavior effectively, an oversight body must look beyond the particular cases of misconduct to systemic issues implicating policy and training."
>
> LASD Office of Independent Review[693]

Authorities must accept that while police officers are individually responsible for their actions, the systems that recruited, trained and supervised them are also responsible. Nevertheless, most of the remedies outlined above are largely reactive, and deal with individual complaints, not systemic failings. Police departments have failed to identify and stop "problem officers" from repeatedly committing misconduct, as well as to tackle the larger systemic issues which give rise to and allow such misconduct to take place, often with impunity.[694]

More proactive ways of identifying misconduct are being explored by some police departments, including so-called "early warning" systems. Such systems consist of a data management tool intended to identify officers whose performance is problematic, and provides intervention, including counseling or training, to correct those problems.[695] AI's survey of internal affairs departments found that eight of 11 responding internal affairs bureaus (73 percent) reported having an early warning system in place, and one reported plans to introduce such a system. The internal affairs departments of Bridgeport, Connecticut and Indianapolis, Indiana reported that they do not have an early warning system. In the four cities studied by AI, San Antonio (which is included in the survey of internal affairs departments), New York and Los Angeles Police Departments have an early warning system, but Chicago Police Department does not. Measuring the effectiveness of such early warning systems, however, is beyond the scope of this report.[696]

Police accountability experts warn that such systems should incorporate several types of data and not rely solely on citizen complaints, which may only represent a portion of misconduct because of underreporting. For example, the Pittsburgh early warning system requires input from computerized records of each officer's disciplinary, training and complaints history (including unsustained complaints and data on civil lawsuits), as well as data on all arrests, traffic stops, use of force incidents[697] and race, including alleged use of racial epithets.[698]

In light of the findings of this report indicating that LGBT individuals, including LGBT individuals of color, homeless people, sex workers, youth and immigrants, are targeted for police misconduct, police departments should be vigilant about identifying discrimination and misconduct against members of these communities. AI believes that while many early warning systems seek mainly to identify violent behavior, it is also important for police departments to be able to identify patterns of individual or systemic discriminatory treatment, including indications of an officer's homophobia, transphobia or racial bias.

One of the methods of tracking information for an early warning system is through complaints filed. Five departments out of 29 (17 percent) responding to AI's survey reported that they document the gender identity of complainants. Four departments out of 29 (14 percent) reported that they document sexual orientation.[699] AI notes that while tracking sexual orientation or gender identity or expression of all complainants may reveal discriminatory patterns

---

[693] Office of Independent Review, First Report, October 2002.

[694] For example, a Chicago law clinic professor told AI that the clinic had successfully brought several police brutality lawsuits, and found that some officers had around 30 complaints against them in preceding years. AI interview with Craig Futterman, University of Chicago, Legal Aid Clinic, Chicago, 14 November 2003.

[695] Samuel Walker, Geoffrey P. Alpert, and Dennis J. Kenney, "Early Warning Systems: Responding to the Problem Police Officer," *National Institute of Justice, Research in Brief*, July 2001.

[696] For example, LAPD has reportedly had great difficulty in creating a computerized early warning system which fulfils the requirements of the consent decree with the Department of Justice. "Keep Up Pressure on LAPD," *Los Angeles Times*, 24 May 2004.

[697] For example, some systems incorporate data collected from traffic stops, where police departments have begun tracking the race and gender of persons stopped, as well as reasons for the stop in response to allegations of racial profiling.

[698] The Pittsburgh Police Department's early warning system was set out through a Consent Decree reached with the Justice Department in April 1997 to improve procedures in the department. See below for further discussion of Consent Decrees.

[699] Memphis, Tennessee; Manchester, New Hampshire; Lexington, Kentucky; and Bridgeport, Connecticut reported documenting both gender identity and sexual orientation of complainants. Los Angeles, California reported documenting gender identity of complainants.

beyond those cases where overt homophobic or transphobic slurs are used, formally requiring sexual orientation or gender identity or expression of complainants to be recorded may dissuade LGBT individuals from coming forward to make a complaint. If individuals feel comfortable sharing information on their sexual orientation or gender identity, then such information should be tracked and monitored.

AI believes that in order to identify systemic issues of discrimination, police departments must not only track complaints alleging discriminatory treatment and abuse, but should work with advocacy groups in order to better identify problems and solutions to these, and should provide an independent oversight body with the ability to periodically review data with a view to identifying patterns of discriminatory treatment and abuse.

8.6.3
INDEPENDENT AND EXTERNAL CIVILIAN OVERSIGHT

AS PUBLIC OPINION INCREASINGLY has expressed concern about the ability of law enforcement to self-regulate and deal appropriately with unethical conduct, some form of independent oversight has been instituted in many cities across the U.S.[700] As part of its survey of police departments in the largest city in each state, AI asked whether some form of external review mechanism was in place. While the majority of respondents have such a body, seven out of 29 responding cities (24 percent) indicated to AI that they do not have an external review process. The police departments that reported they do not have external review mechanisms are Birmingham, Alabama; Wilmington, Delaware; Jacksonville, Florida; Atlanta, Georgia; Lexington, Kentucky; Jackson, Mississippi; and Manchester, New Hampshire.

There are many different models of external review, including systems where review boards with civilian investigators investigate complaints and issue recommendations, and those in which the police investigate complaints which are then reviewed by an outside civilian body. In nearly all cases, the external review systems have an advisory function, and the Chief of the Police Department remains responsible for deciding on discipline.[701] An exception to this is San Francisco's Office of Citizen Complaints (OCC), which is publicly funded, has 15 investigators, subpoena power and authority to discipline—including firing—officers.[702]

For the four cities studied, the following systems are reportedly in place. It should be noted that AI is unable to conduct a thorough review of the effectiveness of the systems in each city; however, AI notes with concern that not all of the following systems represent independent, external civilian oversight:

- **Chicago:** The Office of Professional Standards (OPS) was created in 1974. It is part of the Chicago Police Department but is staffed by civilians. The vast majority of cases investigated by OPS are found "not sustained," meaning that OPS could not determine whether the incident took place as alleged by the complainant. OPS does not have subpoena power, does not hold public hearings and, if it makes policy recommendations, they are not made public. The OPS files a monthly report to the Police Board, composed of nine civilians appointed by the mayor. The Board reportedly often exonerates officers and usually does not explain the reasoning behind its rulings.[703]

---

[700] See: http://www.nacole.org/. Click on "Citizen review of Police Complaints" on the bottom left-hand side, which directs you to a presentation. In the first paragraph she mentions there are about "100 agencies and slowly growing," and attributes the numbers to Samuel Walker, Police Accountability 6 (2001). Samuel Walker, *Police Accountability—The Role of Civilian Oversight*, 1st Edition, University of Nebraska, Omaha (2001).

[701] See: *Rights for All* (AI Index: AMR 51/035/1998), 1 October 1998.

[702] Kevin Allen, director of OCC, quoted in Hazel Trice Edney, "The Challenge of Policing Police Brutality," *Sacramento Observer*, 21 January 2004.

[703] See *Shielded from Justice: Police Brutality and Accountability in the United States*, Human Rights Watch, June 1998. See also: "Accounting for the Police," *The Chicago Reporter*, November 2004; *Summary of Amnesty International's Concerns on Police Abuse in Chicago* (AI Index: AMR 51/168/1999), October 1999.

- **Los Angeles:** The Office of the Inspector General (OIG) was created as a form of civilian oversight following the Christopher Commission report. The OIG is authorized to have complete and unrestricted access to all LAPD documents, to obtain direct and prompt access to any LAPD or Police Commission employee, and to subpoena witnesses and compel the production of any materials. The Inspector General audits, investigates and oversees the Police Department's handling of complaints of misconduct by police officers.[704]

- **New York:** Two external agencies play a role in monitoring and overseeing the conduct of NYPD officers: the Commission to Combat Police Corruption (CCPC)[705] and the Civilian Complaint Review Board (CCRB).[706] The Board may receive, investigate, hear, make findings and recommend action on complaints against police officers alleging use of excessive or unnecessary force, abuse of authority, discourtesy or the use of offensive language.[707] The CCRB reports its findings and recommendations to the Police Commissioner and issues semi-annual reports. The Board is not authorized to discipline officers.

- **San Antonio:** Once San Antonio's Police Department's Internal Affairs Unit has completed an investigation, the case is forwarded to the Chief's Advisory Action Board. The Board consists of seven police officers and two civilians: they review the case and present its findings to the Chief of Police. Captain Geraldine Garcia, Professional Standards Commander of San Antonio Police Department's Internal Affairs Unit, told AI that while civilian input is important, she would not be supportive of an external civilian review board.[708]

AI surveyed 24 Civilian Complaint Review Boards that exist in the largest city of each of the 50 states and the District of Columbia and received completed surveys from nine.[709] Survey responses indicated a lack of focus on and expertise in LGBT issues, raising concerns about the ability of external review boards to respond to and adequately investigate complaints made by this population. Only three of the nine responding agencies[710] (33 percent) report that they have any practices to recruit LGBT individuals. Only two of the responding nine agencies (22 percent) reported having a LGBT liaison.[711] One of these two agencies[712] was also the only one to report that it offered training for staff on LGBT issues. One agency[713] did not indicate regular training, but noted that its staff had received a presentation by an LGBT organization. Furthermore, only one out of the nine (11 percent) responding external review boards[714] has a policy on how to handle complaints filed by LGBT individuals.

Criticism on a more general level has been expressed at a number of external review boards for failing to live up to expectations of their mandate. In many instances, this critique appears in part to be reflective of limitations on external review boards' power, funds, staff and access to information. In several cities these limitations have created

---

[704] AI interview with Andre Birotte and Nicole Bershon, Office of Inspector General, 29 January 2004. See also: §573 of the Charter of the City of Los Angeles.

[705] The CCPC was established as a permanent entity charged with monitoring and evaluating anti-corruption efforts within the NYPD following the recommendations of the Mollen Commission. The CCPC is completely independent of the NYPD. Its four Commissioners, appointed by the Mayor, direct a full-time staff, including a number of attorneys, and prepare audits and conduct studies reviewing and assessing the NYPD's anti-corruption initiatives.

[706] Five members are selected by the mayor, five members are designated by the City Council, and three are recommended by the Police Commissioner. All 13 Board members are civilians and must be approved by the Mayor.

[707] Civilian Complaint Review Board, Status Report: January to June 2003.

[708] AI interview with Captain Geraldine Garcia, Professional Standards Commander, Lt. Robert Hartle, Internal Affairs Director, Sgt. J.D. McKay, Internal Affairs Unit, San Antonio Police Department, 5 December 2003.

[709] Completed surveys were submitted by the external review boards of Washington, D.C.; Honolulu, Hawaii; Boise, Idaho; Baltimore, Maryland; Omaha, Nebraska; Albuquerque, New Mexico; New York, New York; Salt Lake City, Utah; and Milwaukee, Wisconsin.

[710] These agencies are Washington, D.C.; Salt Lake City, Utah; and Milwaukee, Wisconsin. The Milwaukee Fire and Police Commission indicated that it makes an effort to ensure LGBT representation on its board.

[711] Salt Lake City, Utah and Milwaukee, Wisconsin.

[712] Salt Lake City, Utah.

[713] Washington, D.C.

[714] Albuquerque, New Mexico.

a severe backlog of cases and a reduction in cases fully investigated.[715] Many external investigatory bodies have no power to order witnesses to appear, and their investigations are thwarted if the police or others refuse to cooperate.[716]

AI is further concerned that many civilian oversight systems do not have the authority to make policy recommendations. While some bodies that have such authority have made regular constructive policy recommendations, others have reportedly failed or been unable to use such powers effectively.[717]

- **New York:** Although the CCRB has the authority to make recommendations for system-wide policy changes, to date, the Board has made little use of these powers. The CCRB has publicized only three policy recommendations over the past 11 years, addressing the practice of strip searching detainees who have been charged with minor violations, the use of no-knock search warrants, and officers' refusal to provide their name and/or badge number.[718]

Oversight agencies have been criticized for failing to effectively communicate the results of their investigations, in some cases because they are restricted from giving out detailed information on specific cases. However, some oversight agencies do provide public reports with statistical breakdowns of the number and types of complaint, and include a breakdown of the race of the complainant and officer. The publication of such data is something that should be required in all cases.

Only 10 out of 29 police departments responding to AI's survey (34 percent) indicated that data on complaints against individual officers was publicly available, indicating a need for greater accountability and transparency. Civil rights groups and others have also reported difficulty in obtaining data that should be available under public records acts, such as information on shootings, compensation payments and lawsuits. While some police departments provide statistical information on the number of complaints investigated and the number of officers disciplined each year, the amount of data varies, and rarely provides the kind of information which would shed light on the misconduct against and accountability for victims belonging to marginalized groups, such as LGBT individuals, individuals of color or youth.

INDEPENDENT MONITORS AND OMBUDSMEN AUDITS

AI NOTES THAT SOME AUTHORITIES have appointed independent monitors to monitor the internal disciplinary process of police departments. They may be permanent and review systemic issues within the department, rather than individual cases. They may also undertake "integrity audits": stings or spot checks where undercover agents test practices and procedures in random or select locations. This type of operation may be effective in identifying systemic weaknesses and abuses. Independent monitors or ombudsmen should therefore have sufficient resources to carry out policy analysis and research, in order to identify policy reforms to address systemic patterns of abuse.

---

715 According to L.A.'s Inspector General, resource limitations preclude OIG from conducting a review of the disposition of a sampling of complaints of police misconduct. AI interview with Andre Birotte and Nicole Bershon, Office of Inspector General, 29 January 2004. In New York, the CCRB reportedly continues to suffer from a significant lack of funding and resources, and is chronically understaffed. In 2003, the Board reported that a 21 percent increase in complaints since 2002 coupled with staff reductions and hiring caps would impact the timeliness of investigations. *CCRB Performance*, New York City Civilian Complaint Review Board, 2003, available at: http://www.nyc.gov/html/ccrb/html/about.html.

716 38 percent of external review bodies reportedly had subpoena power in 1997. See: *Rights for All* (AI Index: AMR 51/035/1998), 1 October 1998, Ch. 3, p 48, fn 65.

717 For example, although the L.A. OIG is charged with examining LAPD policies and practices and making policy recommendations to the Police Commission, resource constraints reportedly preclude the office from fulfilling this aspect of its mission. AI interview with Andre Birotte and Nicole Bershon, Office of Inspector General, 29 January 2004. Examples of bodies which have made constructive policy recommendations include the San Diego County citizens review board, the San Francisco Office of Citizen Complaints and the Denver Public Safety Review Commission. See: *Rights for All* (AI Index: AMR 51/035/1998), 1 October 1998.

718 Christopher Dunn and Donna Lieberman, "A Review in Name Only," *The New York Times*, 19 July 2003.

8.7
PROSECUTIONS AND LAWSUITS

IN THE U.S., very few criminal cases involving excessive use of force or discriminatory practices are brought against individual police officers.[719] The standard of proof in a criminal case is high and often rests on the word of the victim (who may also be charged with an offense) against that of the accused officer. It can therefore be difficult to obtain sufficient evidence to convict unless police witnesses come forward, which is hampered by the existence of the "code of silence," as discussed above. Observers point out that prosecutors often do not prosecute police officers, because police and prosecutors depend on each other in their daily work life and these connections may hinder their ability to function impartially in the role of prosecution.[720] Independent "special prosecutors" have been suggested as one way of ensuring that prosecutions are undertaken in the most effective manner.[721] Another shortcoming of criminal lawsuits is that even successful prosecutions have usually only been able to prove the guilt of individual officers, rather than systemic failings.[722] The Department of Justice may also bring federal criminal charges against law enforcement officials; however, of the thousands of complaints of police brutality filed with the Justice Department each year, only a small proportion result in prosecutions.

Individuals may also bring civil claims against individual law enforcement officers and, under some circumstances, municipalities, for monetary compensation.[723] While civil lawsuits may provide financial compensation, they are unlikely to be filed by the most marginalized individuals in a community and rarely serve to hold either police departments or individual officers accountable. Although cities in some cases pay out large sums of money in damages in settlements or judgments the money is usually paid out of a general city or county fund. Furthermore, in many cities, civil lawsuits are not kept track of or recorded in officers' files, meaning that vital information needed to monitor officers' behavior is lost.

The Police Accountability Act, incorporated into the Violent Crime Control and Law Enforcement Act of 1994 (Crime Control Act), gave the Justice Department the authority to bring civil actions in federal courts against police departments accused of engaging in a "pattern or practice" of abuses.[724] As of July 2005, pattern or practice investigations of 14 agencies were ongoing.[725] This is an important remedy which has led to a significant reform program being drawn up in police departments, in most cases formulated as Consent Decrees.[726] Consent Decrees entered over the past 10 years have addressed a number of issues, including excessive use of force; search and seizure policies and practices, including strip searches, racial profiling and bias; discrimination on the basis of religion; accountability mechanisms such as internal investigation structures and practices; and the development and implementation

---

[719] Although there are no comprehensive national statistics on the number of criminal prosecutions against police officers, the scarcity of police prosecutions has been amply documented in research studies, media reports and civil lawsuits. For example, see: Tina Daunt & Matt Lait, "Special Prosecutor Urged for Police Abuse," *The Los Angeles Times*, 5 May 1999; Nancie Katz, "DA Defends Record in Cop Case," *New York Daily News*, 20 February 2004.

[720] AI interviews with Howard Saffold, Positive Anti-Crime Thrust, Chicago, 27 February 2004; Cara Thaxton, Victim Advocacy Coordinator, and Lisa Tonna, Director of Advocacy and Legislative Affairs, Center on Halsted/Horizons Community Services, Chicago, 23 February 2004. See also: David M. Hicks, DA, Richmond, Virginia, quoted by Hazel Trice Edney, "The Challenge of Policing Police Brutality," *Sacramento Observer*, 21 January 2004. "The Failure to Breach the Blue Wall of Silence: The Circling of the Wagons to Protect Police Perjury," *Washburn Law Journal*, 39 Washburn L.J. 211, Winter 2000.

[721] AI interviews with Craig Futterman, University of Chicago, Legal Aid Clinic, Chicago, 14 November 2003; Sylvia Beltran and Alex Sanchez, Homies Unidos, 27 January 2004. See also: Shannon McCaffrey, "Rights Panel Urges Special Prosecutor for Some NYPD Cases," Associated Press, 13 May 2000.

[722] See for example: Asit S. Panwala, "Confronting Issues in Criminal Justice: Law Enforcement and Criminal Offenders: The Failure of Local and Federal Prosecutors to Curb Police Brutality," *Fordham Urban Law Journal*, 30 Fordham Urb. L.J.639, 643-50 (January 2003).

[723] Federal law, codified at 42 U.S.C.A. § 1983 (2000); commonly known as "Section 1983."

[724] Violent Crime Control and Law Enforcement Act of 1994, codified at 42 U.S.C. § 14141.

[725] Including Charleston, WV; Cleveland, OH; Detroit, MI; Eastpointe, MI; City of Miami, FL; New Orleans, LA; New York City, NY; Portland, Maine; Prince George's County, MD; Providence, RI; Riverside, CA; Schenectady, NY; and Tulsa, OK.

[726] Without admitting to any violations, localities often agree to a settlement by a court order known as a "consent decree," or a "settlement agreement" enforceable by the court. Police departments subject to consent decrees or settlement agreements include: Los Angeles Police Department, CA (consent decree, 2001); District of Columbia Metropolitan Police Department (settlement agreement, 2001); Highland Park Police Department, IL (settlement agreement, 2001), Cincinnati Police Department, OH (settlement agreement, 2002).

of "early warning systems" designed to track and address problem officers, areas or practices. Unfortunately, the Justice Department does not have the resources to investigate more than a small proportion of problem agencies.

Finally, AI believes that alternatives to official systems of accountability should be considered alongside official systems. In light of the particular needs of marginalized populations and communities as discussed in this report, other approaches to accountability should also be considered, including potentially granting powers to civilian oversight bodies to facilitate mediation or Alternative Dispute Resolution between complainants and police.[727] Mediation has also been brought forward by scholars in the field of police accountability.[728] Such processes may not be appropriate in serious cases of police misconduct, or in cases where a clear pattern of abuses has been documented around a particular unit or area.

---

[727] This suggestion is contained in Article 7 of the UN Declaration of Basic Principles of Justice for Victims of Crime and Abuse of Power.

[728] Samuel Walker, Carol Archbold, and Leigh Herbst, *Mediating Citizen Complaints Against Police Officers: A Guide for Police and Community Leaders*, at http://www.policeaccountability.org/mediatingcitzcomplaints.pdf. Useful information about mediating citizen complaints can be found on the website of the Washington, D.C., Office of Citizen Complaint Review: www.occr.dc.gov.

9

IDENTITY-BASED DISCRIMINATION AND POLICE ABUSE

"Within the lesbian community I am Black, and within the Black community I am a lesbian. Any attack against Black people is a lesbian and gay issue, because I and thousands of other Black women are part of the lesbian community. Any attack against lesbians and gays is a Black issue because thousands of lesbians and gay men are Black. There is no hierarchy of oppression."

Audre Lorde[729]

AS AI'S FINDINGS INDICATE, police abuse and the forms this takes are often specific to the different aspects of the victim's identity, such as sexual orientation, race, gender or gender identity, age or economic status. Identities are complex, multi-layered and intersectional, such that a person may be targeted for human rights violations based on a composite of identities that that person seems to represent. The targeting of lesbian, gay, bisexual and transgender people for discriminatory enforcement of laws and their treatment in the hands of police needs to be understood within the larger context of identity-based discrimination, and the interplay between different forms of discrimination—such as racism, sexism, homophobia and transphobia—create the conditions in which human rights abuses are perpetuated. This chapter will provide a brief overview of the larger context of some forms of identity-based discrimination facing individuals within the LGBT community in the United States.

As noted earlier in this report, much of AI's research has clearly demonstrated that discrimination, the systematic denial of rights to certain people, is a grave human rights abuse and can often lead to further human rights abuses.[730] Discrimination dehumanizes its victim, who is deemed someone who can be treated inhumanely. Institutional discrimination feeds impunity, denies justice and can incite violence against targeted people or groups. Discriminatory practices and policies have tremendous consequences for targeted groups not only in terms of the nature of their ill-treatment by government agents or society at large, but also in terms of their access to redress and equal protection under the law. Discrimination also often leads to a lack of official action, such as investigations into alleged abuses, which further reinforces impunity.

This report confirms that in the U.S., LGBT people continue to be targeted for human rights abuses by the police based on their real or perceived sexual orientation or gender identity. Furthermore, the report shows that within the LGBT community, transgender individuals, people of color, young LGBT people, immigrant and homeless individuals, and sex workers experience heightened risk of police abuse and misconduct. Reports to AI indicate that individuals from these populations within the LGBT community are more likely to experience negative interactions with police. Several factors contribute to exposing these populations to high risks as targets for serious human rights abuses.

---

[729] As cited in David M. Donahue, *Lesbian, Gay, Bisexual and Transgender Rights: A Human Rights Perspective.* Amnesty International USA, GLSEN and the University of Minnesota Human Rights Center (2000). Lorde, Audre. "There is No Hierarchy of Oppression," *Interracial Books for Children Bulletin,* Vol. 14: No. 3 & 4, P. 9 (1983).

[730] See: *Crimes of hate, conspiracy of silence: Torture and ill-treatment based on sexual identity* (ACT 40/016/2001), June 2001.

TRANSGENDER PEOPLE

Transgender people, often seen as threatening to a gendered social order, are some of the most discriminated-against members of the LGBT community, sometimes encountering prejudice from within the lesbian, gay and bisexual community.[731] The lack of legal recognition and protection of the full human rights of transgender people, including their economic, social and cultural rights, combined with endemic prejudice, leaves them prone to discrimination. The right of access to the most basic areas of daily life, such as employment, housing and health services, are rights under the ICESCR. Nearly 70 percent of transsexual people in some cities in the U.S. are reportedly unemployed or underemployed.[732] Reports indicate that a significant proportion of the transgender community is homeless, particularly transgender persons of color and immigrants.[733] Homeless transgender people face difficulties accessing homeless shelters that are safe for them.[734] Lacking access to safe shelter, they often face life on the streets, which gives rise to a set of risk factors. To make money for food and rent, some transgender individuals may resort to engaging in illegal activity, further increasing the likelihood of encounters with law enforcement.

Violence and discrimination against transgender people by police can be seen as enforcement of socially constructed boundaries of gender inflicted on those who transgress social "norms" regarding "gender appropriate" conduct and presentation. As this report documents, transgender and gender variant people may come into contact with police simply for being who they are. Reportedly, the likelihood and the quality of police interactions are affected by how visible an individual's perceived gender variance is.[735] Further compounding this issue is that an individual's lower socioeconomic status may play a role in how he or she is treated by the police, since low-income transgender men and women may not be able to afford the hormones, surgical procedures or make-up and wigs which enable them to "pass" and therefore be more likely to escape police attention.

The impact of pervasive discrimination against transgender people is compounded further for those who endure other prejudices due to their race, ethnicity, age or socioeconomic and/or immigration status. Reports to AI indicate that transgender people of color are discriminated against on the basis of race and gender identity, and are especially at risk of police abuse.

COMMUNITIES OF COLOR

In its 1998 report *Rights for All*, Amnesty International found that "members of racial minorities bear the brunt of police brutality and excessive force in many parts of the U.S."[736] Reported abuses include racist language, harassment, ill-treatment, unjustified stops and searches, false arrests, use of excessive force, unjustified shootings and torture.[737] The systemic racism inherent in U.S. policing was also noted by the U.N. Special Rapporteur on Racism,

---

731 Patrick Letellier and Yoseñio V. Lewis, *Economic Empowerment for the Lesbian Gay Bisexual Transgender Communities, A Report by the Human Rights Commission City and County of San Francisco*, 30 November 2000.

732 Patrick Letellier and Yoseñio V. Lewis, *Economic Empowerment for the Lesbian Gay Bisexual Transgender Communities, A Report by the Human Rights Commission City and County of San Francisco*, 30 November 2000, p64 & 65. *The Washington Transgender Needs Assessment Study*, Us Helping Us and People Into Living, Inc., 24 August 2000; available at: http://www.gender.org/resources/dge/gea01011.pdf, conducted by Jessica Xavier in the District of Columbia from September 1998 to May 2000. See also: National Center for Transgender Equality, http://nctequality.org/Homelessness.asp.

733 AI interviews with Anonymous, Attorney, Los Angeles, 30 January 2004; and with La Opportunidad, Los Angeles, 30 October 2003. Shannon Minter and Christopher Daley, *Trans Realities: A Legal Needs Assessment of San Francisco Transgender Communities*, San Francisco: National Center for Lesbian Rights and Transgender Law Center, 2003, np.

734 See Homeless section for more information.

735 AI interview with Anonymous Transgender Service Provider, Los Angeles, 2 October 2003.

736 See: *United States of America: Rights For All* (AI Index: AMR 51/35/98), 1998.

737 See for example: Commission on Civil Rights, *Revisiting Who Is Guarding the Guardians?: A Report on Police Practices and Civil Rights in America*, November 2000; *United States of America: Race, Rights and Police Brutality* (AI Index: AMR 51/147/99), 21 September 1999; Kwame Dixon and Patricia Allard, *Police Brutality and International Human Rights in the USA; The Report on Hearings Held in Los Angeles, California, Chicago, Illinois and Pittsburgh, Pennsylvania Fall 1999*, Amnesty International (2000); David A. Harris, *Driving While Black: Racial Profiling on Our Nation's Highways; An American Civil Liberties Union Special Report*, American Civil Liberties Union (June 1999); *United States of America: Rights for All* 38, (AI Index: AMR 51/35/98), October 1998; *United States of America: Police Brutality and Excessive Force in the New York City Police Department* (AI Index: AMR 51/36/96), 1 June 1996; National Association for the Advancement of Colored People and Criminal Justice Institute at Harvard Law School, *Beyond the Rodney King Story: An Investigation of Police Conduct in Minority Communities*, NAACP (1995) .

Racial Discrimination, Xenophobia and other Related Intolerances in his report on the United States, which found that law enforcement officers disproportionately used excessive force against people of color.[738] Although the national debate on police misconduct affecting communities of color has focused primarily on African American and Latino communities, police abuse of Native Americans and individuals of Asian descent is also prevalent.[739] Racial profiling of citizens and visitors of Middle Eastern and South Asian descent, and others who appear to be from these areas, has substantially increased since the attacks of 11 September 2001.[740]

The targeting of LGBT people of color by law enforcement mirrors the systemic racism found in policing in the USA in general. A survey conducted by the Policy Institute of the National Gay and Lesbian Task Force found that police brutality/criminal justice issues ranked among the top 10 concerns for black LGBT people in the USA.[741] The Audre Lorde Project Community Center conducted a survey of lesbian, gay, bisexual, two spirit and transgender (LGBTST) people of color in New York City in 2000, receiving 112 responses. Of these, 51 individuals reported they had experienced police violence, defined as "any abuse of power committed by the police including physical abuse, verbal abuse, failure to provide competent services, illegal stop and seizure, unjustifiable removal from public property or any other form of disrespect."[742] Furthermore, the survey also found that Asian Pacific Islanders and multiracial people, while constituting only 23 percent of the respondents, made up 66 percent of persons reporting physical assaults by police officers.[743]

Women of color may also be affected by race-based policing.[744] Reports to AI indicate that transgender women of color are more likely to be targeted by police, and that young LGBT individuals of color are targeted in ways specific to their age as well as to their race, sexual orientation, or gender identity or expression; for example, through curfew regulations or under gang ordinances.[745] AI heard reports that LGBT people of color are frequently stopped and questioned by police regarding their presence in traditionally LGBT-identified areas such as Hollywood and West Hollywood in Los Angeles.[746]

Throughout this report, AI's findings indicate that race continues to be a motivating factor in presumptions of criminality, and that racism compounds the homophobic and transphobic treatment of LGBT people of color by police. Incidents reported to AI strongly suggest that racism, homophobia and transphobia are mutually reinforcing and have profound impact on an LGBT individual's experience of police abuse.

---

[738] Implementation of the Programme of Action for the Second Decade to Combat Racism and Racial Discrimination, Report by Mr. Maurice Glélé-Ahanhanzo, Special Rapporteur on contemporary forms of racism, racial discrimination, xenophobia and related intolerance, on his mission to the U.S., 9 to 22 October 1994, submitted pursuant to Commission on Human Rights resolutions 1993/20 and 1994/64, E/CN.4/1995/78/Add.1, 16 January 1995, available at: http://www.unhchr.ch/Huridocda/Huridoca.nsf/0/8f7ece900c396f738025671c004e745a?Opendocument.

[739] See: United States of America: Rights for All 38, (AI Index: AMR 51/35/98), October 1998.

[740] Threat and Humiliation: Racial Profiling, Domestic Security, and Human Rights in the United States of America, Amnesty International, September 2004.

[741] Juan Battle, Cathy J. Cohen, Dorian Warren, Gerard Ferguson and Suzette Audam, Say it Loud, I'm Black and I'm Proud: Black Pride Survey 2000, Policy Institute of the National Gay and Lesbian Task Force, 25 March 2002, p.26.

[742] The Audre Lorde Project, Police Brutality Against Lesbian, Gay, Bisexual, Two Spirit and Transgender People of Color in New York City, draft report at 23 July 2000 (on file with Amnesty International Research Department).

[743] The Audre Lorde Project, Police Brutality Against Lesbian, Gay, Bisexual, Two Spirit and Transgender People of Color in New York City, draft report at 23 July 2000 (on file with Amnesty International Research Department).

[744] The Bay Area Police Watch, which operates a police misconduct hotline in San Francisco, reported that of police misconduct calls received from lesbians, 36 percent were from women identified as African American or Latina. AI interview with Malaika Parker, Director, Bay Area Police Watch, San Francisco, 27 October 2003.

[745] AI interviews with Lora Branch, City of Chicago Department of Public Health, Chicago, 26 February 2004; Jesse Ehrensaft-Hawley, FIERCE!, New York City, 12 February 2004; Members of Youth Drop-In, Streetworks, New York City, 5 March 2004.

[746] AI interview with Ujima Moore, Amassi, 29 January 2004; GLASS focus group discussion, 29 October 2003.

YOUNG LGBT PEOPLE

Young LGBT people face a number of challenges stemming from society's reaction to their age and their sexual orientation and/or gender identity. A number of these factors lead to young LGBT individuals being more likely to interact with law enforcement. Various reports have indicated that societal homophobia and transphobia, rejection from family, domestic violence, ensuing homelessness, substance abuse, mental illness and harassment in schools may cause some youth to resort to engaging in illegal activity, and all play a part in rendering LGBT youth vulnerable to police interaction, which can often subsequently lead to misconduct and abuse. These issues are exacerbated for transgender youth and LGB youth of color and immigrants.[747] Amnesty International has received reports from many communities that police unjustly target young black, Latino or Asian males, especially in inner cities, and automatically view them as potential criminal suspects.

Reportedly, LGBT-identified youth are "coming out" in greater numbers and at earlier ages than previous generations.[748] In recent years, LGBT youth service providers are noticing a significant increase in young people identifying as transgender.[749] One particular study found that transgender youth are increasingly using hormone treatment, sex reassignment surgery and name change as means towards positively affirming their gender identity.[750] A recent survey of high school youth in Massachusetts found that 5.5 percent self-identified as gay, lesbian or bisexual and/or reported same-sex sexual contact.[751]

Although more youth are "coming out" earlier, LGBT youth nevertheless often face rejection at home and stigmatization in schools and institutions. Most LGBT and gender variant youth experience significant harassment in school. In a 2003 national study, over 84 percent of LGBT youth reported that they are frequently subjected to homophobic slurs and 44.7 percent of LGBT youth of color report being verbally harassed because of both their sexual orientation and race/ethnicity.[752] Advocates report that young LGBT people are more likely than those who do not identify as LGBT to miss school; 28.6 percent of LGBT students reported missing at least one day of school in the previous month because they felt unsafe. The rate was even higher (35.1 percent) among LGBT youth of color who felt unsafe at school because of their sexual orientation, their race or both.[753] Missing school is a "status offense"[754] which places LGBT youth in the path of law enforcement agencies that are charged with apprehending "truant" youth.

---

[747] Massachusetts Department of Education. *Massachusetts High School Students and Sexual Orientation, Results of the 1999 Youth Risk Behavior Survey*, Boston, MA: The Dept, 1999, at http://www.state.ma.us/gcgly/yrbsfl99.html. Savin-Williams, RC. "Verbal and physical abuse as stressors in the lives of lesbian, gay male, and bisexual youths: associations with school problems, running away, substance abuse, prostitution, and suicide," *J Consult Clin Psychol* 1994; 62:261-69.

[748] Ryan C, Futterman D. "Lesbian and Gay Youth: Care and Counseling," *Adolescent Medicine State-of-the-Art Review*, v. 8, no. 2; Philadelphia: Hanley & Belfus (1997), cited in Jessie Gilliam, "Respecting the Rights of GLBTQ Youth, A Responsibility of Youth-Serving Professionals," *Transitions*, Vol. 14, No. 4, June 2002, at: www.advocatesforyouth.org.

[749] Pagliaro S., Gipson M. "Effective HIV/STD and Teen Pregnancy Prevention Programs for Young Women of Color," Washington, DC: Advocates for Youth, 2000.

[750] Charlene Leach, "Transgender Youth and the Role of Service Providers," *Transitions*, Volume 14, No. 4, June 2002, at: http://www.advocatesforyouth.org/publications/transitions/transitions1404_9.htm.

[751] This number is a low estimate, as it does not include transgender and questioning youth or those who fear "coming out." *Massachusetts Department of Education. Massachusetts High School Students and Sexual Orientation, Results of the 1999 Youth Risk Behavior Survey*. Boston, MA: The Dept, 1999, at http://www.state.ma.us/gcgly/yrbsfl99.html.

[752] The Gay, Lesbian and Straight Education Network (GLSEN), *The 2003 National School Climate Survey: The School Related Experiences of Our Nation's Lesbian, Gay, Bisexual and Transgender Youth*, 1 April 2005. See also: Human Rights Watch, *Hatred in the Hallways: Violence and Discrimination Against Lesbian, Gay, Bisexual and Transgender Students in U.S. Schools*, May 2001, at http://hrw.org/reports/2001/uslgbt/toc.htm.

[753] The Gay, Lesbian and Straight Education Network (GLSEN), *The 2003 National School Climate Survey: The School Related Experiences of Our Nation's Lesbian, Gay, Bisexual and Transgender Youth*, 1 April 2005. See also: Kosciw JG, Cullen MK. *The School-Related Experiences of Our Nation's Lesbian, Gay, Bisexual, and Transgender Youth: The GLSEN 2001 National School Climate Survey*. New York: GLSEN (2001); Vanessa Eisemann, "Protecting the Kids in the Hall: Using Title IX to Stop Student-on-Student Anti-Gay Harassment," *Berkeley Women's Law Journal*, 31 January 2000; *Massachusetts State Youth Risk Behavior Survey*, Massachusetts Department of Education HIV/AIDS Program (1999).

[754] A "status offense" is misbehavior which would not be criminal if committed by an adult (e.g., truancy).

LGBT youth are at a heightened risk of violence at the hands of their family members.[755] In one survey of LGBT youth of color, 61 percent testified that they had been victims of violence by family members.[756] Rejection by family members is particularly problematic for LGBT immigrant youth who may be dependent on family members for legalizing their immigration status, and the lack of such papers may negatively impact interactions with law enforcement officials (See **Immigration**, below).[757] A Rhode Island study found that nearly half of LGBT youth end up having to leave the home because of their families' reaction to their sexual orientation or gender identification.[758] Some end up in the foster care system; others become precariously housed or homeless.[759] LGBT youth in the foster care system and homeless shelters reportedly experience verbal harassment and, in some instances, physical or sexual abuse because of their sexual orientation or gender identity.[760]

It has been estimated that in some U.S. cities up to 40 percent of homeless youth are gay, lesbian, bisexual or transgender.[761] Once on the streets, these youth are at increased risk for rape, beatings and sexually transmitted infections, including HIV and AIDS.[762] LGBT youth who are homeless may commit offenses such as sex work and theft in order to survive life on the street, which invariably increases their contact with law enforcement.[763] One study found that up to half of the gay and bisexual young men forced out of their homes due to sexual orientation engage in sex work to support themselves.[764] An advocate in Chicago told AI that a significant percentage of homeless LGBT youth in Chicago are involved in sex work.[765]

Few studies have focused on the experiences of LGBT youth of color. What studies do exist show that LGBT youth of color face stigma related to both race and sexual orientation or gender identity and expression, and often do not have access either to any social support systems or systems equipped to handle their particular needs.[766] This stigma places LGBT youth of color at even greater risk for substance use, violence and high-risk sexual behavior. Youth of color may not identify as LGBT, which can be a barrier to providing needed social services. Most models of LGBT identity development are based on the experiences of white middle- and upper-middle-class lesbians and gays.[767] Reports to AI indicate that young LGBT immigrants are especially at risk of police misconduct, since LGBT

---

[755] *Domestic Violence in Lesbian, Bisexual, Gay and Transgender Communities: A Fact Sheet*, Women's Human Rights Program, Amnesty International USA, found at: http://www.amnestyusa.org/women/violence/domesticviolence_lgbt.html.

[756] *Transitions*, Volume 14, No. 4., June 2002, cited in *Domestic Violence in Lesbian, Bisexual, Gay and Transgender Communities: A Fact Sheet*, Women's Human Rights Program, Amnesty International, USA, found at: http://www.amnestyusa.org/women/violence/domesticviolence_lgbt.html.

[757] Susan Hazeldean and Pradeep Singla, *Out in the cold: The Challenges of Representing Immigrant Lesbian, Gay, Bisexual, and Transgender Youth*, An Urban Justice Center Report, June 2002.

[758] Rhode Island Task Force on Gay, Lesbian, Bisexual and Transgendered Youth, "School Shouldn't Hurt: Lifting the Burden from Gay, Lesbian, Bisexual and Transgendered Youth," March 1996.

[759] People who are precariously housed are in danger of becoming literally homeless because they have no place of their own to live or their current housing situation is tenuous.

[760] Urban Justice Center, *Justice for All? A Report on Lesbian, Gay, Bisexual and Transgendered Youth in the New York Juvenile Justice System* 16 (2001). See also *Youth in the Margins*, at 15 (See Lambda Legal Defense and Education Fund, *Youth in the Margins: A Report on the Unmet Needs of Lesbian, Gay, Bisexual, and Transgender Adolescents in Foster Care* 11 (2001) AI interview with Carl Siciliano, Ali Forney Center, New York City, February 13, 2004.

[761] Ryan C and Futterman D. *Social and developmental challenges for lesbian, gay, and bisexual youth* SIECUS Report 2001; *Challenges faced by homeless sexual minorities: comparison of gay, lesbian, bisexual, and transgender homeless adolescents with their heterosexual counterparts*, Cochran BN, Stewart AJ, Ginzler JA, Cauce AM, American Journal of Public Health 92.5 (2002) p. 773-776; Victim Services/Traveler's Aid, "Streetwork Project Study" 1991 cited by The Ali Forney Center, Housing for Homeless LGBT Youth.

[762] Transitions. Volume 14, No. 4. June 2002, cited in *Domestic Violence in Lesbian, Bisexual, Gay and Transgender Communities: A Fact Sheet*, Women's Human Rights Program, Amnesty International, USA, found at: http://www.amnestyusa.org/women/violence/domesticviolence_lgbt.html.

[763] Savin-Williams, RC. "Verbal and physical abuse as stressors in the lives of lesbian, gay male, and bisexual youths: associations with school problems, running away, substance abuse, prostitution, and suicide." J Consult Clin Psychol 1994; 62:261-69; Ryan C, Futterman D. "Lesbian and Gay Youth: Care and Counseling," *Adolescent Medicine State-of-the-Art Review*, v. 8, no. 2, Philadelphia: Hanley & Belfus, 1997.

[764] Savin-Williams, R., "Theoretical Perspectives Accounting for Adolescent Homosexuality," *Health Care*, 9(2):95-104, 1988.

[765] AI interview with Night Ministry, Chicago, 18 February 2004.

[766] See http://www.safeschoolscoalition.org/RG-glbt_youth_of_color.html for listing of resources for LGBT youth of color.

[767] Ryan C and Futterman D. *Social developmental challenges for lesbian, gay, and bisexual youth*. SIECUS Report 2001; 29(4).

youth who are fleeing persecution and abuse in their home countries often arrive with no support network and end up homeless and destitute.[768] Young LGBT immigrants of color reportedly also are more likely to be targeted by the police, and are profiled for stops and searches, or as gang members.[769]

POVERTY AND HOMELESSNESS IN THE USA

Contrary to the popular myth of the "affluent gay community," reports indicate that the LGBT community earns, on average, less than the general population. One study found that gay men frequently earn less than their heterosexual counterparts.[770] The 2000 Census found that average income of persons in same-sex couples was $29,272 compared with the national average of $42,228, with five percent of same-sex households reporting income below the poverty line.[771] Pervasive discrimination combined with lack of legal protection puts many of the most marginalized populations within the LGBT community at critical risks for poverty and homelessness.

According to a national estimate, each year, approximately two to three million individuals experience homelessness in the United States, with children not accompanied by an adult accounting for approximately five percent of this number.[772] People of color comprised 65 percent of the homeless population while accounting for only 31 percent of the general population.[773] It is estimated that up to 40 percent of homeless youth are gay, lesbian, bisexual or transgender.[774] Reports indicate that a significant proportion of the transgender community is homeless, particularly transgender persons of color and immigrants.[775] Advocates report that a number of homeless LGBT individuals become homeless as a consequence of domestic violence and familial issues surrounding their sexual orientation or gender identity.[776]

Reportedly, homeless or domestic violence shelters often do not welcome and are unsafe for LGBT people.[777] AI has received reports that the transgender community, in particular, incurs discrimination and abuse in the shelter

---

[768] AI interviews with Clients of GLASS Mobile Unit, Los Angeles, October 2003; Julia Garcia, La Opportunidad, Los Angeles, 30 October 2003.

[769] AI interview with Namita Chad, DRUM, New York City, 9 March 2004; Audre Lorde Project, New York City, 10 March 2004.

[770] M.V. Lee Badgett, Ph. D., *Income Inflation: The Myth of Affluence Among Gay, Lesbian and Bisexual Americans*, A Joint Publication of the Policy Institute of the National Gay and Lesbian Task Force and the Institute for Gay and Lesbian Strategic Studies (1998).

[771] "Poverty Rate Rises, Household Income Declines," *Census Bureau Reports, United States Department of Commerce News*, 24 September 2002, at: http://www.census.gov/Press-Release/www/2002/cb02-124.html; www.gaydemographics.org.

[772] This estimate does not take into account those who do not contact a homeless assistance provider. *Ending Chronic Homelessness: Strategies for Action*, U.S. Department of Health and Human Services, March 2003, available at: http://aspe.hhs.gov/hsp/homelessness/strategies03/; *A Status Report on Hunger and Homelessness in America's Cities*, The U.S. Conference of Mayors, December 2002.

[773] National Coalition for the Homeless with contributions from Minnesota Advocates for Human Rights, *ICERD Shadow Report, RACIAL AND ETHNIC DISCRIMINATION IN THE UNITED STATES, The Status of Compliance by the United States Government with the International Convention on the Elimination of All Forms of Racial Discrimination*, 21 September 2000, at: http://www.woatusa.org/cerd/toc.html; *A Status Report on Hunger and Homelessness in America's Cities*, The U.S. Conference of Mayors, December 2002.

[774] Ryan C and Futterman D. *Social and developmental challenges for lesbian, gay, and bisexual youth*, SIECUS Report 2001; Cochran BN, Stewart AJ, Ginzler JA, Cauce AM. "Challenges faced by homeless sexual minorities: comparison of gay, lesbian, bisexual, and transgender homeless adolescents with their heterosexual counterparts," *American Journal of Public Health* 92.5 (2002) p. 773-776; Victim Services/Traveler's Aid, "Streetwork Project Study," 1991, cited by The Ali Forney Center, Housing for Homeless LGBT Youth.

[775] AI interviews with Carol Soebel, Los Angeles, 30 January 2004; Julia Garcia, La Opportunidad, Los Angeles, 30 October 2003. See also: Shannon Minter and Christopher Daley, Trans Realities: *A Legal Needs Assessment of San Francisco Transgender Communities*, *San Francisco:* National Center for Lesbian Rights and Transgender Law Center, 2003.

[776] AI interviews with Dean Spade, Attorney, Sylvia Rivera Law Project, New York City, 19 February 2004; Carl Siciliano, Executive Director, Ali Forney Center, New York City, 13 February 2004.

[777] AI interview with Clients of Picture the Homeless, New York City, 16 February 2004.

and temporary housing systems and is often refused access to domestic violence shelters.[778] A number of organizations working with homeless LGBT youth, such as the Ali Forney Center in New York and the Night Ministry in Chicago, have reported that LGBT youth do not have equal access to shelter and housing as they are often harassed and abused in such settings.[779] The discriminatory treatment of homeless LGBT individuals in accessing shelters and housing is in violation of a state's responsibilities to prevent discrimination in the access of services under both the ICESCR and the ICCPR.

Many states have specific laws and policies penalizing homeless individuals for engaging in conduct such as sleeping, eating and congregating in public. This can increase the likelihood of a homeless person coming into negative contact with the police. Reports to AI indicate that the increased focus on policing "quality of life" ordinances, such as those criminalizing the consumption of alcohol, storage of belongings, and urination in public spaces, tend to be discriminatorily applied towards communities that, due to poverty and homelessness, have no choice but to engage in such activities in public spaces. AI is concerned that the increased focus on such activities inherently has the effect of "criminalizing" homelessness.[780] LGBT homeless individuals may be specifically targeted by law enforcement for discriminatory application of "quality of life" legislation or other police abuse due to homophobia or transphobia, and reports indicate that discrimination on the basis of race, sex or age further informs such misconduct.

SEX WORK

Due to the criminalization of sex work, sex workers are at greater risk of suffering abuse and mistreatment at the hands of law enforcement.

While advocates emphasize that for some adult sex workers, there is a level of control and choice in whether and how to engage in sex work, economic and social conditions may limit decision-making capacity for others. For example, studies in several cities have found a very high incidence of homelessness or precarious housing among sex workers.[781]

Stigmatization of and discrimination against LGBT people, particularly transgender individuals, people of color, immigrants and youth, in accessing human rights such as education, housing and work can limit their choices and may, in some instances, be contributing factors in the decision to engage in sex work.[782] Ending discrimination and promoting economic and social rights of LGBT individuals are therefore important to address sex work and the violence and abuse often associated with it.

---

[778] AI interviews with Dean Spade, Attorney, Sylvia Rivera Law Project, New York City, 13 February 2004; Patrick Markee, Senior Policy Analyst, Coalition for the Homeless, New York City, 18 February 2004; Pauline Park, Co-Chair, NYAGRA, New York City, 11 February 2004; Michelle Sosa, Positive Health Project, New York City, 25 February 2004. According to National Coalition for the Homeless, most homeless shelters are segregated by sex, and if they accept transgender residents, require that they be housed with members of the sex they were assigned at birth. Transgender women who identify and live as women but were born male report that male residents harass, sexually proposition and sometimes assault them. Transgender men who identify and live as men but were born female are sometimes placed in men's shelters that do not have privacy in bathrooms (no stall doors) or in showers. Gender-based dress codes are also a significant problem, especially for transgender youth in shelters who may face discipline for dressing according to their gender identity. See: http://www.nationalhomeless.org/civilrights/transgender.html.

[779] AI interviews with Heather Bradley, Night Ministry, Chicago, February 2004; Carl Siciliano, Ali Forney Center, New York City, 13 February 2004; Justine Sullivan, Streetworks, New York City, 5 March 2004.

[780] The National Law Center on Homelessness and Poverty reported that in "criminalizing" homelessness, cities pursue four primary types of action: 1. enacting and/or enforcing restrictions on homeless people's use of public spaces for activities such as sleeping or sitting; 2. enacting and/or enforcing restrictions on panhandling; 3. conducting police "sweeps" designed to remove homeless people from specific areas; and 4. targeting homeless people by selectively enforcing laws such as those designed to discourage vagrancy. See: *Mean Sweeps: A Report on Anti-Homeless Laws, Litigation and Alternatives in 50 United States Cities*, National Law Center on Homelessness and Poverty, 1996. A 2002 New York survey found that 61 percent of homeless individuals had been issued a summons or arrested for engaging in conduct occasioned by their housing status, such as sleeping in a public place: *Pattern and Practice: Systemic Violations of the Civil Rights of Homeless New Yorkers by the NYPD, Picture the Homeless*, 7 November 2002.

[781] Past or current homelessness was reported by 84 percent of respondents in a San Francisco study: Farley Melissa and Howard Barkan, *Prostitution, Violence Against Women and Posttraumatic Stress Disorder*, 1998. See also: Raphael Jody and Deborah L. Shapiro, *Sisters Speak Out: The Lives and Needs of Prostituted Women in Chicago,"* Center for Impact Research, August 2002; *Revolving Door, An Analysis of Street-Based Prostitution in New York City*, The Urban Justice Center, Sex Workers Project, 2003.

[782] 88 percent of sex workers interviewed in a San Francisco study stated they wanted to leave sex work. Many voiced a need for services such as a home or safe place (78 percent) or job training (73 percent). Farley Melissa and Howard Barkan, *Prostitution, Violence Against Women and Posttraumatic Stress Disorder, Women and Health*, 27 (3): 37-49, Haworth Press, Inc. (1998).

The U.N. Special Rapporteur on the Sale of Children, Child Prostitution and Child Pornography has noted that LGBT children by reason of social exclusion and discrimination are more vulnerable to sexual exploitation, and further noted that transgender youth may be especially vulnerable to entering into prostitution.[783]

AI heard reports of sexual, physical and verbal abuse against LGBT individuals perceived to be sex workers by police. The most serious abuses reported to AI in particular were of transgender individuals, individuals of color, immigrants, young people and homeless individuals who engage in sex work. AI also heard reports of widespread arbitrary arrests of individuals profiled as sex workers, on the basis of their sex, gender and gender expression, race or ethnicity, and immigration status. Transgender individuals are reportedly frequently profiled as sex workers, and young LGBT people of color are also assumed to be sex workers in some locations.

The illegality of prostitution can be an obstacle to accessing justice for sex workers who have been subjected to abuse by the public or the police. Many sex workers face discrimination by society as a whole, and particularly the criminal justice system. The nature of their work creates specific dangers and stigmatization. Acts of violence against them are taken less seriously, sex workers are blamed for putting themselves at risk, and the perpetrators often escape with impunity.[784] Amnesty International believes all individuals are entitled to the fulfillment of their human rights and redress against abuse.

IMMIGRANTS

The United States Census Bureau reported in 2002 that close to one in five U.S. residents (56 million) are either foreign-born or first generation immigrants.[785] Although the Census does not document how many immigrants identify as either lesbian, gay, bisexual or transgender, reports from advocates suggest that there are a number of LGBT immigrants living in the United States, many of whom have fled persecution in their countries of origin based on their sexual orientation or gender identity or expression.[786]

In 1990, the U.S. granted its first asylum claim based on sexual orientation and in 1994, Attorney General Janet Reno proclaimed that the holding of that case was precedent for asylum claims based on sexual orientation through an Executive Order.[787] However, reports to AI indicate that many LGBT immigrants, particularly the most marginalized populations such as youth and transgender individuals, do not attempt to gain legal asylum rights despite the danger they face if deported to their home countries, either because they are unaware of this right or because they are afraid of revealing their sexual orientation or gender expression or identity to authorities.[788]

State and local police are authorized to notify federal immigration officials about foreign nationals in their custody who have committed crimes.[789] Prior to the *Lawrence* decision, this could have included those LGBT immigrants who

[783] Report on the Rights of the Child by Juan Miguel Petit, Special Rapporteur on the Sale of Children, Child Prostitution and Child Pornography, E/CN.4/2004/9, 5 January 2004, para 118, para 123.

[784] Pickup, Francine, with Williams, Suzanne and Sweetman, Caroline. 2001. *Ending Violence Against Women. A challenge for development and humanitarian work.* Oxfam Publishing, Oxford, p. 15.

[785] *Profile of the Foreign-Born Population in the United States: 2000*, United States Census Bureau, found at: http://www.census.gov/prod/2002pubs/p23-206.pdf.

[786] AI interviews with Nohelia Canales and Richard Coggan, L.A. Anti-Violence Project, Los Angeles, d28 January 2004; eight Outreach Workers, APICHA, New York City, 30 March 2004; Vanessa Edwards Foster, Local and National Transgender Activist, Houston, 30 November 2003. See: *Crimes of hate, conspiracy of silence: Torture and ill-treatment based on sexual identity* (AI Index: ACT 40/016/2001), June 2001.

[787] See: Matter of Toboso-Alfonso, 20 I. & N. Dec. 819 (BIA 1990), Gen. Order No. 1895-94 (19 June 1994); see also: David Johnston, "Ruling Backs Homosexuals on Asylum," *The New York Times*, 17 June 1994, at A12.

[788] Testimony of Trishala Deb at the Racial Profiling Hearings, 3 October 2004; AI interviews with Clients of GLASS Mobile Unit, Los Angeles, October 2003; Anonymous Transgender Service Provider, Los Angeles, 2 October 2003; Michelle Sosa, Positive Health Project, New York City, 21 November 2002.

[789] In 1996, the Illegal Immigration Reform and Immigrant Responsibility Act of 1996 (IIRIRA) increased immigration authority and opened the door to enforcement of immigration laws by state and local law enforcement agencies.

would have been convicted under "sodomy" statutes, rendering many LGBT people at a heightened risk for removal from the U.S. However, a number of cities and municipalities across the U.S. adopted polices intended to foster trust between law enforcement agencies and immigrants by prohibiting police from inquiring about the immigration status of crime victims, witnesses or others who seek assistance from the police.[790] Law enforcement agencies have not always honored such safeguards in the past,[791] and Amnesty International has received recent reports alleging that law enforcement officers have threatened individuals with deportation and inquired into their immigration status, in violation of such policies.[792] The U.S. Congress is currently considering enactment of the Clear Law Enforcement for Criminal Alien Removal Act ("CLEAR Act"),[793] which would require state and local police to enforce immigration laws or risk losing federal funding. Amnesty International opposes the CLEAR Act, and believes it creates an atmosphere of fear and distrust among immigrant populations that could prevent utilization of and cooperation with local and state police.[794]

In the aftermath of the attacks on 11 September 2001, the federal government turned primarily to immigration regulations in its efforts to combat terrorism.[795] Advocates argue that policies and laws such as the National Entry and Exit Registration System (NSEERS),[796] the USA Patriot Act and the CLEAR Act, coupled with increasing scrutiny of immigrants and asylum seekers, have had the effect of "criminalizing" immigrants and increasing fear of authorities within immigrant communities.[797] AI is concerned that such policies create a hostile climate against immigrants within which it is permissible for law enforcement and non-state actors alike to abuse and commit crimes against immigrants with impunity.

Reports indicate that LGBT immigrants in the U.S. face significant challenges based on their immigration status, race, sexual orientation and/or gender identity or expression, as well as because of language barriers, which increase their vulnerability to police misconduct. AI's research suggests that LGBT immigrants of color are not only treated in a manner similar to that described with respect to communities of color as a whole, but are also subject to particular forms of police misconduct specifically related to their immigration status and are further impacted due to their sexual orientation or gender expression. Advocates in Washington, D.C., told AI that LGBT immigrants "have a generally negative experience with the police here," and noted that it is not clear whether their experiences are colored by language differences, their undocumented status, their sexual orientation, their gender identity or expression or permutations of these factors working together.[798] Therefore it becomes more important that advocates and officials alike understand how all of these identities and factors impact an individual's interaction with law enforcement.

---

[790] Los Angeles Special Order 40, passed in 1979, states, "no officer of the Los Angeles Police Department shall cooperate with the INS to inquire about the immigration status of any individual." Report of the Rampart Independent Review Panel: A Report to the Los Angeles Board of Police Commissioners Concerning Special Order 40, 1 February 2001, at www.ci.la.ca.us/oig/Special_Order_40_708061_v1.pdf; New York's Executive Order 41 prohibits police from inquiring about the immigration status of crime victims, witnesses or others who seek assistance from the police, Executive Order No. 41 at Section 49(c).

[791] For example, the "Rampart scandal" in Los Angeles also brought attention to the singling out of immigrants as targets for abuse by Community Resources Against Street Hoodlums (CRASH) officers. Compiling lists in the thousands, joint LAPD/INS sweeps were reported to have arrested and deported immigrants because they witnessed abuse by LAPD officers or acted as alibi-witness for people who had been framed.

[792] Namita Chad, DRUM, New York City, 9 March 2004; Jih-Fei Cheng, APICHA, New York City, 8 March 2004; Patricia Castillo, Executive Director, The Peace Initiative, San Antonio, 2 December 2003; First Defense Legal Aid, Chicago, 24 February 2004.

[793] CLEAR Law Enforcement for Criminal Alien Removal Act, H.R. 2671, 108th Cong. (2004).

[794] Amnesty International, Urge Your Representative to Oppose the Proposed CLEAR Act, Action 10419, available at: http://www.amnestyusa.org/actioncenter/actions/action10419.rtf.

[795] See: United States of America: Amnesty International's Concerns Regarding Post September 11 Detentions in the USA (AI Index: AMR 51/044/2002), 14 March 2002.

[796] In 2002, the U.S. Government implemented a policy requiring men aged 16 and over from 24 Muslim and Middle Eastern countries and North Korea to register with immigration authorities. As a result, over 13,000 men were placed in deportation proceedings. See Letter from Amnesty International to Attorney General John Ashcroft, dated 10 January 2003, available at http://www.amnestyusa.org/news/2003/usa01102003-3.html. NSEERS has now been suspended: Associated Press, "U.S. to End Registration Program," The Washington Post, 2 December 2003, at A11.

[797] Mark Engler and Saura Sarkar, "The Renewed War on Immigrants," ZMagazine, zmag.org, April 2003, Volume 16 Number 4, available at: http://zmagsite.zmag.org/Apr2003/engler0403.html.

[798] AI interview with Catalina Sol and Dilcia Molina, La Clinica del Pueblo, Washington, D.C., 20 November 2003.

AI has received reports of police officers threatening immigrants, including LGBT immigrants and individuals perceived to be illegal immigrants, with deportation. Discriminatory targeting of immigrants by law enforcement, including on the basis of sexual orientation or gender identity and expression, would violate international standards prohibiting discrimination. Authorities must ensure that individuals are not removed to countries where they may be at serious risk of human rights abuses.[799]

---

[799] AI has documented grave human rights abuses including torture and other forms of ill-treatment towards the LGBT community around the world. See: *Crimes of Hate, Conspiracy of Silence: Torture and Ill-Treatment Based on Sexual Identity* (AI Index: ACT 40/016/2001), which documented cases from across the world of persecution based on sexual orientation and gender identity.

10

RECOMMENDATIONS

ADDRESSING THE ISSUE OF POLICE ABUSE AND MISCONDUCT requires a holistic and integrated approach that recognizes the interrelation and interplay between different forms of discrimination, and how they create the social conditions in which identity-based human rights abuses can thrive. AI's findings clearly demonstrate that the issue of police brutality cannot be tackled without looking at the social, economic and cultural human rights issues that are at the roots of this problem; these must include those issues affecting the LGBT community, particularly its most targeted populations, such as transgender people, young people, homeless individuals, immigrants and sex workers. It is the interaction of all of these factors that elicits discrimination, violence and other abuses with impunity. States are responsible for addressing all of these factors in order to protect all sectors of society. Police abuse is an issue that emphasizes the indivisibility and interdependence of human rights. The findings of this report indicate that there is a need to take action to deal with widespread discrimination and abuse in the realm of policing, yet there is also the need for other actors in society, including national, state and local governmental entities, to take steps to address the pervasive discrimination that LGBT people in the U.S., particularly those most marginalized within the LGBT community, continue to face in society.

ACCOUNTABILITY

Federal, state and local authorities should take immediate action to prevent human rights violations by police officers. They should make clear that abuses by officers—including torture, brutality and ill-treatment—will not be tolerated; that officers will be held accountable for their actions; and that those responsible for abuses will be brought to justice.

- Authorities should condemn any act of torture or ill-treatment and other cruel, inhuman or degrading treatment based on actual or perceived sexual orientation or gender identity or expression.

- Authorities should ensure that all allegations and reports of police abuse and misconduct are promptly and impartially investigated. All officers responsible for abuses should be adequately disciplined and, where appropriate, prosecuted.

- Authorities should suspend law enforcement officers who are placed under investigation for human rights violations pending the outcome of the disciplinary or judicial proceedings against them.

- Verbal abuse or slurs by police officers based on real or perceived sexual orientation or gender identity or expression must not be tolerated, and officers should be appropriately disciplined and, if appropriate, mandated training.

- Special measures should be implemented to ensure that people who have been victims of torture or ill-treatment based on sexual orientation or gender identity or expression have access to the means of gaining redress and the right to an effective remedy, including compensation.

- There should be greater transparency in internal investigation of complaints of misconduct and abuse made against the police. Complainants should be regularly kept informed of the progress of these investigations. Police departments should also provide information on the internal disciplinary process by publishing regular statistical data on the number and type of complaints filed, the outcome of the investigation and disciplinary action. They should publish regular statistics on the number of complaints of abuse and misconduct based on real or perceived sexual orientation or gender identity.

- All police departments should have effective early warning systems to identify and deal with officers involved in human rights violations or other abuses. They should establish clear reporting systems and keep detailed records of every officer's conduct in order to identify and take remedial action with respect to any patterns of abuse, including racial bias or bias based on sexual orientation or gender identity or expression. Complaints should be tracked and early warning systems should be utilized not only to monitor the performance of individual officers, but should also be mined for systemic manifestations of discriminatory behavior and abuses.

- All police departments should issue clear guidelines requiring officers to report abuses, and offices with chain-of-command controls should be held responsible for enforcing those guidelines. There should be strong penalties for failing to report or for covering up misconduct.

COMPLAINT MECHANISMS

- Information about complaints procedures should be prominently displayed in all police stations. Police departments must conduct extensive outreach to educate LGBT individuals on how to access complaint mechanisms.

- Complaint procedures should be straightforward and should not require a complainant to provide a sworn statement.

- Police authorities should accept anonymous and third-party complaints of police misconduct and abuse.

- Police authorities should examine why individuals from marginalized communities are not coming forward to make complaints, and should assess how such mechanisms can be amended to better serve individuals who most need them.

- Local authorities should take effective measures to ensure that people who bring complaints of ill-treatment against police officers are protected against intimidation. Such measures should include the careful scrutiny by the prosecuting authorities of police charges that detainees have resisted state authority, particularly those which are filed only after complaints of police ill-treatment are brought.

INDEPENDENT AND EFFECTIVE EXTERNAL OVERSIGHT

- Local, state and federal authorities should establish effective, independent oversight bodies for their respective police agencies, with powers to investigate and review complaints against the police as well as broader policy issues and patterns of concern, and to issue detailed public reports.

- Oversight bodies and internal oversight agencies should recruit diverse staff and management, and include women, LGBT individuals and people of color.

- Oversight bodies should conduct outreach to marginalized and disenfranchised communities to ensure that their concerns are heard.

- Oversight bodies should be trained in handling complaints pertaining to LGBT individuals, sex workers, youth and other marginalized communities and should report on incidents and patterns.

- City and county authorities should be required to forward information on civil lawsuits alleging police misconduct to the police department and relevant oversight bodies. They should regularly make public information on the number of lawsuits filed, as well as judgments and settlements.

- The U.S. government should collect data about the incidence of police abuse and misconduct at the local, state and federal levels, and should monitor patterns of misconduct for the purpose of directing federal resources toward redressing these.

- A national database of officers dismissed for misconduct should be established so that they cannot transfer from jurisdiction to jurisdiction.

- The federal government should provide resources and technical assistance to state and local law enforcement agencies to improve their complaint procedures, internal discipline and training programs.

TRAINING

- The U.S. government, state and local authorities should enact legislation requiring that human rights education be made an integral part of law enforcement training. Police training should be based on human rights standards and aimed at ensuring the highest standards of professional conduct. Departments should review their training curriculum to ensure that human rights are appropriately integrated. Commitment to human rights training should be reflected in police plans and budgets.

- All police departments should introduce training programs that include LGBT sensitivity training. Such training should reinforce that police misconduct and abuse against LGBT persons will not be tolerated. All police departments must ensure that as part of this training, issues and policies relating to the transgender community are covered.

- Officers should be required to address transgender individuals by either the name on their identification or the name they regularly use if they have not had their identification corrected to reflect gender identity. In investigative circumstances an officer may respectfully ask gender- and name-related questions. Once those questions have been answered, an officer must refer to an individual by the name he or she regularly uses.

- All police departments should develop specific policies and provide training on:

  ○ How to respond to and investigate hate crimes based on sexual orientation or gender identity or expression;

  ○ How to respond to and investigate sexual assault against LGBT individuals;

  ○ How to respond to and investigate LGBT domestic violence;

  ○ How to respectfully address transgender individuals (officers should also receive training on the difficulties that transgender individuals may experience in obtaining identification that matches gender presentation and how to respond in such situations);

  ○ Searches of transgender individuals;

  ○ Detention policies and procedures for LGBT individuals.

- Training should be provided to all ranks from the highest to the lowest and should be given at periodic intervals, not just at the start of the job.

- Training should pay due attention to the obligation to respect the human rights of marginalized groups, including LGBT persons, people of color, youth, women, homeless individuals, sex workers, immigrants and refugees.

- External experts and instructors should be engaged for the purposes of training police officers in the area of human rights. Representatives of organizations made up of, working with, or advocating on behalf of LGBT individuals and communities should be involved in and compensated for training, and direct exchanges between police officers and representatives of such organizations should take place during training.

- Law enforcement agencies' training curricula must be informed by, and where possible should be developed in collaboration with, LGBT individuals and organizations, especially those with particular expertise in certain areas; for example, LGBT family and interpersonal violence.

RECRUITMENT

- U.S. authorities should promote diversity in the composition of agencies responsible for the administration of justice, including LGBT individuals, women and people of color. Authorities must ensure that their anti-discrimination policies prohibit discrimination on the basis of sexual orientation and gender identity.

COMMUNITY ACCOUNTABILITY AND OUTREACH

- Local authorities should work proactively to build an effective relationship with their communities, and take steps to ensure that law enforcement is responsive to the needs of all the members of their communities, including the most marginalized groups. Those efforts should include exploring and supporting complementary community-informed models to traditional policing.

- Local police should maintain systems for effective consultation with relevant community leaders and groups, including LGBT community leaders and organizations, and should engage proactively in outreach to the most marginalized communities.

- Police authorities should appoint LGBT liaison officers, both in central command and in precinct stations.

PROFILING AND SELECTIVE ENFORCEMENT

- Authorities must ensure that laws regulating sex work are not selectively enforced on the grounds of gender identity or expression. In the absence of specific evidence or probable cause for suspicion, transgender individuals must not be profiled as sex workers.

- Transgender individuals should not be arrested or detained solely for using a bathroom appropriate to their gender identity or expression.

- Authorities must ensure that morals regulations, such as those against lewd conduct, are not selectively enforced on the grounds of sexual orientation or gender identity. Authorities must ensure that any measures taken to enforce morals regulations are not discriminatory, either de jure or de facto.

- Federal and state governments should review all legislation that could result in the discrimination, prosecution or punishment of individuals solely for their sexual orientation or gender identity. This includes lewd conduct legislation founded on notions of conduct "offensive" to third parties or other vague elements that currently provide opportunities for discriminatory application against LGBT individuals. Such legislation must be amended to specifically describe the conduct prohibited and to explicitly require monitoring and oversight of enforcement practices in order to prevent selective enforcement.

- Use of undercover operations as a means of enforcement of lewd conduct ordinances may lead to discriminatory enforcement, entrapment, and arbitrary arrest and detention. Such undercover enforcement methods should be conducted according to strict protocols and under strict supervision precluding entrapment or should be discontinued.

- Local law enforcement agencies should be required to document arrests made pursuant to statutes criminalizing lewd conduct or other "morals regulations" according to their perception of the gender or gender identity, sexual orientation and race of any participants, as well as the location and time such arrests were made. This data should be analyzed for the purpose of identifying any patterns of discriminatory application of the law.

- Policing operations should be reviewed to ensure that they are not targeted in a discriminatory fashion, including operations involving the enforcement of quality of life regulations and policies.

- Authorities should take steps to ensure equal enjoyment of economic, social and cultural rights by LGBT people, including LGBT youth. This should include supporting affirmative action initiatives to address the obstacles LGBT people face in realizing their rights to adequate housing and to accessible and appropriate health services.

- U.S. authorities should ensure that officials policing demonstrations adhere to international standards. Restrictions on freedom of association and peaceful assembly of LGBT organizations and individuals should not be applied in an arbitrary or discriminatory manner.

- States should adopt legislation and educational authorities should implement policies to prevent homophobic assaults and other "bullying" in schools. Such initiatives must have the best interest of the child in mind, and should not resort to excessively punitive measures.

SEARCHES

- LGBT persons should not be subjected to cruel, inhuman or degrading treatment in the course of police investigations or detentions, including manual frisks or searches of persons in order to determine genitally determined sex or whether an individual has breasts.

- Under no circumstances should individuals be subjected to strip searches in public space, either on the street or in police detention centers in view of officers not directly involved with the search or other detainees.

- If a frisk or search is necessary under governing legal standards, transgender persons should be searched by two officers of the gender(s) requested by the transgender individual, consistent with maintenance of physical integrity and human dignity of the person. If a transgender individual does not specify a preference, then the search should be conducted by officers of the same gender presentation (e.g., a transgender female expressing no preference should be searched by a female officer).

- The notion of exigent circumstances requiring immediate search without concern for an individual's preference as to the gender of the officer who will search them must be strictly construed. Presence of prostheses or apparel designed to alter body shape should not be used as a justification for performing a search, and should be returned to individuals immediately after any search is performed.

DETENTION

- No individual should be required to disclose his or her sexual orientation or gender identity upon detention in police custody. However, individuals should be respectfully offered an opportunity to do so privately. If an individual elects to do so, no further "proof" of sexual orientation or gender identity should be required. Confidentiality with respect to an individual's sexual orientation or gender identity must be maintained by law enforcement and custodial officers at all times.

- U.S. authorities must ensure that safe housing is provided for LGBT individuals while in detention.

- Authorities should immediately begin consultations with transgender organizations to identify best practices for policies in making housing decisions in a detention facility. AI recommends that when deciding where to house a transgender detainee, authorities should take into consideration the transgender individual's opinion as to where it would be safest for them to be detained in gender-segregated facilities. The individual's assessment should be central, if not necessarily determinative, as to where they should be housed.

- Administrative segregation in police custody should avoid further marginalizing LGBT people or rendering them at further risk of torture or ill-treatment. If safety concerns require that lesbian, gay, bisexual or transgender people be held separately from other detainees, they must be afforded the same degree of access to resources and services, including restroom and other facilities, and their detention should not be prolonged as a result.

- LGBT people in custody should have adequate access to medical care appropriate to their needs. Women should have access to female medical staff, and transgender individuals should have access to medical staff of the gender of their choice.

POLICE RESPONSE TO CRIMES AGAINST LGBT INDIVIDUALS

- Authorities should make clear that the targeting of LGBT people for violence is a crime and will not be tolerated.

- Authorities must exercise due diligence in preventing, investigating, prosecuting and punishing crimes committed against LGBT individuals, including LGBT people of color, youth, immigrants, homeless individuals and sex workers.

- Federal, state and local authorities should ensure that prompt, thorough and impartial investigations are conducted into all reports of violence against LGBT individuals, whether perpetrated by law enforcement officials or private individuals. All allegations should be properly investigated, the perpetrators brought to justice and adequate redress provided to the victims.

- U.S. authorities must ensure that police are trained to protect those who are attacked on the grounds of their race/ethnicity, sexual orientation or gender identity. Authorities should provide training to all police, both veterans and new recruits, to enable them to deal effectively with allegations of violence against LGBT individuals.

- Specific written directives and training should be given to law enforcement officials on how to identify and investigate transphobic and homophobic crimes, and ensure the greatest degree of protection possible to LGBT communities.

- Clear guidelines must be issued to law enforcement agencies, stating that deterring LGBT individuals from reporting acts of violence will not be tolerated and insisting on duties of law enforcement officials to investigate acts of violence against LGBT individuals, whether perpetrated within their family or community, or in custody.

- Hate crime statutes, where they exist, should address hate crimes based on actual or perceived sexual orientation and gender identity or expression, and emphasize documentation, public education and training initiatives aimed at hate crime prevention. Under no circumstances should penalty enhancements provide for the death penalty.

- All law enforcement authorities should undertake comprehensive data collection on hate crimes based on sexual orientation or gender identity. Such documentation must include provision for documentation of violence based on multiple identities. Detailed and comprehensive statistics should be regularly published.

- The FBI should include hate crimes based on gender identity or expression as part of their efforts to monitor hate crimes in the U.S.

- Authorities should create working groups of representatives from the LGBT community, including the most marginalized, and law enforcement officials to coordinate efforts to address violence motivated by homophobia or transphobia.

DOMESTIC VIOLENCE

- The U.S. government should ensure that statutes governing domestic violence do not impede investigation and prosecution of cases of intimate partner violence among LGBT persons.

- The U.S. government must act with due diligence to prevent, and protect LGBT individuals from, domestic violence by ensuring that laws against family violence and abuse, rape, sexual assault and other violence give adequate protection to LGBT individuals, and respect their integrity and dignity.

- Law enforcement agencies must conduct prompt investigations of all reports of LGBT domestic violence, and ensure that officers are thoroughly trained on how to investigate allegations of domestic violence. Such training must include how identify the abuser. Officers should not arrest both parties in order to avoid having to undertake a thorough assessment.

- Appropriate protective and support services should be provided for survivors. States should provide emergency services to LGBT victims of violence. These could include crisis intervention services; transportation from the victim's home to a medical center, shelter or safe haven; immediate medical attention; emergency legal advice and referral; crisis counseling; financial assistance; childcare support; and specific services for individuals of minority or immigrant communities. LGBT-specific services should be available.

GENERAL RECOMMENDATIONS

- Governments should promote the human rights of all persons regardless of their sexual orientation or gender identity.

- Governments should support the recommendations by UN/IGO treaty bodies to end human rights violations on the grounds of sexual orientation and gender identity.

- The U.S. government should immediately ratify the International Covenant on Economic, Social, and Cultural Rights, CEDAW and the CRC. The U.S. government should withdraw reservations to ICCPR and CAT.

- The U.S. government should fully implement requirements under ICERD and cooperate fully with relevant international monitoring bodies on the implementation of measures taken against racism.

- The U.S. government should recognize that discrimination against LGBT people, both in law and in practice, is a key contributory factor to the torture and ill-treatment of LGBT people. In order to combat human rights abuses against LGBT people, governments should periodically review, evaluate and revise their laws, codes and procedures to ensure that they do not discriminate against LGBT people, and to enhance their effectiveness in eliminating discrimination against LGBT people. The U.S. government should remove provisions that allow for or condone discrimination against LGBT people.

- The U.S. government should secure greater legal protection against transphobic and homophobic abuse by ensuring that national laws prohibit all forms of discrimination based on sexual orientation and gender identity or expression.

- State and local authorities should bar discrimination in basic areas of life—housing, employment, health services and public accommodations—to include discrimination based on sexual orientation and gender identity, and must ensure that LGBT individuals have access to these services.

GLOSSARY OF TERMS

IN MATTERS OF GENDER AND SEXUALITY, the terms people use and identify with can vary widely from culture to culture. In this report the phrase "lesbian, gay, bisexual or transgender (LGBT)"is used because they are the English terms most commonly used in the international human rights discourse. However, this is in no way intended to ignore the diversity of other terms and identities, nor to deny the cultural connotations attached to these terms.

Bisexual
A person who is sexually/emotionally attracted to both sexes.

Cross-dresser
A person who chooses sometimes to wear clothing conventionally associated with another gender. They may or may not adopt a different gender identity when cross-dressing.

Gay
The term gay is sometimes used to encompass all LGBT people, but it is more commonly used to refer to men whose primary sexual and emotional attraction is to other men.

Gender
Refers to a social construction of femininity or masculinity that varies in time and place and is constructed through learned, rather than innate, behavior.

Gender Expression
Refers to things like clothing and behavior that manifest a person's sense of oneself as male or female. This can include dress, posture, hairstyle, jewelry, vocal inflection, speech patterns, and social interactions.

Gender Identity
Gender identity refers to a person's deeply felt sense of identification of their gender, in relation to the social construction of masculinity or femininity. A person may have a male or female gender identity, with the physiological characteristics of the same or different sex. Gender identity is different from sexual orientation.

Gender Variant Individuals
Used in this report to describe individuals who transgress social "norms" regarding "gender appropriate" conduct and presentation whether or not they identify with the gender associated with their sex assigned at birth. Gender variant individuals can be heterosexual, lesbian, gay, bisexual or transgender.

Hate crimes
Used in this report to describe crimes that are motivated by discrimination on grounds such as race, sexual orientation or gender identity or expression. Over past decades, the problem of violence motivated by discrimination in the US has resulted in the introduction of the "hate crimes" legislation. This legislation may make a criminal act motivated by discrimination a distinct crime in the criminal code, or it enhances penalties for a crime when it is motivated by discrimination.

Heterosexual
A person who is sexually and emotionally attracted primarily to people of the opposite sex.

Homosexual
A person who is sexually and emotionally attracted primarily to people of the same sex.

Homophobia
Used in this report to describe prejudice against lesbians, gay men and bisexual people.

Lesbian
A woman whose primary sexual and emotional attraction is to other women.

Morals regulations
Regulations used to prohibit public sexual expression or conduct, including offenses such as lewd conduct and public lewdness and other behavior seen as offending public morals.

Quality of life policing
Quality of life policing is the term popularly applied to a law-enforcement strategy that seeks to maintain public order by aggressively enforcing laws against minor offenses, for example, public drunkenness, loitering, vandalism, littering or public urination.

Queer
As used in the US context of identity politics, is an umbrella term for a range of sexual orientations and gender identities that include lesbian, gay, bisexual and transgender.

Sex
A person's sex refers to their biological or anatomical identity as male or female. Although often used interchangeably, gender and sex do not have the same meaning.

Sexual Orientation
Refers to the direction of an individual's sexual/emotional attraction, whether to individuals of a different sex (heterosexual), same-sex (homosexual) or both sexes (bisexual).

Transgender
Used as an umbrella term for people whose gender identity and/or gender expression differs from the sex they were assigned at birth, including cross-dressers, female or male impersonators, pre-operative or post operative or non-operative transsexuals. Transgender people may define themselves as female-to-male (FTM, assigned a female biological sex at birth but who have a predominantly male gender identity) or male-to-female (MTF, assigned a male biological sex at birth but who have a predominantly female gender identity); others consider themselves as falling outside binary concepts of gender or sex. Transgender people may or may not choose to alter their bodies hormonally and/or surgically: the term is not limited to those who have the resources for and access to gender reassignment through surgery. Transgender is not about sexual orientation; transgender people may be heterosexual, lesbian, gay or bisexual.

Transphobia
Used in this report to describe prejudice against transgender people.

Transsexual
A transsexual person is someone who experiences conflict between their biological sex and their gender identity. A transsexual person may sometimes undergo sex reassignment surgery so that his/her physical sex corresponds to his/her gender identity.

Transvestite

In the U.S. context, transvestite is an out-of-date description most often referring to men who wear clothes conventionally associated with another gender.

Two-Spirited

Derived from interpretations of Native American languages used to describe people who displayed both characteristics of male and female[800] or that embodied both the male and female spirit. Two-Spirit people were highly valued in many pre-colonial Native American cultures because they brought harmony and balance and were honored to be able to sit in both male and female camps. Today, the term Two-Spirit is claimed by many gay, lesbian, bisexual and transgender Native American people to identify themselves.[801]

---

[800] Two-Spirited People, Project Interaction, McGill University, available at: www.mcgill.ca/interaction.mission/twospirit/, visited 4/5/05.

[801] Equity Services: Identifying Allies Language and Definitions, University of Manitoba, available at: http://www.umanitoba.ca/admin/human_resources/equity/allies/language.html, visited 4/5/05.

B

THE HUMAN RIGHTS OF LGBT PEOPLE
INTERNATIONAL AND DOMESTIC LAW AND STANDARDS

THE INTERNATIONAL COMMUNITY has adopted human rights standards applying to all nations, including the United States. These standards are based on the principle that the protection and fulfillment of human rights are international responsibilities, and not exclusively matters of internal or domestic concern.

International human rights law instruments and standards, applying to all people and communities, have proliferated since the drafting of the Universal Declaration of Human Rights. However, the LGBT community has struggled to realize the basic rights provided for in existing standards. In spite of this, to date, the international community has largely failed to agree upon and adopt protections specific to sexual orientation or gender identity. This section provides an overview of the related content of two areas of international law particularly relevant to the fulfillment of LGBT rights: international instruments and standards related to law enforcement policing and to prohibiting identity-based discrimination. This section will also examine U.S. anti-discrimination laws.

1

INTERNATIONAL LAW AND STANDARDS
POLICING

The international standards used for regulating policing mainly come from Conventions and Treaties, as well as codes, including the United Nations' Code of Conduct for Law Enforcement Officials,[802] Basic Principles on the Use of Force and Firearms by Law Enforcement Officials[803] and the Standard Minimum Rules for the Treatment of Prisoners.[804] The former legally bind the United States where it has ratified the instrument in question. In instances where the United States has signed but not ratified a treaty, it is obliged to refrain from acts that would defeat the

---

[802] Code of Conduct for Law Enforcement Officials, G.A. res. 34/169, annex, 34 U.N. GAOR Supp. (No. 46) at 186, U.N. Doc. A/34/46 (1979), available at: http://www1.umn.edu/humanrts/instree/i1ccleo.htm.

[803] Basic Principles on the Use of Force and Firearms by Law Enforcement Officials, Eighth United Nations Congress on the Prevention of Crime and the Treatment of Offenders, Havana, 27 August to 7 September 1990, U.N. Doc. A/CONF.144/28/Rev.1 at 112 (1990), available at: http://www1.umn.edu/humanrts/instree/i2bpuff.htm.

[804] Standard Minimum Rules for the Treatment of Prisoners, adopted 30 August 1955 by the First United Nations Congress on the Prevention of Crime and the Treatment of Offenders, U.N. Doc. A/CONF/611, annex I, E.S.C. res. 663C, 24 U.N. ESCOR Supp. (No. 1) at 11, U.N. Doc. E/3048 (1957), amended E.S.C. res. 2076, 62 U.N. ESCOR Supp. (No. 1) at 35, U.N. Doc. E/5988 (1977), available at: http://www1.umn.edu/humanrts/instree/g1smr.htm.

object and purpose of that treaty.[805] While the declarations, standards and principles listed below are not legally binding on states, these instruments were articulated by the General Assembly and other United Nations bodies in which the United States actively participates, and represent the moral authority of the international community. AI believes that they should also represent the attainable, aspirational standards of every law enforcement agency throughout the world.

1.1

HUMAN RIGHTS TREATIES

The following human rights treaties contain standards and protections relevant to the treatment of individuals by law enforcement officials:

The **International Covenant on Civil and Political Rights**[806] (ICCPR), to which the United States is a party, sets out a range of rights for individuals, including the right of every human being not to be arbitrarily deprived of life.[807] The ICCPR stipulates that everyone has the right to "liberty and security of the person," as well as to freedom from "arbitrary arrest and detention" and "torture, cruel, inhuman or degrading treatment or punishment."[808] The Human Rights Committee's General Comment 20 states that the aim of Article 7 of the ICCPR is "...to protect both the dignity and the physical and mental integrity of the individual."[809] The Covenant does not contain any definition of the acts covered by Article 7, and the Human Rights Committee does not "...consider it necessary to draw up a list of prohibited acts or to establish sharp distinctions between the different kinds of punishment or treatment; the distinctions depend on the nature, purpose and severity of the treatment applied." The prohibition under this article relates "... not only to acts that cause physical pain but also to acts that cause mental suffering [emphasis added] to the victim." The ICCPR also requires that anyone deprived of his or her liberty be treated with humanity and with respect for the inherent dignity of the human person.[810]

Amnesty International has previously found that sexual abuse of women in prison violates the right to be treated with respect for human dignity, the right to privacy and the right to be free from torture, cruel, inhuman or degrading treatment or punishment enshrined in the ICCPR.[811] Sexual harassment and abuse by law enforcement officials also violates the right to be treated with respect for human dignity, the right to privacy, the right to liberty and security of the person, and the right to equal protection under the law, all enshrined in the ICCPR.[812]

---

[805] Art. 18(a), Vienna Convention on the Law of Treaties, 1155 U.N.T.S. 331, 8 I.L.M. 679, *entered into force* 27 January 1980. Although the United States has not ratified the Vienna Convention on the Law of Treaties, the Department of State has stated that it regards particular articles of the Convention as codifying customary international law. United States Restatement of the Law (3rd), Foreign Relations Law of the United States, Part 3 – International Agreements, Introductory Note. The United States Restatement of the Law (3rd), Foreign Relations Law of the United States, an unofficial but authoritative digest of U.S. law, also "accepts the Vienna Convention as, in general, constituting a codification of the customary international law governing international agreements, and therefore as foreign relations law of the United States even though the United States has not adhered to the Convention." United States Restatement of the Law (3rd), Foreign Relations Law of the United States, Part 3 – International Agreements, Introductory Note. Part 3, Chapter 2, §312, subparagraph 3 of the Restatement addresses the obligations of states that have, prior to the entry into force of an international agreement, signed that agreements. Source notes accompanying the subparagraph indicates that it "follows" Article 18 of the Vienna Convention. According to the Introductory Note to Part 3 of the Restatement, sections are said to "follow" the Convention where the text of the section is the same as the Convention except for minor grammatical and clarifying changes. Part 3, Chapter 2, §312 comment (i) indicates that a state's obligations as a signature to a treaty continue "until the state has made clear its intention not to become a party or if it appears that entry into force will be unduly delalyed." United States Restatement of the Law (3rd), Foreign Relations Law of the United States, Part 3, Chapter 2, §312, Comment (i).

[806] ICCPR, G.A. res. 2200A (XXI), 21 U.N. GAOR Supp. (No. 16) at 52, U.N. Doc. A/6316 (1966), 999 U.N.T.S. 171.

[807] Art 6, ICCPR, G.A. res. 2200A (XXI), 21 U.N. GAOR Supp. (No. 16) at 52, U.N. Doc. A/6316 (1966), 999 U.N.T.S. 171, *entered into force* 23 March 1976.

[808] Articles 7, 9, ICCPR, G.A. res. 2200A (XXI), 21 U.N. GAOR Supp. (No. 16) at 52, U.N. Doc. A/6316 (1966), 999 U.N.T.S. 171.

[809] General Comment 20 on Article 7 of the ICCPR adopted by the Human Rights Committee (44th session, 1992) replacing General Comment 7.

[810] Art. 10, ICCPR, G.A. res. 2200A (XXI), 21 U.N. GAOR Supp. (No. 16) at 52, U.N. Doc. A/6316 (1966), 999 U.N.T.S. 171, *entered into force* 23 March 1976.

[811] See: *Not Part of My Sentence: Violations of the Human Rights of Women in Custody* (AI Index: 51/01/99), 1999.

[812] Arts. 10, 17, 9 and 14, ICCPR, G.A. res. 2200A (XXI), 21 U.N. GAOR Supp. (No. 16) at 52, U.N. Doc. A/6316 (1966), 999 U.N.T.S. 171, *entered into force* 23 March 1976.

Article 26 of the ICCPR prohibits discrimination, stating that "[a]ll persons are equal before the law and are entitled without any discrimination to the equal protection of the law. In this respect, the law shall prohibit any discrimination and guarantee all persons equal and effective protection against discrimination on any ground such as race, color, sex, language, religion, political or other opinion, national or social origin, property, birth or other status."[813] Targeting of incarcerated individuals because of their sexual orientation or gender identity violates their right to be free from discrimination, as enshrined in the ICCPR.

The **Convention Against Torture and Other Cruel, Inhuman or Degrading Treatment or Punishment,** (CAT) to which the United States is a party, in prohibiting absolutely the use of torture and other cruel, inhuman or degrading treatment or punishment by law enforcement officials (and other state agents), prescribes that education and information regarding the prohibition of torture be fully included in the training of law enforcement personnel.[814] Under international law, rape of a prisoner by correctional staff is considered to be an act of torture.[815]

The U.S. is a party to the **International Convention on the Elimination of All Forms of Racial Discrimination** (ICERD), which obliges each state party to refrain from any "act or practice of racial discrimination against persons, groups of persons or institutions and to ensure that all public authorities and public institutions, national and local, shall act in conformity with this obligation."[816] ICERD further guarantees "the right to security of person and protection by the State against violence or bodily harm, whether inflicted by government officials or by any individual group or institution."[817] An act or practice may be defined as racial discrimination under the Convention by its discriminatory effect on a particular group, even if not intentional.[818]

The United States has signed but not ratified the **Convention Eliminating All Forms of Violence Against Women** (CEDAW). Amnesty International includes transgender women in the definition of women, and thus they are under the protection of CEDAW. CEDAW includes a number of rights and freedoms, including the right not to be subjected to gender-based violence.[819] CEDAW safeguards the human rights of women, obliging states to "take all appropriate measures, including legislation, to modify or abolish existing laws, regulations, customs and practices which constitute discrimination against women"[820] and "to repeal all national penal provisions which constitute discrimination against women."[821] Furthermore, CEDAW requires signatory states to take affirmative

[813] Article 26, ICCPR, G.A. res. 2200A (XXI), 21 U.N. GAOR Supp. (No. 16) at 52, U.N. Doc. A/6316 (1966), 999 U.N.T.S. 171, *entered into force* 23 March 1976.

[814] Article 10 (1) Convention against Torture and Other Cruel, Inhuman or Degrading Treatment or Punishment, G.A. res. 39/46, [annex, 39 U.N. GAOR Supp. (No. 51) at 197, U.N. Doc. A/39/51 (1984)], *entered into force* 26 June 1987.

[815] In a report to the United Nations Commission on Human Rights, then United Nations Special Rapporteur on Torture, Professor Kooijmans, noted that "since it was clear that rape or other forms of sexual assault against women in detention were a particularly ignominious violation of the inherent dignity and the right to physical integrity of the human being, they accordingly constituted an act of torture." UN Commission on Human Rights, UN Doc E/CN.4/1992/SR.21, 21 February 1992, paragraph 35.

[816] Article 2, ICERD, 660 U.N.T.S. 195, *entered into force* 4 January 1969 and ratified by the U.S. on 24 June 1994.

[817] Art. 5(b), ICERD, G.A. res. 2106 (XX), Annex, 20 U.N. GAOR Supp. (No. 14) at 47, U.N. Doc. A/6014 (1966), 660 U.N.T.S. 195, *entered into force* 4 January 1969.

[818] Art. 1(1), ICERD, G.A. res. 2106 (XX), Annex, 20 U.N. GAOR Supp. (No. 14) at 47, U.N. Doc. A/6014 (1966), 660 U.N.T.S. 195, *entered into force* 4 January 1969.

[819] CEDAW, *General Recommendation 19*, UN GAOR, 1992, Doc. No. A/47/38.

[820] Article 2(f), Convention on the Elimination of All Forms of Discrimination Against Women, G.A. res. 34/180, U.N. GAOR Supp. (No. 46) at 193, U.N. Doc. A/34/180, *entered into force* 3 September 1981. CEDAW has been signed, but not ratified, by the United States.

[821] Article 2(g), Convention on the Elimination of All Forms of Discrimination Against Women, G.A. res. 34/180, U.N. GAOR Supp. (No. 46) at 193, U.N. Doc. A/34/180, *entered into force* 3 September 1981. CEDAW has been signed, but not ratified, by the United States.

steps to address such conduct, including modifying social patterns to address and eliminate prejudices based on the idea of stereotyped roles for men and women.[822]

Through CEDAW committee meetings, the need for gender-sensitive training of law enforcement personnel has frequently been stressed in the context of ending violence against women.[823] In relation to women, the most striking instance of U.S. resistance to international human rights commitments is its failure to ratify CEDAW.[824] As of 18 March 2005, CEDAW had been ratified by 180 countries, over 90 percent of the member states of the UN.[825]

The United States is a signatory to the **International Covenant on Economic, Social and Cultural Rights** (ICESCR), which holds that sexual abuse violates rights such as the right to the highest attainable standard of physical and mental health.[826] Furthermore, the ICESCR mandates that states guarantee all of the rights enunciated in the Covenant without discrimination of any kind.[827]

Although U.S. laws and policies are in many respects consistent with the above standards, they are frequently violated in practice, as illustrated by the cases described in this report. By failing to take adequate measures to prevent or punish human rights violations by law enforcement officials, U.S. authorities are in breach of their international human rights obligations.

The fact that some abuses against LGBT individuals are perpetrated by private individuals rather than agents of the state does not absolve the authorities of their responsibility: the state may be held accountable under international human rights standards when these abuses persist owing to the complicity, acquiescence or lack of due diligence of the authorities. The term "due diligence" describes a threshold of efforts which a state must undertake to fulfill

---

[822] Articles 2 and 5, Convention on the Elimination of All Forms of Discrimination Against Women, G.A. res. 34/180, U.N. GAOR Supp. (No. 46) at 193, U.N. Doc. A/34/180, *entered into force* 3 September 1981. CEDAW has been signed, but not ratified, by the United States. Committee on the Elimination of Discrimination Against Women, *Declarations, Reservations, Objections and Notifications of Withdrawal of Reservations Relating to the Convention on the Elimination of All Forms of Discrimination Against Women*, U.N. Doc. CEDAW/SP/2000/2 (2000).

[823] The Beijing Declaration and Platform for Action, Fourth World Conference on Women, 15 September 1995, A/CONF.177/20 (1995) and A/CONF.177/20/Add.1 (1995) Paragraph 125 (f), Actions to be Taken by Governments states in part, "Implement the Convention on the Elimination of All Forms of Discrimination against Women, taking into account general recommendation 19 adopted by the Committee on the Elimination of Discrimination against Women, at its 11th session; Promote an active and visible policy of mainstreaming a gender perspective in all policies and programs related to violence against women and actively encourage, support and implement measures and programs aimed at increasing the knowledge and understanding of the causes, consequences and mechanisms of violence against women among those responsible for implementing these policies, such as law enforcement officers, police personnel and judicial, medical and social workers, as well as those who deal with minority, migration and refugee issues, and develop strategies to ensure that the revictimization of women victims of violence does not occur because of gender-insensitive laws or judicial or enforcement practices…" and the Committee on the Elimination of Discrimination against Women, General Recommendation 19, Violence against women, (11th session, 1992), U.N. Doc. A/47/38 at 1 (1993), reprinted in *Compilation of General Comments and General Recommendations Adopted by Human Rights Treaty Bodies*, U.N. Doc. HRI/GEN/1/Rev.6 at 243 (2003) recommends in Recommendation 24 (b) & (f) that there be "…[g]ender-sensitive training of judicial and law enforcement officers and other public officials is essential for effective implementation of the Convention…" and "…education and public information programs to help eliminate prejudices which hinder women's equality."

[824] The U.S. government signed the treaty in 1980, shortly after it was adopted by the United Nations. Signature is a procedure that formally expresses a country's willingness to become a party that is obliged to implement a treaty's provisions. By signing, a government binds itself not to do anything that would defeat the object and purpose of the treaty, pending the decision whether to ratify it. Ratification is the procedure that makes a treaty binding and makes the government subject to international scrutiny of its implementation of the treaty's obligations.

[825] U.N. Division for the Advancement of Women, Department of Economic and Social Affairs, http://www.un.org/womenwatch/daw/cedaw/states.htm.

[826] Art. 12, International Covenant on Economic, Social and Cultural Rights, G.A. res. 2200A (XXI), 21 U.N.GAOR Supp. (No. 16) at 49, U.N. Doc. A/6316 (1966), 993 U.N.T.S. 3, *entered into force* 3 January 1976.

[827] Art. 2(2), International Covenant on Economic, Social and Cultural Rights, G.A. res. 2200A (XXI), 21 U.N.GAOR Supp. (No. 16) at 49, U.N. Doc. A/6316 (1966), 993 U.N.T.S. 3, *entered into force* 3 January 1976.

its responsibility to protect individuals from abuses of their rights.[828] Due diligence includes taking effective steps to prevent such abuses, to investigate them when they occur, to prosecute the alleged perpetrators and bring them to justice through fair proceedings, and to provide adequate compensation and other forms of redress. It also means ensuring that justice is dispensed without discrimination of any kind.

1.2

DECLARATIONS, STANDARDS AND PRINCIPLES

ARTICLE 2 of the **U.N. Code of Conduct for Law Enforcement Officials** ("Code"), adopted by the U.N. General Assembly in 1979, provides that law enforcement officials shall respect and protect human dignity and maintain and uphold the human rights of all persons."[829] The Code stipulates that law enforcement officials should not inflict, instigate or tolerate any act of torture or other cruel, inhuman or degrading treatment or punishment.[830] Under Article 3, "Law enforcement officials may use force only when strictly necessary and to the extent required for the performance of their duty."[831] Article 8[832] of the Code requires a chain of command that is responsive and supportive of human rights. States must also act with due diligence to ensure that all parts of the population are protected equally under Article 2 of the Code.[833] The Code specifies that police agencies should be representative of and responsive and accountable to the community as a whole. Law enforcement officials who have reason to believe that a violation has occurred, or is about to occur, shall report the matter.[834] Furthermore, The Guidelines for the Effective Implementation of the Code prescribe that effective mechanisms must be established to ensure the internal discipline and supervision of law enforcement officials.[835]

The **Declaration of Basic Principles of Justice for Victims of Crime and Abuse of Power**[836] ("Declaration") requires police and other personnel concerned with victims to treat victims with compassion and respect for their dignity and to ensure their safety.[837] The Declaration mandates that police receive training to sensitize them to the needs of victims.[838] Overall, in protecting and serving the community, police shall not unlawfully discriminate on the basis of race, gender, religion, language, color, political opinion, national origin, property, birth or other status.[839]

---

[828] The UN Special Rapporteur on violence against women, its causes and consequences, has stated that a "[s]tate can be held complicit where it fails systematically to provide protection from private actors who deprive any person of his/her human rights. UN Doc. E/CN.4 /1996/53, para. 32.

[829] U.N. Code of Conduct for Law Enforcement Officials, G.A. res. 34/169, annex, 34 U.N. GAOR Supp. (No. 46) at 186, U.N. Doc. A/34/46 (1979).

[830] U.N. Code of Conduct for Law Enforcement Officials, G.A. res. 34/169, annex, 34 U.N. GAOR Supp. (No. 46) at 186, U.N. Doc. A/34/46 (1979).

[831] U.N. Code of Conduct for Law Enforcement Officials, G.A. res. 34/169, annex, 34 U.N. GAOR Supp. (No. 46) at 186, U.N. Doc. A/34/46 (1979).

[832] U.N. Code of Conduct for Law Enforcement Officials, G.A. res. 34/169, annex, 34 U.N. GAOR Supp. (No. 46) at 186, U.N. Doc. A/34/46 (1979).

[833] U.N. Code of Conduct for Law Enforcement Officials, G.A. res. 34/169, annex, 34 U.N. GAOR Supp. (No. 46) at 186, U.N. Doc. A/34/46 (1979), article 2.

[834] U.N. Code of Conduct for Law Enforcement Officials, G.A. res. 34/169, annex, 34 U.N. GAOR Supp. (No. 46) at 186, U.N. Doc. A/34/46 (1979), article 8.

[835] U.N. Code of Conduct for Law Enforcement Officials, G.A. res. 34/169, annex, 34 U.N. GAOR Supp. (No. 46) at 186, U.N. Doc. A/34/46 (1979), preambular paragraph 8(d) and articles 7 and 8; Principles on Force & Firearms, principles 22-26.

[836] Declaration of Basic Principles of Justice for Victims of Crime and Abuse of Power, G.A. res. 40/34, annex, 40 U.N. GAOR Supp. (No. 53) at 214, U.N. Doc. A/40/53 (1985).

[837] Declaration of Basic Principles of Justice for Victims of Crime and Abuse of Power, G.A. res. 40/34, annex, 40 U.N. GAOR Supp. (No. 53) at 214, U.N. Doc. A/40/53 (1985).

[838] General Assembly Resolution 40/34 of 29 November 1985.

[839] Article 2, UDHR, G.A. res. 217A (III), U.N. Doc A/810 at 71 (1948); Articles 2 and 3, ICCPR, G.A. res. 2200A (XXI), 21 U.N. GAOR Supp. (No. 16) at 52, U.N. Doc. A/6316 (1966), 999 U.N.T.S. 171, *entered into force* Mar. 23, 1976; Articles 2 and 5, ICERD, G.A. res. 2106 (XX), Annex, 20 U.N. GAOR Supp. (No. 14) at 47, U.N. Doc. A/6014 (1966), 660 U.N.T.S. 195, *entered into force* 4 January 1969; Articles 1 and 2, *U.N. Code of Conduct for Law Enforcement Officials,* G.A. res. 34/169, annex, 34 U.N. GAOR Supp. (No. 46) at 186, U.N. Doc. A/34/46 (1979).

Furthermore, when violations of human rights have occurred, all parts of the population are to have equal access to remedies.[840] Last, any investigations into violations shall be prompt, competent, thorough and impartial.[841]

The **Basic Principles on the Use of Force and Firearms by Law Enforcement Officials** ("Basic Principles") provide that:

> Law enforcement officials, in carrying out their duty, shall as far as possible apply non-violent means before resorting to the use of force and firearms. They may use force and firearms only if other means remain ineffective or without any promise of achieving the intended result. Whenever use of force and firearms is unavoidable, law enforcement officials shall:
>
> a. Exercise restraint in such use and act in proportion to the seriousness of the offence and the legitimate objective to be achieved;
>
> b. Minimize damage and injury and respect and preserve human life;
>
> c. Ensure that assistance and medical aid are rendered to any injured or affected persons at the earliest possible moment"[842]

The Basic Principles also call on governments to ensure that "arbitrary or abusive use of force and firearms by law enforcement officials is punished as a criminal offense under their law."[843]

The **Body of Principles for the Protection of All Persons under Any Form of Detention or Imprisonment** ("Body of Principles") contains safeguards to prevent arbitrary arrest and detention and to ensure humane treatment of detainees.[844] The detainee must be given access to a telephone in order to contact a parent or guardian if underage and at all times must be allowed to seek counsel as soon as detained.[845] Within a short time after being detained, there must be a determination by a judicial authority as to the probable cause for the arrest and detention to protect individuals from arbitrary arrest or detention.[846] Training and clear guidelines shall be made available on all matters of police activities affecting human rights to all law enforcement officers.[847] Provisions shall be made

---

[840] Principles 4 and 8, Declaration of Basic Principles of Justice for Victims of Crime and Abuse of Power, G.A. res. 40/34, annex, 40 U.N. GAOR Supp. (No. 53) at 214, U.N. Doc. A/40/53 (1985).

[841] Principle 6, Declaration of Basic Principles of Justice for Victims of Crime and Abuse of Power, G.A. res. 40/34, annex, 40 U.N. GAOR Supp. (No. 53) at 214, U.N. Doc. A/40/53 (1985); Principle 9, Principles on the Effective Prevention and Investigation of Extra-Legal, Arbitrary and Summary Executions, E.S.C. res. 1989/65, annex, 1989 U.N. ESCOR Supp. (No. 1) at 52, U.N. Doc. E/1989/89 (1989); Article 13, Declaration on the Protection of All Persons from Enforced Disappearances, G.A. res. 47/133, 47 U.N. GAOR Supp. (No. 49) at 207, U.N. Doc. A/47/49 (1992). Adopted by General Assembly resolution 47/133 of 18 December 1992.

[842] Basic Principles on the Use of Force by Law Enforcement Officials, Eighth United Nations Congress on the Prevention of Crime and the Treatment of Offenders, Havana, 27 August to 7 September 1990, U.N. Doc. A/CONF.144/28/Rev.1 at 112 (1990).

[843] Principle 7, Basic Principles on the Use of Force by Law Enforcement Officials, Eighth U.N. Congress on the Prevention of Crime and the Treatment of Offenders, Havana, 27 August to 7 September 1990, U.N. Doc. A/CONF.144/28/Rev.1 at 112 (1990).

[844] Body of Principles for the Protection of All Persons under Any Form of Detention of Imprisonment, G.A. res. 43/173, annex, 43 U.N. GAOR Supp. (No. 49) at 298, U.N. Doc. A/43/49 (1988).

[845] Principles 15-19, Body of Principles for the Protection of All Persons under Any Form of Detention or Imprisonment, G.A. res. 43/173, annex, 43 U.N. GAOR Supp. (No. 49) at 298, U.N. Doc. A/43/49 (1988).

[846] Principles 10,11 and 32, Body of Principles for the Protection of All Persons under Any Form of Detention or Imprisonment, G.A. res. 43/173, annex, 43 U.N. GAOR Supp. (No. 49) at 298, U.N. Doc. A/43/49 (1988).

[847] Principle 3, Body of Principles for the Protection of All Persons under Any Form of Detention or Imprisonment, G.A. res. 43/173, annex, 43 U.N. GAOR Supp. (No. 49) at 298, U.N. Doc. A/43/49 (1988); Rules 46 and 47, Standard of Minimum Rules for the Treatment of Prisoners, adopted 30 August 1955, by the First United Nations Congress on the Prevention of Crime and the Treatment of Offenders, U.N. Doc. A/CONF/611, annex I, E.S.C. res. 663C, 24 U.N. ESCOR Supp. (No. 1) at 11, U.N. Doc. E/3048 (1957), amended E.S.C. res. 2076, 62 U.N. ESCOR Supp. (No. 1) at 35, U.N. Doc. E/5988 (1977); Article 6(3), Declaration on the Protection of All Persons from Enforced Disappearances, G.A. res. 47/133, 47 U.N. GAOR Supp. (No. 49) at 207, U.N. Doc. A/47/49 (1992). Adopted by General Assembly resolution 47/133 of 18 December 1992; Principles 1, 11, and 19, Basic Principles on the Use of Force by Law Enforcement Officials, Eighth United Nations Congress on the Prevention of Crime and the Treatment of Offenders, Havana, 27 August to 7 September 1990, U.N. Doc. A/CONF.144/28/Rev.1 at 112 (1990).

for the receipt and processing of complaints against law enforcement officials regarding violations of human rights submitted by members of the public, and the existence of those provisions shall be publicized.[848]

The **Standard Minimum Rules for the Treatment of Prisoners** ("Standard Rules") sets forth standards for the humane treatment of prisoners.[849] While these standards are not binding on States, they do set out what is generally accepted as "good principle and practice in the treatment of prisoners and the management of institutions."[850] For instance, Rule 17(1) calls for the provision of suitable clothing, which "shall in no manner be degrading or humiliating." It is also important that people in detention have adequate access to bathroom and bathing facilities if they are detained for more than just a few minutes[851] and that they have food served to them on a regular basis.[852] The detainee must also be given access to a telephone in order to contact a parent or guardian if underage and at all times must be allowed to seek counsel as soon as the person is detained.[853]

The **International Human Rights Standards for Law Enforcement**, a pocket book by the United Nations High Commissioner for Human Rights, is a series of standards that are compiled into one document for law enforcement agencies to ensure that they are acting within the requirements of international law. The standards specify that "[l]aw enforcement officials shall at all times fulfill the duty imposed upon them by law, by serving the community and by protecting all persons against illegal acts, consistent with the high degree of responsibility required by their profession."[854] The standards also indicate that, "[t]he recruitment, hiring, assignment and promotions policies of police agencies shall be free from any form of unlawful discrimination."[855] The "pocket book" also outlines several ways for law enforcement agencies to include the community into its work in the form of community policing.[856]

---

[848] Articles 9 and 13, Declaration on the Protection of All Persons from Enforced Disappearances, G.A. res. 47/133, 47 U.N. GAOR Supp. (No. 49) at 207, U.N. Doc. A/47/49 (1992). Adopted by General Assembly resolution 47/133 of 18 December 1992; Principles on Summary Execution, principle 9; Principles on Force & Firearms, principle 23; Principles of Detention or Imprisonment, principle 33; SMR, rule 36.

[849] Standard of Minimum Rules for the Treatment of Prisoners, adopted 30 August 1955, by the First United Nations Congress on the Prevention of Crime and the Treatment of Offenders, U.N. Doc. A/CONF/611, annex I, E.S.C. res. 663C, 24 U.N. ESCOR Supp. (No. 1) at 11, U.N. Doc. E/3048 (1957), amended E.S.C. res. 2076, 62 U.N. ESCOR Supp. (No. 1) at 35, U.N. Doc. E/5988 (1977).

[850] Art. 1, Standard Minimum Rules for the Treatment of Prisoners, adopted 30 August 1955 by the First United Nations Congress on the Prevention of Crime and the Treatment of Offenders, U.N. Doc. A/CONF/611, annex I, E.S.C. res. 663C, 24 U.N. ESCOR Supp. (No. 1) at 11, U.N. Doc. E/3048 (1957), amended E.S.C. res. 2076, 62 U.N. ESCOR Supp. (No. 1) at 35, U.N. Doc. E/5988 (1977).

[851] Art. 15 of Standard Minimum Rules for the Treatment of Prisoners, adopted 30 August 1955 by the First United Nations Congress on the Prevention of Crime and the Treatment of Offenders, U.N. Doc. A/CONF/611, annex I, E.S.C. res. 663C, 24 U.N. ESCOR Supp. (No. 1) at 11, U.N. Doc. E/3048 (1957), amended E.S.C. res. 2076, 62 U.N. ESCOR Supp. (No. 1) at 35, U.N. Doc. E/5988 (1977).

[852] Art. 20 of Standard Minimum Rules for the Treatment of Prisoners, adopted 30 August 1955 by the First United Nations Congress on the Prevention of Crime and the Treatment of Offenders, U.N. Doc. A/CONF/611, annex I, E.S.C. res. 663C, 24 U.N. ESCOR Supp. (No. 1) at 11, U.N. Doc. E/3048 (1957), amended E.S.C. res. 2076, 62 U.N. ESCOR Supp. (No. 1) at 35, U.N. Doc. E/5988 (1977).

[853] Art 92 and 93 of Standard Minimum Rules for the Treatment of Prisoners, adopted 30 August 1955 by the First United Nations Congress on the Prevention of Crime and the Treatment of Offenders, U.N. Doc. A/CONF/611, annex I, E.S.C. res. 663C, 24 U.N. ESCOR Supp. (No. 1) at 11, U.N. Doc. E/3048 (1957), amended E.S.C. res. 2076, 62 U.N. ESCOR Supp. (No. 1) at 35, U.N. Doc. E/5988 (1977).

[854] Art. 1, Code of Conduct for Law Enforcement Officials, G.A. res. 34/169, annex, 34 U.N. GAOR Supp. (No. 46) at 186, U.N. Doc. A/34/46 (1979).

[855] Articles 2, 3, and 26, ICCPR, G.A. res. 2200A (XXI), 21 U.N. GAOR Supp. (No. 16) at 49, U.N. Doc. A/6316 (1966), 993 U.N.T.S. 3, *entered into force* 3 January 1976; preambular paragraphs 5, 8, 9 and 10, and articles 2(1)(e), 2(2), and 5(e), ICERD, 660 U.N.T.S. 195, *entered into force* 4 January 1969; preambular paragraphs 3, 9, and 14, and articles 2(d)-(f), 3, 5(a), and 7(b), CEDAW, G.A. res. 34/180, 34 U.N. GAOR Supp. (No. 46) at 193, U.N. Doc. A/34/46, *entered into force* 3 September 1981; and preambular paragraph 8(a), U.N. Code of Conduct for Law Enforcement Officials, G.A. res. 34/169, annex, 34 U.N. GAOR Supp. (No. 46) at 186, U.N. Doc. A/34/46 (1979).

[856] Principle 25, Basic Principles on the Use of Force & Firearms by Law Enforcement Officials, Eighth United Nations Congress on the Prevention of Crime and the Treatment of Offenders, Havana, 27 August to 7 September 1990, U.N. Doc. A/CONF.144/28/Rev.1 at 112 (1990). These include: Establish a partnership between police and law-abiding members of the community. Adopt a community relations policy and plan of action. Recruit from all sectors of the community. Train officers to deal with diversity. Establish community outreach and public information programs. Liaise regularly with all groups in the community. Build contacts with the community through non-enforcement activities.

The standards contained in the "pocket book" indicate that superior officials shall be held responsible for the actions of police under their command if the superior knew or should have known of abuses but failed to take action.[857] Similarly, under the Basic Principles on the Use of Force and Firearms by Law Enforcement Officials, superior officers shall be held responsible for abuses if they knew or should have known of their occurrence, and did not take action.[858] According the Basic Principles, obedience to superior orders shall not be a defense for violations committed by police.[859]

1.3

STANDARDS PROTECTING SEXUAL ORIENTATION AND GENDER IDENTITY IN INTERNATIONAL LAW [860]

EVERYONE, regardless of their sexual orientation or gender identity or expression, is guaranteed the fullest enjoyment of their civil, political, social, economic and cultural rights under international law.[861] Lesbian, gay, bisexual and transgender individuals, like all other persons, are entitled to equality before the law. International law guarantees all persons the rights to life,[862] to privacy,[863] to health,[864] to liberty of movement[865] and to freedom of expression[866] and association,[867] as well as freedom from arbitrary arrest and detention,[868] and from cruel, inhuman or degrading treatment and punishment.[869] The U.N. Human Rights Committee has urged states not only to repeal laws criminal-

---

[857] Principle 24, Basic Principles on the Use of Force & Firearms by Law Enforcement Officials, Eighth United Nations Congress on the Prevention of Crime and the Treatment of Offenders, Havana, 27 August to 7 September 1990, U.N. Doc. A/CONF.144/28/Rev.1 at 112 (1990).

[858] Principle 24, Basic Principles on the Use of Force and Firearms by Law Enforcement Officials, Eighth United Nations Congress on the Prevention of Crime and the Treatment of Offenders, Havana, 27 August to 7 September 1990, U.N. Doc. A/CONF.144/28/Rev.1 at 112 (1990).

[859] Principle 26, Basic Principles on the Use of Force and Firearms by Law Enforcement Officials, Eighth United Nations Congress on the Prevention of Crime and the Treatment of Offenders, Havana, 27 August to 7 September 1990, U.N. Doc. A/CONF.144/28/Rev.1 at 112 (1990).

[860] See also: Amnesty International, *The Human Rights of Lesbian, Gay, Bisexual and Transgender People: A Primer to working with the United Nations Treaty Monitoring Bodies and the Special Procedures of the United Nations Commission on Human Rights*, 1 March 2005, AI Index IOR 40/004/2005.

[861] International bodies have made statements specifically noting the human rights of lesbians and gays. Paul Hunt, Special Rapporteur on the right of everyone to the enjoyment of the highest attainable standard of physical and mental health, notes in his report to the 60th session of the Commission of Human Rights, "...the Special Rapporteur has no doubt that the correct understanding of fundamental human rights principles, as well as existing human rights norms, leads ineluctably to the recognition of sexual rights as human rights. Sexual rights include the right of all persons to express their sexual orientation, with due regard for the well-being and rights of others, without fear of persecution, denial of liberty or social interference." E/CN.4/2004/49, 16 February 2004, para.54.

[862] Art. 3, Universal Declaration of Human Rights, G.A. res. 217A (III), U.N. Doc A/810 at 71 (1948); Art, 6(1), International Covenant on Civil and Political Rights, G.A. res. 2200A (XXI), 21 U.N. GAOR Supp. (No. 16) at 52, U.N. Doc. A/6316 (1966), 999 U.N.T.S. 171, *entered into force* 23 March 1976.

[863] Art. 12, Universal Declaration of Human Rights, G.A. res. 217A (III), U.N. Doc A/810 at 71 (1948); Art. 17(1), International Covenant on Civil and Political Rights, G.A. res. 2200A (XXI), 21 U.N. GAOR Supp. (No. 16) at 52, U.N. Doc. A/6316 (1966), 999 U.N.T.S. 171, *entered into force* 23 March 1976.

[864] Art. 12(1), International Covenant on Economic, Social and Cultural Rights, G.A. res. 2200A (XXI), 21 U.N.GAOR Supp. (No. 16) at 49, U.N. Doc. A/6316 (1966), 993 U.N.T.S. 3, *entered into force* 3 January 1976.

[865] Art. 13(1), Universal Declaration of Human Rights, G.A. res. 217A (III), U.N. Doc A/810 at 71 (1948).

[866] Art. 19, Universal Declaration of Human Rights, G.A. res. 217A (III), U.N. Doc A/810 at 71 (1948); Art. 19(2), International Covenant on Civil and Political Rights, G.A. res. 2200A (XXI), 21 U.N. GAOR Supp. (No. 16) at 52, U.N. Doc. A/6316 (1966), 999 U.N.T.S. 171, *entered into force* 23 March 1976.

[867] Art. 20(1), Universal Declaration of Human Rights, G.A. res. 217A (III), U.N. Doc A/810 at 71 (1948); Art. 22(1), International Covenant on Civil and Political Rights, G.A. res. 2200A (XXI), 21 U.N. GAOR Supp. (No. 16) at 52, U.N. Doc. A/6316 (1966), 999 U.N.T.S. 171, *entered into force* 23 March 1976.

[868] Art. 9, Universal Declaration of Human Rights, G.A. res. 217A (III), U.N. Doc A/810 at 71 (1948); Art. 9(1), International Covenant on Civil and Political Rights, G.A. res. 2200A (XXI), 21 U.N. GAOR Supp. (No. 16) at 52, U.N. Doc. A/6316 (1966), 999 U.N.T.S. 171, *entered into force* 23 March 1976.

[869] Art. 5, Universal Declaration of Human Rights, G.A. res. 217A (III), U.N. Doc A/810 at 71 (1948); Art. 7, International Covenant on Civil and Political Rights, G.A. res. 2200A (XXI), 21 U.N. GAOR Supp. (No. 16) at 52, U.N. Doc. A/6316 (1966), 999 U.N.T.S. 171, *entered into force* 23 March 1976.

izing same-sex sexual conduct but also to enshrine the prohibition of discrimination based on sexual orientation into their constitutions or other fundamental laws.[870]

The UN Human Rights Committee, a body of independent experts, monitors state compliance with the ICCPR. An optional protocol to the ICCPR grants the Human Rights Committee competence to examine individual complaints regarding alleged violations of the Convention by States Parties to the protocol. In 1992, this mechanism was used by an Australian citizen, Nick Toonen, to challenge an Australian law criminalizing same-sex relations between adult men. In 1994, the Committee found that the law violated the right to privacy jointly with the right to freedom from discrimination. As AI has observed previously, the Committee noted that reference to "sex" in the non-discrimination clauses of the ICCPR—Articles 2(1) and 26—should be taken as including "sexual orientation," thereby affirming that the rights set out in the ICCPR cannot be denied to any individual because of their sexual orientation.[871] Other UN human rights monitoring bodies have also emphasized that discrimination on the basis of sexual orientation is prohibited under international legal standards.[872]

International instruments have not, to date, expressly referred to transgender individuals.[873] Nevertheless, a number of international bodies have spoken to the human rights of transgender individuals. For example, the European Court of Human Rights has ruled that prohibiting a transsexual person from adopting a feminine name or changing her civil status is contrary to Article 8 of the European Convention on Human Rights, which deals with the right to privacy.[874]

2

U.S. LAWS AND STANDARDS

NEITHER THE UNITED STATES CONSTITUTION nor current federal legislation explicitly provides protection from discrimination against lesbian, gay, bisexual or transgender individuals. The Fourteenth Amendment of the U.S. Constitution, which provides that no state shall "deny to any person within its jurisdiction the equal protection of the laws,"[875] has been held to protect against discrimination based on classifications including race, national origin, gender, and alienage.[876] It has also long been held that, for the purposes of equal protection, the acts of law enforce-

---

[870] See for example, Human Rights Committee, Concluding Observations: Poland, 29/07/99 (UN Doc. CCPR/C/79/Add.110), para.23, 29 July 1999.

[871] See: Human Rights Committee, *Toonen v. Australia* (Views on Communication, No 488/1992, adopted 31 March 1994).

[872] See: Amnesty International, *Crimes of Hate, Conspiracy of Silence: Torture and Ill-Treatment Based on Sexual Identity* 9 (2001), citing to Concluding Observations of the Committee on the Rights of the Child (Isle of Man): United Kingdom of Great Britain and Northern Ireland, 16 October 2000, UN Doc. CRC/C/15/Add.134, para. 22; Concluding Observations of the Committee on the Elimination of Discrimination against Women: Kyrgyzstan, 27 January 1999, UN Doc. A/54/38, paras. 127-8; the right to the highest attainable standard of health (Article 12 of the International Covenant of Economic, Social and Cultural Rights): 11 August 2000, UN Doc. E/C.12/2000/4, CESCR General Comment 14, para. 18.

[873] Although not amounting to international law or standard, the International Conference on Transgender Law and Employment Policy Inc (ICTLEP) adopted the International Bill of Gender Rights (IGBR) in 1995, which sets forth a number of fundamental rights including right to free expression of gender identity, and the right to secure employment. International Conference on Transgender Law and Employment Policy (ICTLEP), The International Bill of Gender Rights (IBGR), 17 June 1995, Houston, Texas, at http://www.pfc.org.uk/gendrpol/gdrights.htm.

[874] See: e.g. *Goodwin v. United Kingdom* (2002) 35 E.H.R.R. 18 ECHR; *I v. United Kingdom* (2003) 36 E.H.R.R. 53 ECHR; and *B v. France*, (1993) 16 E.H.R.R. 1 ECHR. The Committee Against Torture has likewise voiced concern regarding threats and attacks against LGBT activists in Venezuela. *Conclusions and recommendations of the Committee Against Torture:* Venezuela (23 December 2002), CAT/C/CR/29/2, para. 10. *See also,* 61st Session of the United Nations Commission on Human Rights, International Human Rights References to Human Rights Violations on the Grounds of Sexual Orientation and Gender Identity, March – April 2005, E/CN.4/2000/9, para 49, appeal to the government of El Salvador to investigate killings of transvestites in that country, and to take the necessary steps to protect sexual minorities from violence and extra-judicial killings.

[875] U.S. Constitution, Amendment XIV.

[876] Alienage: the state or legal condition of being an alien. See definition at: http://www.hyperdictionary.com/dictionary/alienage.

ment officials are state actions, thus prohibiting discriminatory treatment by police against protected classes of individuals. While it may be argued that the Supreme Court has shown an inclination to provide some protection against discrimination on the basis of sexual orientation, sexual orientation has not, to date, emerged as a protected class under the equal protection clause.[877]

The Fourteenth Amendment applies only to state action and does not proscribe private conduct, "however discriminatory or wrongful."[878] Consequently, there is no U.S. constitutional prohibition against discrimination by private individuals against persons based on their sexual orientation or gender identity. In the absence of relevant non-discrimination legislation, this means that, with regard to the private sector, people can be denied a job, the right to own a house or rent an apartment solely on the basis of their sexual orientation or gender identity.

2.1

STATE LEVEL: SEXUAL ORIENTATION

47 U.S. STATES have adopted a state-level human rights or anti-discrimination statute that bars discrimination in basic areas of life, such as employment, housing and public accommodations on the basis of such identities as race, ethnicity, gender, nationality and religion. Only 16 of these states include a prohibition against discrimination based on sexual orientation.[879] An additional 11 states prohibit such discrimination against state employees.[880] The courts in one other state interpreted its anti-discrimination statute to also prohibit discrimination on the basis of sexual orientation.[881]

2.2

STATE LEVEL: GENDER IDENTITY OR EXPRESSION

ONLY SIX OF 47 state human rights and anti-discrimination statutes include a prohibition against discrimination on the basis of gender identity or expression.[882] Two states protect against discrimination based on gender identity by issuance of an Executive Order (limited to public employment).[883] Seven states have existing laws that have been interpreted in court or commission rulings to provide some level of protection to transgender individuals.[884] Finally, District of Columbia courts have interpreted the District's statute prohibiting discrimination based on "personal appearance" to reach transgender people as well.[885]

---

[877] Romer v. Evans, 517 U.S. 620 (1996).

[878] Shelley v. Kraemer, 334 U.S. 1, 13 (1948).

[879] California, Connecticut, Hawaii, Illinois, Maine, Maryland, Massachusetts, Minnesota, Nevada, New Hampshire, New Jersey, New Mexico, New York, Rhode Island, Vermont, Wisconsin. (As noted by Human Rights Campaign, *The State of the Workplace: For Lesbian, Gay, Bisexual and Transgender Americans, 2004* [2005], available at: www.hrc.org.)

[880] Alaska, Arizona, Colorado, Delaware, Indiana, Kentucky, Louisiana, Michigan, Montana, Pennsylvania and Washington. (As noted by Human Rights Campaign, *The State of the Workplace: For Lesbian, Gay, Bisexual and Transgender Americans, 2004* [2005], available at: www.hrc.org.)

[881] Oregon, see Harris v. Pameco Corp., 170 Or. App. 164, 12 P.3d 524 (Or. App. 2000).

[882] California, Illinois, Maine, Minnesota, New Mexico, Rhode Island. See www.transgenderlaw.org.

[883] Kentucky and Pennsylvania. (As noted by Human Rights Campaign, *The State of the Workplace: For Lesbian, Gay, Bisexual and Transgender Americans, 2004* [2005], available at: www.hrc.org.)

[884] Connecticut, Florida, Illinois, Hawaii, Massachusetts, New Jersey and New York. (As noted by Human Rights Campaign, *The State of the Workplace: For Lesbian, Gay, Bisexual and Transgender Americans, 2004* [2005], available at: www.hrc.org.)

[885] Underwood v. Archer Management Services, 857 F. Supp. 96, 97 (D.C. 1994).

STONEWALLED

2.3

LOCAL LEVEL: SEXUAL ORIENTATION AND GENDER IDENTITY

SOME U.S. CITIES have shown a willingness to extend protections against discrimination in basic areas of life to LGBT people. Amnesty International examined municipal ordinances in the largest city in each of the 50 states. 41 of the largest cities had enacted local human rights ordinances that protect people from discrimination in basic areas of life like employment, housing and public accommodations. 26 cities provided protection from discrimination on the basis of sexual orientation,[886] and 14 include gender identity as a prohibited ground for discrimination.[887] Nationally, at the end of 2003, 285 cities, counties and government organizations provided some level of protection against employment discrimination based on sexual orientation. Of those, 152 extended protections to employment in the private sector as well. A total of 67 cities and counties prohibited workplace discrimination on the basis of gender identity or expression.[888]

---

[886] Phoenix, AZ; Los Angeles, CA; Denver, CO; Wilmington, DE; Atlanta, GA; Honolulu, HI; Chicago, IL; Des Moines, IA; Lexington-Fayette, KY; New Orleans, LA; Portland, ME; Baltimore, MD; Boston, MA; Detroit, MI; Minneapolis, MN; Kansas City, MO; Albuquerque, NM; New York, NY; Columbus, OH; Portland, OR; Philadelphia, PA; Providence, RI; Houston, TX; Seattle, WA; Charleston, WV; Milwaukee, WI.

[887] Los Angeles, CA; Denver, CO; Atlanta, GA; Chicago, IL; Lexington-Fayette, KY; New Orleans, LA; Baltimore, MD; Boston, MA; Minneapolis, MN; New York, NY; Portland, OR; Philadelphia, PA; Houston, TX; Seattle, WA.

[888] Human Rights Campaign, *The State of the Workplace for Lesbian, Gay, Bisexual and Transgender Americans 2004* (2005). Available at: http://www.hrc.org/Content/ContentGroups/Publications1/State_of_the_Workplace/SOTW_03.pdf.

APPENDIX
C

SURVEYS AND INTERVIEWS
WITH LAW ENFORCEMENT OFFICIALS

SURVEYS

A. POLICE DEPARTMENTS

The following police departments returned completed surveys:

1. Birmingham, Alabama
2. Anchorage, Alaska
3. Phoenix, Arizona
4. Los Angeles, California
5. Bridgeport, Connecticut
6. Wilmington, Delaware
7. Jacksonville, Florida
8. Atlanta, Georgia
9. Honolulu, Hawaii
10. Chicago, Illinois
11. Lexington, Kentucky
12. Baltimore, Maryland
13. Boston, Massachusetts
14. Jackson, Mississippi
15. Kansas City, Missouri
16. Omaha, Nebraska
17. Las Vegas, Nevada
18. Manchester, New Hampshire
19. Albuquerque, New Mexico
20. New York, New York
21. Fargo, North Dakota
22. Portland, Oregon
23. Philadelphia, Pennsylvania
24. Memphis, Tennessee
25. San Antonio, Texas
26. Salt Lake City, Utah
27. Virginia Beach, Virginia
28. Seattle, Washington
29. Cheyenne, Wyoming

The following police departments declined or failed to return completed surveys:

1. Little Rock, Arkansas
2. Denver, Colorado
3. Washington, D.C.
4. Boise, Idaho

5. Indianapolis, Indiana
6. Des Moines, Iowa
7. Wichita, Kansas
8. New Orleans, Louisiana
9. Portland, Maine
10. Detroit, Michigan
11. Minneapolis, Minnesota
12. Billings, Montana
13. Newark, New Jersey
14. Charlotte, North Carolina
15. Columbus, Ohio
16. Oklahoma City, Oklahoma
17. Providence, Rhode Island
18. Columbia, South Carolina
19. Sioux Falls, South Dakota
20. Houston, Texas
21. Burlington, Vermont
22. Charleston, West Virginia
23. Milwaukee, Wisconsin

B. INTERNAL AFFAIRS DEPARTMENTS

The following internal affairs departments returned completed surveys:

1. Little Rock, Arkansas
2. Bridgeport, Connecticut
3. Indianapolis, Indiana
4. Boston, Massachusetts
5. Minneapolis, Minnesota
6. Jackson, Mississippi
7. Albuquerque, New Mexico
8. Fargo, North Dakota
9. Portland, Oregon
10. Providence, Rhode Island
11. San Antonio, Texas

The following internal affairs departments declined or failed to return completed surveys:

1. Birmingham, Alabama
2. Anchorage, Alaska
3. Phoenix, Arizona
4. Los Angeles, California
5. Denver, Colorado
6. Wilmington, Delaware
7. Washington, D.C.
8. Jacksonville, Florida
9. Atlanta, Georgia
10. Honolulu, Hawaii
11. Boise, Idaho
12. Chicago, Illinois
13. Des Moines, Iowa
14. Wichita, Kansas
15. Lexington, Kentucky
16. New Orleans, Louisiana
17. Portland, Maine
18. Baltimore, Maryland

19. Detroit, Michigan
20. Kansas City, Missouri
21. Billings, Montana
22. Omaha, Nebraska
23. Las Vegas, Nevada
24. Manchester, New Hampshire
25. Newark, New Jersey
26. New York, New York
27. Charlotte, North Carolina
28. Columbus, Ohio
29. Oklahoma City, Oklahoma
30. Philadelphia, Pennsylvania
31. Columbia, South Carolina
32. Sioux Falls, South Dakota
33. Memphis, Tennessee
34. Houston, Texas
35. Salt Lake City, Utah
36. Burlington, Vermont
37. Virginia Beach, Virginia
38. Seattle, Washington
39. Charleston, West Virginia
40. Milwaukee, Wisconsin
41. Cheyenne, Wyoming

C. CIVILIAN REVIEW BOARDS

The following civilian review boards returned completed surveys[889]:

1. Washington, D.C.
2. Honolulu, Hawaii
3. Boise, Idaho
4. Baltimore, Maryland
5. Omaha, Nebraska
6. Albuquerque, New Mexico
7. New York, New York
8. Salt Lake City, Utah
9. Milwaukee, Wisconsin

The following civilian review boards declined or failed to return completed surveys[889]:

1. Birmingham, Alabama
2. Torrance, California[890]
3. Commerce, California[891]
4. Denver, Colorado
5. Indianapolis, Indiana
6. Charlotte, North Carolina
7. Portland, Oregon
8. Philadelphia, Pennsylvania
9. Memphis, Tennessee
10. Houston, Texas
11. Seattle, Washington

---

[889] AI researchers did meet with and interviewed Staff of the Office of Inspector General for Los Angeles on 29 January 2004, which oversees complaints for the Los Angeles Police Department, although they did not complete a survey.

[890] The Department of Ombudsman reviews and assesses investigations by the LA County Sheriff's Department and the Office of Public Safety.

[891] The Office of Independent Review oversees the Los Angeles County Sheriff's Department

12. Milwaukee, Wisconsin
13. Detroit, Michigan
14. Minneapolis, Minnesota
15. Las Vegas, Nevada

TARGET CITY INTERVIEWS

CHICAGO

- Amnesty International requested a meeting with Philip J. Cline, Superintendent, CPD, by letters of 4 February 2004 and 26 February 2004. Superintendent Cline declined to meet with Amnesty International.

CPD/19th District: Sergeant William Looney, Commanding Officer; and Lieutenant Lynn Kuehn, Community Policing Team Leader, 25 February 2005.

CPD/23rd District: Commander Gary Yamashiroya, Commanding Officer; Officer Jose Rios, LGBT Liaison for the 23rd District; and Sergeant Anthony Scalise, Commanding Officer of the Civil Rights Section for the CPD, 26 February 2004.

LOS ANGELES

- Amnesty International requested a meeting with William J. Bratton, LAPD Chief of Police, by letters of 17 December 2003 and 22 January 2004. Although the office of Chief Bratton indicated that he was unavailable to meet with AI, AI was able to schedule meetings with Assistant Chief of Police Papa, as well as with the two LGBT Liaisons of the LAPD, Officers Jolicoeur and Nielsen. These meetings were all cancelled without offers to reschedule. Despite an additional request to meet with Chief Bratton, dated 4 February 2004, AI was not granted an interview.

LAPD/Hollywood-Wilcox Precinct: Captain Downing, Commanding Officer, 26 January 2004.

LAPD/77th Precinct: Captain Kenneth Garner, Commanding Officer, 26 January 2004.

West Hollywood Sheriff Station: Sergeant Don Mueller, 26 January 2004.

Los Angeles County Sheriff's Department/West Hollywood Station: Captain Long, 29 January 2004.

Los Angeles County Sheriff's Department: Sheriff Baca; Linda Castro; Jeff Prang, 29 January 2004.

NEW YORK

NYPD Administration: Deputy Chief John Gerrish, Office of Management Analysis and Planning; Commissioner James Fyfe, Training; June Roberts, Internal Affairs; Detective Kevin Zatariski, LGBT Liaison to the Commissioner; Assistant Chief Gerald Nelson, School Safety Division; Chief Dennis Blackmon, Hate Crimes Task Force, 24 March 2004.

NYPD/6th Precinct: Dep. Inspector Brian Fitzgerald; Captain Hanley; Deputy Chief John Gerrish, Office of Management Analysis and Planning, 15 March 2004.

NYPD/77th Precinct: Captain Crystal Johnson, Executive Officer for the 77th Precinct; Inspector Owen Monaghan, Office of Management Analysis and Planning; Officer McClain, Community Relations for the 77th Precinct, 22 March 2004.

NYPD/115th Precinct: Dep. Inspector Douglas Rolston, Commanding Officer; Inspector Owen Monaghan, Office of Management Analysis and Planning, 22 March 2004.

NYPD/Midtown South Precinct: Dep. Inspector Brian Conroy, Commanding Officer; Detective Adam Damico, Community Relations; Inspector Owen Monahan, Office of Management Analysis and Planning; Lieutenant Sam Ortiz, 22 March 2004.

SAN ANTONIO

San Antonio Police Department: Chief Albert Ortiz; Dep. Chief Jeffrey Page, 4 December 2003.

San Antonio Police Department, Internal Affairs Bureau: Captain Geraldine Garcia, Professional Standards Commander; Lieutenant Robert Hartle, Internal Affairs Director; Sergeant J.D. McKay, Internal Affairs Unit, 5 December 2003.

San Antonio Police Department: Jane Schaefer, Victim Advocate Services, 3 December 2003.

Bexar County Sheriff's Department: Sheriff Ralph Lopez; Captain Brianne Lunan, 5 December 2003.